G P S
FOR
EVERYONE

Ms. Larijani has successfully combined in one very readable book: a basic description of how the GPS works, its broad applications and rich appendices, including bibliographies, a glossary and acronyms.

Dr. Ivan A. Getting, Founding President, The Aerospace Corporation, and leading force behind development of the Global Positioning System; recipient, President's Medal of Merit (1948), IEEE Founders Award (1989) and Department of Defense Medal for Distinguished Public Service (1997).

GPS — beautifully explained and thoroughly understandable. A welcome presentation of a far-reaching but down-to-earth technology!

Leonard Kleinrock, UCLA Professor of Computer Science; a "father" of the Internet, established Node 1 on Arpanet in 1969; member, National Academy of Engineering; National Research Council Computer Science and Telecommunications Board; IEEE Fellow; Guggenheim Fellow; author, Queueing Systems; recipient, L.M. Ericsson Prize, 12th Marconi Award, ORSA Lanchester Prize, CCNY Townsend Harris Medal.

GPS for Everyone is a compelling, exciting and informative read for professional resource and infrastructure mappers, monitors and managers, as well as for lay readers. After her insightful and helpful book on Virtual Reality, Larijani again engages us with an accurate, clear, timely guide to a high-tech topic. She takes us on a delightful historical and practical journey, using everyday words and amusing sketches, and covers the practical applications in spades. She answers the questions (1) What is GPS? (2) How does it work? (3) What can it do? (4) What can't it yet do? And (5) What's being done to turn (4) into (3)? Once opened, it's a hard book to close until finished!

Barney P. Popkin, Geosciences Team Leader, TetraTech EM, Inc. & Co-Chair, San Francisco Board of Supervisors' Hazardous Materials Advisory Committee.

On water, on land or in the air, know where you are, and know where you're headed! Read this book to know how!

Amy Fuller, crew member, America³, 1st all-women's America's Cup team, 2-time Olympic rower, Olympic silver-medallist.

G P S

FOR

EVERYONE

How the Global Positioning System Can Work for You

L. Casey Larijani

American Interface Corporation
Publishing Division
New York

Cataloging in Publication Data

Larijani, L. Casey

GPS for everyone : how the global positioning system can work for you /
L. Casey Larijani.

    p.   cm.

    Includes bibliographical references, appendices, glossary and index.

    ISBN 0-9659667-5-5

    1. Technology.   2. Navigation.   I. Title

97-77600

This publication is designed to provide accurate and authoritative information in regard to the subject matter covered and is sold with the understanding that neither the author nor the publisher is engaged in rendering technical, legal, accounting or other professional service.

Every effort has been made to ensure the accuracy and completeness of information contained herein, but the author and publisher assume no responsibility for errors, inaccuracies, omissions or inconsistency herein. If legal or other expert assistance is required, the services of a competent professional person should be sought.

Printed in the United States of America on acid-free paper.
Library of Congress Catalog Card Number: 97-77600

American Interface Corporation
Publishing Division
400 East 52nd Street, Suite 11A
New York, New York 10022-6423

First printing.
Cartoons © 1998 Anthony Marynowski.

To my parents,
Julia, whose internal compass was never wrong,
& John, who loved the gadgets.

ACKNOWLEDGMENTS

Professor Walter J. Karplus of the UCLA School of Engineering is responsible for providing crucial insight and support and for getting this project into print. I am sincerely grateful to him for his help and friendship.

I also wish to thank my children and my family for their patience, humor and confidence in the book and in me. Only because they are such a strong, wonderful bunch of human beings am I able to follow my own interests, and I appreciate it. Special thanks are due Jayron, who brought her expertise and eagle eye back east when the manuscript and her mother needed them, and Leila, whose friendship affords me glimpses of an enviable perspective on people, life and work.

Mr. Carl Machover, of Machover Associates Corporation, was instrumental in identifying the market and approach for this type of book, and Mr. Anthony Marynowski chipped in to liven up the text with his cartoons. I thank them heartily.

Acknowledgment must also be extended here to the unnamed engineers and researchers everywhere whose hours of calculations and hard work so long ago led to the development of the Global Positioning System we share today and which I am pleased to present to you.

PREFACE

We can all get lost. Whether hikers, car-poolers, pilots, truckers or stockbrokers, we share this frustrating vulnerability. Today, though, there's a service to help us stay on course. Like soldiers in the Persian Gulf War, who used little devices to pick up satellite signals and pinpoint their positions in the featureless expanse of the desert, civilians around the world can now take advantage of a locator and timing technology developed and fine-tuned by the U.S. Department of Defense. It is the Global Positioning System (GPS) — and it's free and easy to use.

Up until now, reliable, understandable information about GPS has been harder for most people to find than using the devices. So, this book was written as a plain-English, information-rich package simply to tell you about GPS, answer questions you may have and let you know how people everywhere are using it. Everything you need to learn about the technology in order to better take advantage of GPS receivers and techniques is here — in one place — designed so you can quickly learn as much or as little about GPS as you wish.

A unique constellation of satellites — at present, 21 working and 3 spares — is orbiting the earth, arranged so that at least four of them can be sighted above the horizon at any time, from anywhere on earth. Each satellite carries a set of atomic clocks and continuously emits very precise, atomic-time signals that can be picked up by the others and by simple receivers on earth.

Because war gives impetus to innovation, many electronic devices have been spawned by the necessity for military advantage. It is not surprising, then, that the set of GPS satellites evolved from a quest for total earth surveillance. Its effectiveness and utility, however, reach far beyond the spy satellites of the '60s and '70s. People around the world are using it to perform everyday tasks faster, more easily and with much greater accuracy than ever before. It is also becoming the means of making air, land and sea navigation safer.

Widespread use of the Global Positioning System is inevitable because, although GPS itself has cost billions of dollars, its services are free and receivers that pick up its signals are inexpensive. If you are considering the purchase of one of these devices, Chapter 2 and the extensive, understandable glossary at the back of the book will help you sort out the "hype" that accompanies new products.

Even an inexpensive (less than $200) GPS receiver shows accurate-enough latitude and longitude coordinates for where it is so that you, the user, can find your location on a map. You can also choose a location from a map, enter its grid numbers into the device and get step-by-step directions to the place. Specific points along the way can also be stored in the receiver as guideposts for future reference.

Using a concept called time of arrival, the distance from the person holding the receiver and each of the four satellites being used can be calculated. These distances are then mathematically combined for precise locational fixes of latitude, longitude and altitude.

Some of us may have used the time-of-arrival concept during thunderstorms, counting the seconds between seeing a flash of lightning and hearing its clap of thunder. This time span is the Time-Of-Arrival (or TOA) range. Combining this with the known speed of sound (about 1/5 mile per second) people have been able to figure out approximately how far away lightning occurs.

A thousand and one, a thousand and two, ..., a thousand and five!

Wow! That was only a mile away!

Very simply, that is the basis of how GPS works. Distances from four different satellites are very precisely calculated. Where their lines intersect is where you are.

Straightforward positional coordinates are not all that GPS provides. As you will see throughout the book, the use of GPS is also spreading fast as a timing standard. Around the world, clocks are being synchronized to a new, standardized unit of time, precise to 1/9-billionth of a second.

All of this is due to a U.S. government policy change granting free use of the GPS to the world. One of the goals of this open access policy is to provide opportunities for American businesses to supply the world with GPS-related products and services — justified, perhaps, since American taxpayers funded the system. As a result, the commercial market for GPS services has been doubling every two years and currently generates $2 billion per year in business.

It is predicted that GPS-related industries will become a $30-billion business early in the 21st century. GPS devices in stores right now range from simple, generic receivers to multiplexing units that excite the most device-obsessive consumers. The worldwide market for GPS receiver equipment alone is expected to grow to more than $8 billion by the year 2000.

As GPS replaces ground-based radar and microwave traffic-control systems, aviation will become safer, and pilots will chart their own paths. Precise measurements afforded by GPS are helping defend us militarily and satisfy scientific curiosity. Early results of GPS' superior positional capability are better surveys, better maps and more precise measurements of the movement of the earth's crust.

In a world of few truly-global standards, GPS is providing a clean, easy-to-use navigation and time-transfer standard. Everyone, regardless of location or political bent, can reap dividends from the decisions made so long ago by the Department of Defense. Geologists, crime fighters, farmers and network moguls are taking advantage of GPS to measure, solve crimes, fertilize fields and synchronize telecommunications. If you are a hands-on type of person whose interest and curiosity go beyond just gadgetry, a small investment in learning about GPS will greatly increase your appreciation of its potential.

How the material is presented is shown below. Depending on your interests, you may wish to read chapters in nonsequential order.

GPS FOR EVERYONE **How the Global Positioning System Can Work for You**	
Chapters 1-3 *The Basics*	• What the Global Positioning System is; how it works; people and organizations involved. • Receivers used to pick up GPS signals and the differences among them. • Handy checklist for choosing a device. • Differential GPS (DGPS), a nonmilitary means to get around degraded signals; how DGPS works.
Chapters 4-7 *Popular Use* *of GPS*	• How GPS is being used by real people for real things — on land, in the air and on water. • Equipment needed for particular tasks. • How to get the most out of what you buy.
Chapters 8-13 *Technical & Scientific* *Applications*	• GPS precision in defense, mapping, surveying, exploration, geology, geodesy, geography, protecting the environment, predicting earthquakes and synchronizing power and telecommunication lines.
Chapters 14-15 *GPS Markets* *& Costs*	• Issues of costs, politics & standards. • GPS-related activities around the world. • Commercial opportunities for entrepreneurs. • Socio-political implications of use of GPS.
Appendix A *Navigation, Time &* *Technology*	• GPS as the latest advance in the evolutionary history of navigation. • Instruments and techniques used in the past.
Appendix B *Triangulation*	• For readers interested in measurements and calculations, how triangulation works — a simple example.
Appendix C *Vendors & Sources*	• A representative list of equipment manufacturers, suppliers and sources of information — a snapshot of players in the field.
Bibliography	• An extensive resource bibliography to give you a scope of current research and a foundation for further reading.
Glossary	• Jargon-free definitions for over 450 terms. • More than 250 GPS-related acronyms.

BRIEF TABLE OF CONTENTS

TABLE OF CONTENTS

1

GLOBAL POSITIONING SYSTEM
The Basics

In the Bible, the seduced Adam seemed at a loss to answer the first question God asked, "Where are you?" Still trying to figure that out, humankind has been creative, conjuring responses ranging from dry geographical reference to sublimely philosophical discourse. Most of us grasp for answers somewhere in-between.

Philosophical musing is best postponed, perhaps, to other stages of discussion, but finding answers to a more mundane "Where am I?" does not have to wait. Pinpointing exactly where we stand on the face of the earth has become child's play with the help of new, available-to-all global positioning services.

The technology is already here. Drivers using the Global Positioning System (GPS) have an option to jump in their cars, plug in area maps and know exactly where they are. Pilots, charting their own courses, can savor free flight, saving time and fuel as they go, and sailors can navigate through harbors in high-tech mode. Up-to-date hikers are already augmenting the compasses in their gear with transistor-size GPS receivers, and truck drivers are both tracking and being tracked.

It will not be long before universal GPS coordinates serve as postal zip codes. Business cards will list not only telephone and fax numbers and e-mail addresses but will give precise latitude and longitude coordinates for our home and business addresses.

Positioning is not navigation, but the terms are often confused. Strictly speaking, positioning merely provides locational coordinates based on some standardized grid. Navigation goes well beyond that, requiring guidance and steering information, as well.

GPS stands for the U.S. military Global *Positioning* System. Operated by the Air Force, it is a space-based technology that aids navigation. The two, however, have historical links. Three critical leaps occurring in the evolution of the art of navigation provided the critical elements of GPS.

The first of these was the little leap of a signal across a laboratory. The second occurred when people measured the time it took for a signal to leap somewhere to determine how far it had gone. Two of the basics of GPS, radio signals and timing, were thus established.

The impetus for the third leap in the evolution of navigation may have been a mountain. Early use of radio in positioning and navigation used low-frequency signals that lumbered along the lay of the land, making their way over obstacles.

Later applications demanded high-frequency signals. Signals sent at high frequencies, though, are easily blocked. They are effective only if transmitted from places far enough above the earth's surface to transcend its topography.

RADIO SIGNALS   TIMING   SATELLITES

Putting transmitters in space was the next logical leap. Satellites, designated as their carriers, comprise the last critical component of the Global Positioning System.

A Unique Set of Satellites

The Global Positioning System (GPS) is a unique constellation of artificial satellites. Though passive as a system, its individual satellites are working units. Together they comprise the space segment of GPS, the part that provides navigational and timing information to users. Individual satellites, initially designed to last about 7½ years, are replaced as their usefulness declines.

What differentiates GPS from other navigational aids is its complete package of deliverables — i.e., extremely high accuracy, worldwide coverage, all-weather operation and usefulness at high velocities.

global coverage   **precision**

all-weather availability   **high-velocity functionality**

Other positioning systems and navigational aids fail to provide at least one of these features.

How many satellites are needed?

At the start, developers calculated that 18 satellites in well-chosen orbits would provide worldwide coverage, and first trials of GPS used this number. Three more satellites were added as working units, and three were included as spares, orbiting on-call, ready to replace malfunctioning or obsolete units. Thus, references to the number of GPS satellites in the constellation have reflected its historical evolution — 18+3+3, 18+6, 21+3, 24 or a "few dozen."

Although the GPS constellation was considered "complete" at 21 working units and three spares, other satellites are being added. More satellites orbiting increase reliability, readings and accuracy. Recently gained access to signals from GLONASS, Russia's positioning system, will help, too. Its set of 24 satellites brings the candidate satellite pool up to 48. Combined use of both systems delivers the potential for higher levels of accuracy than either system alone.

How far away are they?

All 24 satellites of the Global Positioning System are placed in six very high orbital planes, from low points of about 12,552 statute miles (20,200 kilometers) to high points of about 12,614 statute miles (20,300 kilometers) above the earth. In the literature, heights usually reflect the military preference for nautical over statute miles.

Orbital Heights of Global Positioning System Satellites		
Statute Miles	Nautical Miles	Kilometers
12,552-12,614	10,915-10,961	20,200-20,300

At such high altitudes, the GPS orbits are stable and are not affected by atmospheric drag. The sun and moon have some impact on the orbits of GPS satellites, but it can be calculated and accounted for.

Aside from other uses, high orbits play an important role in arms strategy. They are considered good vantage planes from which to detect heat radiation from the booster flames of missile firings. Explosion-detection systems have been placed aboard many orbiting satellites, including GPS ones. Also, because the GPS satellites are placed so high, a number of them can be seen simultaneously from points on earth. Those close to the horizon may fall within a vertical angle called the mask angle.

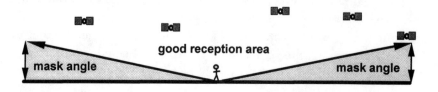

Due to the effects of how signals travel through the troposphere, signals taken from within the mask angle are unreliable for location finding with most receiving devices. For general discussion, the area of the sky over 10 degrees vertical from the horizon is the accepted viewing area. The mask angle for civilian Standard Positioning Service (SPS) receivers is usually defined as 7½ degrees vertical from the horizon. The mask angle for military Precise Positioning Service (PPS) is defined as low as 5 degrees.

How are GPS satellites arranged?

Orbits

An orbit is the path a natural or artificial body in space takes around a celestial object — such as the path the moon or a satellite takes around the earth or the earth takes around the sun. The orbits of the satellites comprising the Global Positioning System are important to its effectiveness and accuracy.

GPS satellites are in geosynchronous orbit with an orbital period of 12 hours — actually, 11 hours and 58 minutes since it is based on the observation of the stars (sidereal hours). This sub-multiple of the earth's 24-hour period means that a GPS satellite has two turns around the earth in its orbital path every 24 hours.

Together, GPS-satellite orbits are so arranged (and tilted at an angle of 55 degrees relative to the equator) that at least four satellites are in view above the horizon at any time. The spatial planes within which the satellites move were established to provide not only good earth coverage but also to ensure the best observable configuration over certain military proving grounds in the U.S.

More than four satellites may be visible, but readings from four are needed to calculate the 3-D position (latitude, longitude and altitude) of a receiver on earth. Enough information may be obtained from three to determine the latitude and longitude (a 2-D position) of a receiver on earth, but not enough to obtain altitude.

Effects of Configuration on Precision

How accurate GPS is depends primarily on two things: the accuracy of the signals themselves and the geometric configuration of the satellites visible in the sky. The influence exerted by inherent signal errors and range errors imposed for selective availability is combined into a factor called the User Equivalent Range Error (UERE). When calculations are done, the UERE becomes part of the equation.

As the satellites orbit, the geometric configuration of the set visible above the horizon changes. The effect that this satellite geometry has on the results obtained from GPS is called the Geometric Dilution of Precision (GDOP). The ideal DOP is zero.

A configuration of one satellite directly overhead with three others equally spaced as low around the horizon as possible (but above the mask angle and without terrain interference) is ideal and produces the most accurate readings. Deviations from the ideal configuration produce results of varying degrees of lesser accuracy. In other words, the precision of readings obtained from anything less than the ideal configuration is "diluted."

BEST GDOP CONFIGURATION   **1 OVERHEAD, 3 LOW**
(but above mask angle)

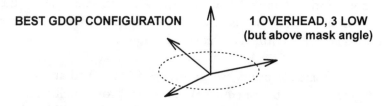

A good receiver determines which configuration of visible satellites provides the combination of signals that produces the best result. It does this when the receiver is turned on. More about satellite orbits and the effects of configuration on accuracy can be found in Appendix A.

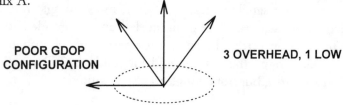

POOR GDOP
CONFIGURATION   **3 OVERHEAD, 1 LOW**

From 2-D to 3-D + Time

The Global Positioning System provides 3-D (latitude, longitude and altitude) location determination and timing. Its broadcast of extremely precise time signals from clocks aboard satellites in orbits that are exactly known is the result of a stellar combination of signaling, tracking and computer technologies. GPS incorporated technologies developed by the Navy's Transit system, which used two frequencies to measure ionospheric propagation delays, and Timation, a system that qualified and tested the use of atomic clocks in space.

Teamed up with velocity-determining capability, GPS is well poised to take over the navigation and time-transfer services for the 21st century. Its 3-D positioning plus time — in effect, 4-D navigation — is phasing out today's costly, specialized navigation systems.

Satellite to User: a Simple Sequence

A simple sequence can be used initially to describe how distance is calculated from satellite signals to a user via receiver:

1. Each satellite sends coded radio signals to a receiver on earth.

    0101000101101010010101001010101010

2. How long they take to arrive is measured.

    0101000101101010010101001010101010

3. The receiver on earth generates an identical set of codes.

    0101000101101010010101001010101010

4. The receiver then calculates the time delay between its own code and the satellite's, i.e., how far the receiver's code has to shift to align with the code received from the satellite. (Their clocks are synchronized.)

    0101000101101010010101001010101010

    0101000101101010010101001010101010

5. Since radio signals travel at the speed of light, the calculated time delay is multiplied by the speed of light to yield the distance traveled by the signal, i.e., the distance between the satellite and user receiver.

This is done for each of the 4-to-12 satellites that are visible and being used. Then, because the exact location of each satellite is known, a number of mathematical procedures are performed by the receiving device to pinpoint the exact location on earth where these distances meet.

One of the procedures, triangulation, is based on geometry and is used extensively for survey mapping and navigation purposes. A simple illustration of triangulation can be found in Appendix B.

Space, Control & Users: Three Distinct Segments of GPS

The entire Global Positioning System consists of the constellation of artificial satellites that transmit signals, a network of ground stations and any number of user receivers. They may be viewed as three distinct subsystems:

- the **space** element — a constellation of satellites that broadcast time signals;

  SATELLITES & COMPONENTS

- the **operational control** segment — a network of earth-based facilities that monitor the GPS satellites' telemetry, tracking, controlling and up-loading, as well as their generation of messages; and

  MASTER CONTROL & MONITORING

- the **user** part — all the people, antennae and passive receiver devices that convert satellite signals into position coordinates.

  USERS & EQUIPMENT

Different kinds of equipment and computer software interfaces facilitate communication and control between the segments — space to user, control station to space, etc.

Space Segment of GPS

The space segment of the Global Positioning System is comprised of 21 working satellites and 3 spares (and potentially more), along with the components included in them. This is the segment from which users receive navigational and timing information.

The satellites are sturdy, reliable and able to operate autonomously (without ground control) for six months. The anticipated service life for newer versions of GPS satellites is about 10 years. Because the GPS constellation has evolved over a long period of time, different "blocks" (i.e., versions) of satellites have been or are part of its configuration. Descriptions of these can be found in Appendix A.

The satellites and spares of the Global Positioning System are arranged in six nearly circular orbits. The orbits are tilted at an angle of 55 degrees relative to the axis of the earth.

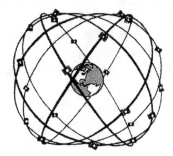

The satellites orbit twice faster than the earth rotates beneath them, making complete rounds every twelve hours. (More accurately, its orbital period is exactly one half of 23 hours and 56 minutes.) Thus, GPS satellites are "semi-synchronous" — i.e., they reappear and pass over the same area on earth every second orbit, or once per day.

Each satellite unit in the Global Positioning System is about the size of a compact car and weighs nearly a ton. Equipped with a pair of extended solar-array panels, it generates almost all the electricity it needs. The surface area of each panel is about seven square meters, and the satellite rotates to obtain maximum power from the sun. During eclipses, nickel-cadmium batteries take over.

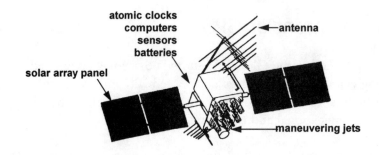

Radio signals, sometimes referred to as signals-in-space (SIS), are broadcast continuously over two frequencies from the satellites. Each satellite also transmits a navigation message (NAVmsg) that contains positioning data and the health status of itself and the other satellites. These data comprise what is called the satellite almanac.

Operational Control Element

The operational control segment of the Global Positioning System is made up of one Master Control Station (MCS) in Colorado (officially called the Consolidated Space Operations Center) and monitoring stations around the world. This is the part of GPS responsible for overall operation of the system. Most users need not know how it works, nor will they have much contact with it. What operational control does is formidable — it predicts satellite orbits, keeps the satellites in them, activates the spare satellites when necessary, calibrates the on-board clocks, checks the batteries and solar panels, monitors all satellite transmissions, controls selective availability and, most importantly, updates the navigation message.

Exact locational measurements are known for all the monitoring stations around the world, each of which houses two of its own atomic clocks. Passively, they continually and automatically track all satellites in view. Because signals from each satellite are picked up by four or five stations, an overlapping abundance of data is collected. The stations (also called pseudo-satellite ground stations) forward their data to the MCS in Colorado. There, sophisticated math processors and computer software models are used to analyze them and perform necessary computations.

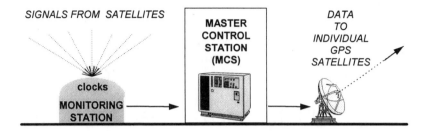

As a rule, monitoring stations are unmanned, and all but one in Hawaii have ground antennae for sending data back to the satellites. Revisions of navigation messages are "uploaded" (sent up) to the satellites via these antennae — once per day, at least.

User Community

Free and easy-to-use, the GPS accommodates a broad spectrum of civilian, scientific and commercial communities. The user segment of GPS includes anyone who captures the transmissions of the GPS satellites in order to determine location, velocity or time. User equipment is also part of this segment.

Who's Who

A standalone technology is rare today. Most emergent technologies are dependent on others and are possible only when each of the individual technologies upon which they rest has matured. Like sections of a good symphony orchestra, all components of a system must be integrated to work well with each other. As the levels of sophistication of individual parts and their management continue to evolve, so does the system.

So it is, also, with people involved in the development of the Global Positioning System.   Many brilliant scientists and engineers have contributed to the success of GPS, but one man, Ivan Getting, sparked early on by the potential of satellite-aided navigation, was instrumental in making it happen.

Who Ran with the Idea — Ivan A. Getting

When the 1957 Soviet launch of Sputnik seized the world's attention, scientists and engineers determined its ever-changing location relative to them by measuring the frequency shift (Doppler effect) of a continuous wave transmitter on the satellite. It quickly dawned on some (at Johns Hopkins Applied Physics Laboratory) that the process could be turned upside down.   In short, if the orbit parameters of a satellite were accurately known, an observer on the surface of the earth, say at sea level, could compute his or her geographical position.   Thus was born the Navy's two-dimensional Transit satellite positioning system.

Transit's response times were slow, but it served well for global positioning and slowly moving observers.   It was not suitable, however, for the position location of fast or maneuvering platforms such as fighter planes, nor did it provide continuous location information since there were occasional signal blackouts.

Getting envisioned a constellation that would provide such high-velocity, near-real-time location information and would do so for an unlimited number of users.   The new system's satellites, circling the earth in precisely-defined orbits, would transmit accurately-timed, unique radio signals.   It was the original "Navstar" system although not named that until 1974, when defense efforts were consolidated. (As its descendant, GPS is sometimes still referred to by laypersons as the Navstar system or Navstar GPS.)

The new system's success would depend upon its meeting very specific requirements.   Global coverage was understood, as was the stipulation that user devices not emit any radio signals that could be tracked by an enemy (i.e., receivers had to be "passive").

In addition, three-dimensional positioning (latitude, longitude and altitude) not only had to be accurate to 15 yards but coupled with response times fast enough for continuous tracking of high-velocity aircraft. The system had to work for any number of users without becoming saturated, and their equipment had to be affordable.

These requirements clearly suggested a LORAN-type solution. It would be one that used the difference in arrival times of signals to determine position, and early studies had shown that signals gathered simultaneously from four satellites would provide enough data to calculate not only accurate, three-dimensional fixes but also corrections for errors in user clocks. This latter advantage was two-fold — accurate time and reduced cost of user equipment.

It was clear to Getting and others that as few as 18 satellites placed in strategic orbits would suffice for global coverage. It was also quite clear that developing such a constellation would take years and require billions of dollars, but Getting's drive and resources were suited to the task.

After being graduated from Oxford with degrees in physics and astrophysics, Ivan Getting spent five years at Harvard, doing research in cosmic rays and nuclear physics. He was later conscripted to develop microwave radar at the famous war-time Massachusetts Institute of Technology (MIT) Radiation Laboratory, where the first LORAN system had been developed. After the war, Getting became a professor at MIT but was again conscripted by the Air Force for a year during the Korean War. He then moved to Raytheon as Vice-President of Research and Development.

In 1960, Getting became founding president of The Aerospace Corporation, a nonprofit company dedicated to providing contractual support needed by the military for strategic projects — principally, military space systems. His early focus there was to both build the company and support the many ongoing military and related space systems. It also included planning for new space systems to satisfy increasingly sophisticated military needs — including global positioning.

Many scientists and engineers from Aerospace, the military services and industry contributed to the system engineering of the Global Positioning System, but getting recognition for such a far-out support system and the needed funding proved an almost insurmountable challenge. Getting's position, however, as President of The Aerospace Corporation and his role as a Senior Scientist of the U. S. Air Force Scientific Board provided platforms for continuing advocacy at high Air Force and Department of Defense (DoD) levels.   His efforts were instrumental in protecting the funding of the program from various attempts to deflect the money to other projects.   In particular, in the early developmental phase, Getting negotiated funds from DoD to demonstrate the enabling technology that would transform his vision into a viable, operational system.

During the Persian Gulf War, GPS was not yet fully operational, but an Air Force/Aerospace collaboration reconfigured the orbits of the then-existing satellites to optimize (in two dimensions, at least) positioning services over the Gulf area. As it turned out, GPS was a major factor contributing to successful attacks on many of Iraq's critical targets — to say nothing about the ability it gave the Army to navigate across stretches of nondescript desert terrain. The experience of troops using GPS during the Persian Gulf War not only influenced how military operations are conducted but stimulated the development of civilian applications of GPS, as well.

Who Owns It, Who Built It, Who Manages It

The U.S. Government owns the Global Positioning System. The concept grew from systems first begun at Aerospace in the 1960s and was honed over the years by various military and government teams. All efforts were subsequently consolidated by the Department of Defense (DoD) and combined with other technical resources (such as the Defense Mapping Agency) to develop GPS as it is today. NATO nations also helped in its development. Currently, GPS is managed for DoD by the Space-Systems Division of the U.S. Air Force Systems Command. Its management team, comprised of personnel from DoD, NATO and other allied nations, works out of the Joint Program Office (JPO) located near Los Angeles.

The Joint Program Office oversees the development and production of GPS satellites and conducts field tests for all GPS equipment and techniques used by the U.S. military. The accuracy, efficiency and usability of equipment and techniques are evaluated under varying conditions using aircraft for testing flight components, instrumented vans for mobile tests and a high-speed track for velocity testing.

U.S. PARTICIPANTS IN THE DEVELOPMENT OF THE GLOBAL POSITIONING SYSTEM

1960 **U.S. military & Department of Defense (DoD)**
NASA
  - satellite systems for positioning

1964 **Navy @ Johns Hopkins U. Applied Physics Lab**
  - operational Transit; studies on variants of Transit

Naval Research Laboratory
  - satellites with stable clocks; Timation

Air Force @ The Aerospace Corporation
  - System 621B with new signaling, 3-D coverage and time transfer

Army
  - candidate techniques for ranging, Doppler measurements and angle determination

1968-9 **Department of Defense (DoD)**
  - Navigation Satellite Executive Steering Group; led to the NAVSTAR GPS definition;
  - Defense Navigation Satellite System (DNSS) program established to consolidate separate efforts into one shared system

present **JOINT PROGRAM OFFICE (GPS JPO)**
  - oversees development and production of new satellites
  - tests military GPS equipment and receivers

Who Can Use It

Simply put, the signals are out there, and anyone with a GPS receiver can get them. Highly accurate positioning, previously available only to the military, is now available to everyone everywhere.

The announced accuracy of the general public's slightly-degraded signal is 100 meters, but it's usually much better. Military users with the right receivers are assured of measurements within 20 meters.

Selective Availability: Mixed Signals

As stated, the highly precise, accurate GPS signal is available only to the U.S. military and select civil users. The signal available to the rest of the world is a different one, deliberately degraded to be less accurate. The civilian-use obstacle to precision GPS is a security feature known as "selective availability."

In the 1970s, before civilians had access to GPS, it was thought that inexpensive Coarse-Acquisition-code receivers would be inaccurate enough (to only about 100 meters) to pose little challenge to the monopoly the military had on precision. However, tests conducted by the GPS Joint Program Office showed 20-to-30-meter accuracies.

These levels were uncomfortably precise for security concerns. Subsequently, the code for general-public use was downgraded, and Selective Availability (SA) was born. Imposed by the Department of Defense, selective availability is a wandering, artificial error, a "dither" imposed upon a precise time signal (ostensibly, to prevent enemies from gaining strategic advantage from high-accuracy positioning).

Dithering is easily turned on or off; a dial at the GPS Master Control Station at Colorado Springs is simply set to zero or a predetermined level. By intentionally varying the precise time of the clocks aboard satellites that broadcast signals to GPS receivers, the DoD, as owner, can control GPS accuracy at will — and it does, for now. As a secondary security measure, slowly changing errors are introduced into orbit information contained in each satellite message, as well.

Precise Positioning & Standard Positioning

Two types of GPS services have evolved: Precise-Positioning Service (PPS) and Standard-Positioning Service (SPS). Military users obtain PPS. Civilian users get SPS, the one subject to Selective Availability. Both are available worldwide.

There are differences between the two types of services. 95% of the time, they perform within the parameters below:

	PRECISE-PS	*STANDARD-PS*
horizontal accuracy	22 meters/72 feet	100 meters/328 feet
vertical accuracy	28 meters/92 feet	156 meters/512 feet
*time-transfer accuracy**	200 nanoseconds	340 nanoseconds
velocity measurement	0.2 meters/second	n/a

*referenced to that kept by the U.S. Naval Observatory.

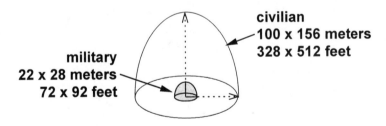

civilian
100 x 156 meters
328 x 512 feet

military
22 x 28 meters
72 x 92 feet

A point in favor of the SPS is that, aside from its imposed error, it is an absolute system, and although its stated accuracy with selective availability turned on is 100 meters (328 feet), users vouch that it is actually better. If selective availability were turned off (as it was during the Gulf War so that soldiers could use off-the-shelf consumer receivers), SPS receivers would obtain much better results.

**Selective Availability
"on"**

100 meters horizontally
156 meters vertically
or
328 feet horizontally
512 feet vertically

**Selective Availability
"off"**

25 meters horizontally
43 meters vertically
or
82 feet horizontally
141 feet vertically

These improved levels for SPS, however, still do not approach the level of precision PPS users always get— 22 meters (72 feet) horizontally and 28 meters (92 feet) vertically. Better results with civilian signals can be obtained with Differential GPS (DGPS), described in Chapter 3.

GPS Signal Codes

Signal codes for Precise Positioning Service (PPS) and Standard Positioning Service (SPS) differ. The precise, military signal is called Precision Code (or P-code); the one provided the rest of the world (the signal subject to altering) is called Coarse/Acquisition (C/A) code. Precision code that has been encrypted has been dubbed Y code.

P code	C/A code	Y code
PGPS (PPS) precise military GPS signals	SGPS (SPS) standard civilian GPS signals	P+AS precise + anti-spoofing (encrypted) GPS signals

Military P-Code

Military P-code is a pseudorandom, week-long number sequence. Transmitted over a wide bandwidth over such a long time, P-code is hard to acquire and less susceptible than civilian code to being "spoofed."

More accurate than C/A code, P-code always provides locational accuracy to well within 30 meters. Although restricted, a number of select civilian users have been given access to this code.

Civilian C/A-Code

With few exceptions, Coarse/Acquisition (C/A) code is the one most people have to use. It is made up of a relatively short sequence of numbers sent on a relatively narrow bandwidth. Under current selective availability, the stated accuracy of the standard signal is within 100 meters. Because the civilian signal is easy to acquire, military users often first pick up C/A code, then transfer to P-code.

Encrypted Y-Code

In 1994, P-code was encrypted into Y-code, available only to users with special deciphering equipment — military receivers with a special chip installed. It is called P-code with AS (anti-spoofing). This added security (and the realization that any enemy of the U.S. sophisticated enough to operate GPS-enhanced weaponry is surely sophisticated enough to acquire and operate differential systems) are leading to the eventual demise of selective availability.

Why now? Changes in the Rules

In 1996, President Clinton announced plans to phase out restrictions on the use of the Global Positioning System by commercial and civilian entities, keeping a promise made by the Reagan administration. In a more freely governed climate, receivers that previously promised no better than 100-meter accuracy would eventually provide accuracy to within 10 meters.

Also, to allay fears of arbitrary shutdown or service charges, the new policy reaffirmed continued free access to the system for at least 10 years. (For readers who are interested, GPS policy details are updated regularly and published in the Federal Radionavigation Plan.)

This change of stance on GPS access has been attributed to a number of factors, not the least of which was common sense. GPS is, after all, a passive system, and it would probably have been only a matter of time before clever persons around the world started picking up GPS signals anyway. Also, if users don't actually interfere with the signal, it falls into a category akin to eavesdropping, something the Federal Communications Commission (FCC) has been reluctant to pursue. No one can really be accused of theft of GPS services, either, since there are no fees or requirements for their use. This latter situation, especially, has propelled the adoption of the technology by private individuals. Application development has proceeded at a quick pace, too — far surpassing the pace it took to build the constellation.

Balancing the needs of the U.S. military with those of civilians and with potential commercial opportunities for American companies was another factor reinforcing proponents' arguments for the change. Even though the watered-down code has been of major benefit worldwide to navigation and communications, it was realized that people will always want more precision. If it were given to them, there would be enormous economic opportunity for those providing the tools. It was also realized that the private sector would not wait, and efforts to monopolize precision-control would be thwarted.

Differential systems have shown that restrictions can be circumvented by anyone intent on doing so. Engineers can figure out differences between exactly known locations and GPS ballpark fixes and make corrections. Their solution — signal-correction techniques providing accuracy rivaling the Pentagon's — undermined reigning justification of selective availability as a security measure.

The Department of Defense prefers keeping more precise service from the general population until protection mechanisms are securely in place. It has maintained that turning off selective availability would be an irrevocable step that would place the U.S. at a disadvantage during wartime. In any case, if the U.S. President is convinced it is necessary, the military will always be able to blur signals and/or use the existing GPS radio wave bands (L1 at 1575.42 MHz and L2 at 1227.6 MHz) to carry command information.

Global Navigation Satellite System

GNSS is an acronym for Global Navigation Satellite System, the term used by the International Civil Aviation Organization (ICAO) to cover all navigation systems using satellite information to determine onboard position. A number of systems qualify for inclusion under GNSS, but by the end of 1996, only two had registered with the International Frequency Registration Board: the U.S.-military-owned Global Positioning System and GLONASS, the Global Orbiting Navigation Satellite System of the Federation of Russia.

The U.S. has offered GPS as a component of the International GNSS, and the ICAO accepted it in 1993 as the first phase of a system proposed for use by all nations. Soon-to-be-replaced USSR officials then offered free and unrestricted use of GLONASS.

An important part of this evolution towards an international system is the development and subsequent implementation of standards. To be addressed and resolved on a global basis are the many technical and bureaucratic differences that exist among countries.

Currently, groups establishing standards for GPS and GLONASS include the International Civil Aviation Organization (ICAO), the Federal Aviation Administration (FAA) and the International Maritime Organization (IMO). They are also working out differences that remain among nations wanting to use the service.

Russia's GLONASS

GLONASS stands for GLObal 'naya NAvigatsionnaya Sputnikovaya Sistema, Russia's version of a space-based time and location-finding or navigation constellation. Begun in the mid-1970s, GLONASS is a descendant of Tsikada, an early two-dimensional positioning system. Like the Transit system, from which GPS has evolved, Tsikada's effectiveness was limited to relatively low-velocity applications.

GLONASS initially used fewer satellites (about 12) than GPS to provide global coverage. It now has 24 but, unlike the 6-orbital-plane, 4-satellite-each arrangement of GPS, GLONASS satellites are arranged in 3 orbital planes of 8 satellites each. Their orbits are tilted at an angle slightly larger (about 10 degrees more) relative to the axis of the earth than GPS's. Expansion plans include a new generation of satellites, a network of differential ground stations and wider choices of user equipment.

Like GPS, the current GLONASS distinguishes between the military and civilian populations, providing separate types of signals for the two; however, no selective-availability-type of degradation is imposed on civilian signals. Military and civilian users both obtain accuracies of about 10-25 meters without having to resort to special techniques.

To sum up, aside from having evolved differently, the notable differences between GPS and GLONASS are:

- GLONASS does not have selectively degraded signals. Users are provided uniform reliability and optimal precision at all times. The basic GLONASS time codes allow better determination of location than GPS' selective-availability C/A code.

- GLONASS' higher orbital inclination provides better coverage of the earth's surface in the high latitudes. GPS provides better coverage around the equator.

Development and refinement of GLONASS user devices are proceeding slowly in the Confederation of Independent States (CIS) compared to what is being done in the U.S. It is unlikely, therefore, that affordable, technologically advanced receivers will be in the hands of many Russian consumers in the near future.

U.S. companies and manufacturers around the world are already building and marketing devices with GPS/GLONASS-compatible receiving antennae and electronics. These units, by acquiring and processing signals transmitted by both systems, are able to achieve accuracies not possible from either system alone.

2

GPS RECEIVERS

For most people, a receiver is simply a piece of equipment that can pick up signals from somewhere. But receiving devices and their components vary widely, depending on who is doing the talking and on the probable use of the unit. Sometimes, adapters are used to convert one type of receiver to another so that it can function in different ways.

A distinguishing feature of a GPS receiver is the type of signal code it is able to recognize. On the ground floor of capability are general-purpose, commercial receivers that process C/A code. These are the types currently sold in electronics stores and through catalogs. Above them are military-specification receivers that pick up P-code (as well as C/A code). Then there are military receivers that can do all that *and* decipher Y-code. Specially designed receivers also exist for export, for GLONASS and for combined GPS/GLONASS use. Information about these is included in a later section of this chapter.

Since the receiver does all the work, using the Global Positioning System is quite easy. One needs only to become comfortable with the type he or she intends to use.

GNSS RECEIVERS

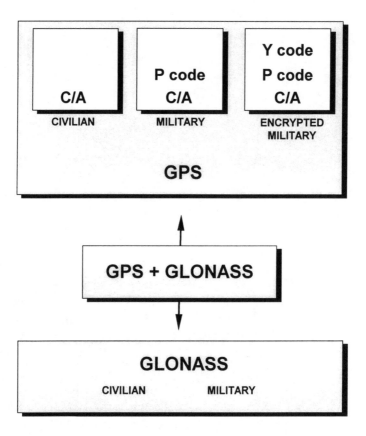

Sizes of GPS receivers range from a miniaturized unit smaller than a bouillon cube to a 70-pound unit aboard a U.S. Navy ship. During the Persian Gulf War, coalition forces carried thousands of handheld GPS receivers into the field. Tank crews, not yet supplied with panel-mounted units, taped their handheld receivers onto the consoles.

General-use categories of GPS receivers include handheld receivers, backpack (or manpack) units, slot- and datacards, vehicle systems, marine devices, miniature components, airborne systems and fixed-station sites. These are described in more detail later in this chapter.

GPS RECEIVER CATEGORIES

HANDHELD UNITS

CELL-PHONE SIZED UNITS

PCMCIA SLOT CARDS

CREDIT-CARD-SIZE UNITS
FOR LAPTOP COMPUTERS

VEHICLE UNITS

RECEIVER UNITS FOR
IN-VEHICLE NAVIGATION,
INTELLIGENT
TRANSPORTATION
SYSTEMS

MANPACK UNITS

LIGHTWEIGHT, PORTABLE
RECEIVERS TO BE CARRIED
BY AN INDIVIDUAL

MARINE EQUIPMENT

SYSTEMS USED FOR
ON-WATER NAVIGATION

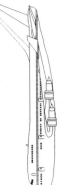

MINIATURIZED UNITS

PRODUCTS FOR USE AS
COMPONENTS OF OTHER DEVICES
SUCH AS MISSILES OR PERSONAL ITEMS

AIRBORNE SYSTEMS

UNITS & ACCESSORIES
DESIGNED FOR
IN-FLIGHT USE

FIXED-STATION UNITS

RECEIVER UNITS
PERMANENTLY INSTALLED
AT A SITE

Getting the GPS Signal

Using a GPS receiver requires direct lines of sight, i.e., nothing between you and the patches of sky where satellites are present. More available lines of sight to more satellites allow a receiver to select from among them the configuration of four that will provide the most accurate positioning information. GPS data collected in dense, urban areas, thus, are usually less reliable than results obtained in suburban or rural areas.

How Long It Takes

Turning On Your GPS Receiver

For each type of receiver, there is a "Time-to-First-Fix" (TTFF) — how long it takes after a user first turns on the receiver until he or she actually gets positional coordinates. The exact time needed to verify the status of the satellites and stabilize a position depends on the receiver's design. A ballpark figure for consumer-electronics receivers is 15-20 minutes.

TIME-TO-FIRST-FIX

Warm up clock and stabilize frequency → about 6 minutes
Acquire signals and download NAVmsg → up to 12.5 minutes
Extract ephemeris data for satellite set → from 30 sec. to 3 minutes

---

Cold starts include turn-on, clock warm-up and stabilization of the frequency. Acquiring the signals involves a receiver's searching for them, then selecting the set of satellites that will perform best. Downloading the navigation-message (NAVmsg) data (comprising the satellite almanac) is usually done from the closest satellite but can be done from any one. It is then stored in the receiver.

Orbital (ephemeris) data for the chosen satellites are extracted from the downloaded NAV-msg. They comprise very accurate information about the position of each satellite and its velocity. A five-channel or multiplex receiver can extract orbital data in as little as 30 seconds to a minute. A double-channel receiver usually takes about two minutes. A single-channel receiver takes the longest to obtain this vital information — up to three minutes. When this is done, the receiver has enough data to calculate positional coordinates and is considered "primed" for that session. The receiver stores the orbital information obtained during the first session for future use, greatly reducing the time it takes on subsequent tries to lock into a good set of satellites. Within about 50 miles from the site of original priming, future warm-ups can take as little as three to five minutes.

Turning Off the Receiver

Even if the receiver is turned off, the satellite-orbital data remain valid — to a point. A new "cold start" is required each time the unit gets damaged, shows signs of memory loss, is turned off for any prolonged period of time or is moved 300 miles or more from the location of its first (or previous) fix. Depending on conditions, the receiver may have to be reinitialized after shorter moves, also.

What It Takes

A Receiving Device

As stated before, devices for use with the Global Positioning System get radio-signal code from the GPS satellites and generate identical code. Timing alignment will differ for the two sets. It is from this that the distance between the receiver and satellite is determined.

Inside a receiver are computer chips that control and command the receiver through its operations. A processor interprets the signals and displays results numerically or graphically. Units that display locational and timing information based on GPS signals are called GPS receivers or GPS User Equipment (UE).

Outwardly, GPS devices may sport different looks, but the basic components of most are the same. Standard consumer models of GPS receivers have an external L-band antenna, an internal phase-modulated radio-signal receiver, an internal data processor and an external interface (which includes a display and/or user control buttons). Some receivers have slots for inserting specialized databases and/or maps. Some units lack a display; these "black-box" models consist of only a receiver and antenna that can be hooked up to the screen of another device.

Receivers can be integrated with many types of navigational systems. They can also be coupled with transmitters and/or cellular-phones, i.e., converted into transceivers so that users may not only receive information but, subsequently, relay it somewhere else.

A sequencing receiver tracks satellites one-by-one, in sequence. Another type, a continuous, multichannel receiver, tracks a number of satellites simultaneously. Each is suited to particular applications or accuracy requirements.

If a standard, consumer-type unit is labeled "differential-ready" or "DGPS-ready," it can be used to work around selective availability — but only if a differential beacon receiver and antenna are added on. Some models have built-in DGPS capability. These features are described more fully later in the chapter.

Antenna

The antenna of a GPS unit is the wire or metal conductor used to pick up the energy of the radio-signals being sent from the satellites — not usually of great concern to people using them. However, the design and placement of antennae on both receivers and satellites affect the levels of precision obtained.

The choice of antenna can mean the difference between a portable unit working in a moving vehicle or not. It can also affect whether it performs well under less-than-optimal conditions — under tree cover, on water or in urban canyons, for example.

The receiver's mounting, its cable and the antenna itself can all impede or contribute to the reception of signals. Basically, a poor choice of antenna compromises the quality of reception possible from a good receiver.

Antennae are either passive or active. A passive antenna merely receives signals and, if removable, can be moved only a very limited distance from the receiver. An active antenna is able to amplify the signals it receives and relay them as far as 25 feet through a cable to a receiver. Anyone considering using an external antenna, on top of a car or boat, perhaps, is better off with an active one.

A civilian GPS or DGPS receiver may be fitted with what is called a flat-patch, quadrifilar or H-field antenna. Hand-held receivers generally have flat-patch (microstrip) or quadrifilar (helix) antennae. There are a number of significant differences between them.

Flat-patch, microstrip antennae are small, flat and internal. A device with this type of antenna is usually lightweight and more manageable than one fitted with a quadrifilar-helix one. But, because a flat-patch antenna must be held parallel to the sky to work; it does not do well with signals from satellites low on the horizon.

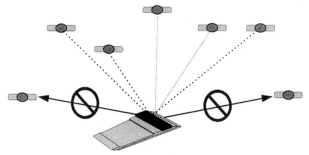

FLAT-PATCH MICROSTRIP

The flat-patch microstrip is, however, better able to detect signals from satellites directly overhead than a quadrifilar-helix antenna.

On the other hand, a quadrifilar-helix antenna is swivel-mounted onto the receiver, which allows a user to adjust its angle for better reception and allows better viewing of the display screen.

Consumer-grade receivers with quadrifilar-helix antennae cannot detect signals from directly overhead, but they are able to detect signals from satellites very low on the horizon (sometimes even below the mask angle of 10 degrees).

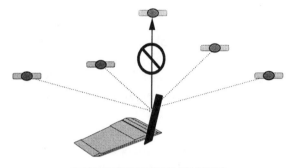

QUADRIFILAR HELIX ANTENNA

Professional surveyors and geodesists require high-end, industrial-strength systems with heavy-duty choke-ring antennae. A choke-ring antenna, which looks like an Olympic-event discus perched upon a pole, can weigh up to ten pounds. Lighter versions are available for use with field packs. Telescoping poles are used to extend antennae above forest canopy or obstructions.

Antennae are bombarded from many directions with signals sent over different radio frequencies. The radio bands over which GPS signals are sent are referred to as L1 and L2 (or Link-1 and Link-2) bands. GPS receivers have L-band antennae, but the antenna itself does not distinguish among signal frequencies to isolate the two GPS ones. Filtering is done by a receiver component called a down converter.

Down Converter

L1 carries both Coarse/Acquisition (C/A) code and Precision (P) code. L2 carries P-code. Receivers are designed to decipher either one of these or both.

	L1 (Link-1)	L2 (Link-2)
Type of Code Transmitted	C/A & P	P
Frequency	1575.42 MHz	1227.6 MHz
General Category of Receiver	civilian	military

In a C/A-code receiver, the down converter filters out everything outside the 1575.42 MHz band. In a P-code receiver, the converter first splits the incoming signals. From one half of the signals it filters out all but the 1575.42 MHz band, and from the other half all signals except the precise, P-code ones at 1227.6 MHz. These are the signals that are made to work with the receiver's internal frequencies.

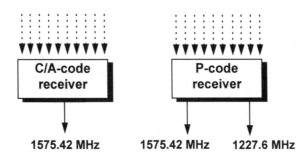

Computers

Computers play a role in all three segments of the GPS — in space (in the satellites themselves), in the control segment and in user equipment. At the GPS Master Control Station, very fast computers are used to process the millions of lines of complex code needed to analyze data and provide updates to the navigation messages transmitted by the satellites. Truck-fleet owners place stand-alone computers in their vehicles to collect data, monitor the fleet and connect to other systems.

Laptop computers linked to GPS devices are becoming critical tools for today's technically astute soldier. Orientation, terrain mapping and firing at targets out of the line of sight are now easier since GPS coordinates provide exact bases for locations, targets and trajectories.

Each receiver, even a hand-held one, contains a processor — a small computer — to control the way the receiver acquires signals, tracks them and then performs calculations on ("processes") the data it receives. The processor must be able to manipulate, transfer and store all the data quickly. How and where it displays the results of its computations depend on how the unit is being used. Results can also be re-routed to other devices, for example, to fishfinders, phones or weapon controllers.

The receiver's computer memory stores data that will be used again, including information about the satellites and details of waypoints. Although memory needs power, it is not affected by simply removing old batteries to replace them. If the batteries wear out or the power is interrupted, its contents are usually safe for a while. How long depends on the receiver — from a few minutes to a couple of hours.

Power

The power for a GPS receiver may be obtained from batteries, standard plugs (via adapter) or both. They may also draw power from the "platform" of devices to which they are connected. Regardless, a separate built-in battery keeps the receiver's internal clock going and babysits the data held in its computer memory.

Portable handheld units usually use general-purpose alkaline or lithium batteries. Units for aircraft, automobiles and boats use either platform power or standard power with adapters.

Input

A receiver needs input (data and commands) so it has something to do and something to work with. The receiver also needs a means for entering the data and commands — an input device.

This may be a keyboard, mouse, pointer, push-button, dial or even microphone. Signals from space are input, and so are the commands a user issues by pushing buttons on the receiver itself.

If a receiver is connected to another piece of equipment, such as an instrument on an aircraft panel or a fishfinder, the interfaces of those instruments can provide input to the GPS receiver, as well. Computer keyboards can be used to enter data and information on disk for later transfer to a GPS receiver.

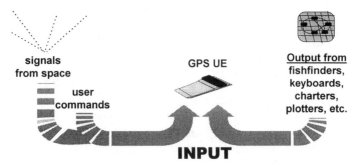

What You Get — Output

The large amounts of data that are received and processed by a GPS receiver (the input) are converted into information that is relayed in some way, as output, to a user. The most common display device is a small LCD screen on the face of the receiver. Output may also be channeled into other devices with different delivery systems.

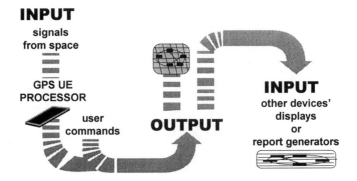

If a receiver is being hooked up to another device such as a fishfinder, the data will be displayed as well as is possible by that device's display.   For example, audio devices will produce only sounds; a low-resolution screen will produce low-resolution pictures.

Visual Displays

A typical consumer GPS receiver shows the results of its calculations on a small display screen. Looking at the screen, a user sees numbers, words, pictures and/or maps.

Northstar

Most of the displays are made up of combinations of black-and-white (or black-and-green) digits or lines, which do not require a lot of computer power or speed to generate. The quality and readability of what appears vary, however, because the little processors in GPS receivers work fast and hard but cannot both perform heavy-duty calculations and produce high-quality images quickly.

Expensive, high-end models, however, do display more complex, full-color graphics. Large, active-matrix, color LCD screens, driven by powerful computer chips, allow a user to combine many functions and view them as a single screen of information. They may also be programmed to include animation or simulations.

These digits or lines can represent speed, direction, surfaces, boundaries or geographical coordinates — presenting the user with a machine-generated view.

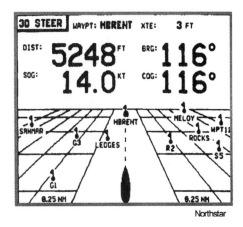

Northstar

What the display shows and how it shows it can often be customized for specific purposes or to suit a user's taste. Parameters can be set for how much computation should be done, how much detail is displayed or how the information should be presented. A user may want to convert American measurements into metric units, for example, or miles per hour (mph) into knots (kts). Most devices also allow switching among nautical, statute and international miles.

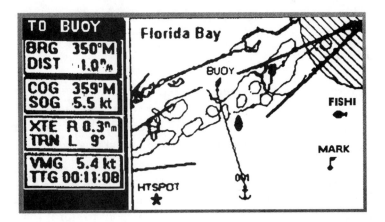

Commonplace graphic aids may be enlisted to enhance the display — the color red for heat and blue for cold, moving lines for flow, a picture of a compass for direction, etc. However, color displays are generally harder to read in sunlight than are monochrome, and many digitized maps have not been designed for color; so, it is up to a user to decide whether the feature is worth buying.

Virtual-Image, Head-Up Displays

The information typically appearing on a receiver screen can be superimposed as a transparent virtual image on a vehicle windshield or mirror, on a helmet faceplate or on a pair of glasses or goggles. This type of head-up display gives information to a user by augmenting what he or she sees without requiring the distraction of having to look away from the task at hand.

A GPS/virtual-imaging system in a car would use the windshield (or part of it) as a transparent screen upon which faint images are electronically projected. The overall effect is somewhat like a very fine etching on crystal. Mapping and navigational software would generate images specific to the route taken, triggered by the GPS receiver registering their coordinates.

Military units fitted with GPS- and computer-driven devices can enter coordinates for field positions within their arena and view virtual images of troop movements at those locations — relayed via a central control station to their receiver screens. Commanders can view virtual images in stealth mode through "private-eye" devices.

Audio Displays

Visual displays are the preferred choice of many users because, for most persons, their eyes are their primary information gatherers. However, stereoscopic surround-sound works well as an information conduit, especially when visual clues are minimal or absent.

Audio capability is being combined with the directional functions of GPS. Since it is a natural tendency to turn towards sounds we hear, spatial sound can be used to coax a person to turn towards a particular direction.

Sound also sharply raises a person's spatial awareness — in itself, important to navigation. Beneficiaries of sight-independent displays include not only visually-impaired persons but soldiers in the field and the whole avionics industry.

Audio-augmented directional cues are used extensively in cockpits and control towers. What is picked up by radar is reinforced by directional aural clues, giving a pilot in a potentially dangerous situation more to work with than visual blips. (See Chapter 5, "Aids for the Disabled," for more about GPS and surround-sound systems.)

Tactile Displays

A tactile (or proprioceptive) display — one that relays information through a person's sense of touch or pressure — can be hooked up to a GPS receiver so that action is triggered when certain coordinates are registered. Electrical stimuli, heat thermodes or inflatable air bladders are some of the means used to communicate information to a user.

Tactile displays may be suitable, for example, for relaying information to persons who can neither hear nor see. Proprioceptors may also be effectively embedded into law-enforcement devices to remind persons of any geographically-specific limitations placed on their missions or paroles.

Basic Receiver-Unit Configurations

Recent interest in receivers has piqued with the removal of restrictions on access to the GPS and the introduction to the market of multifunction devices at consumer prices. Vendor literature for marine, aviation and land products is easily obtained and lists scores of models and hundreds of receiver devices in all price ranges.

It is not the purpose here, therefore, to describe specific brands of receivers in detail. Instead, generic descriptions of the basic types of GPS units, their components and configurations are presented, along with a checklist of things a potential buyer may want to consider.

What is standard in one model may be optional in another. Buyers should assess which features are really needed — and, perhaps, more importantly, which are not.

Hand-Held GPS Receiver

The hand-held unit is the most popular and most affordable type of receiver. Most models are very easy to use, even for the novice, because the receiver does almost all the work.

The antenna receives the GPS timing signals from at least four satellites. The radio receiver inside the hand-held unit decodes the signals (generating identical code), then determines ranging codes, generates measurements and demodulates the message data.

The data processor uses equations to determine location specifics (computing its own latitude, longitude, elevation and time) and sends the data to a user interface (usually a display screen). If a map or information card has been inserted, its information is integrated.

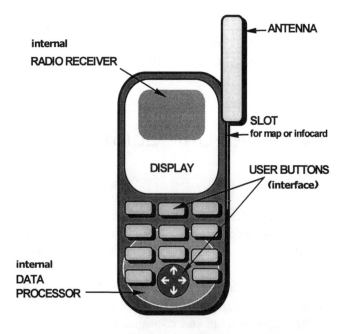

A display or other control device is used for communication with the user. He or she either reads numerical settings or views graphics of the results on a display and can enter data via buttons or keyboard. If the receiver has data-capture features, it stores a log of the output.

Auto & Truck GPS Receivers

The type of GPS receiver equipment that an individual might install in his or her car differs from the typical hand-held unit. Vehicular receivers are meant to be used with accessories such as an outside antenna, a dashboard-mounted map display and slots for inserting digital datum cards or CDs.

GPS units for private cars can be installed discreetly as part of the dashboard panel, and their outside antennae are not very heavy or large. Configurations for vehicles used in professional field work, however, are more industrial looking, have sturdy components and sport noticeable, roof-mounted antennae.

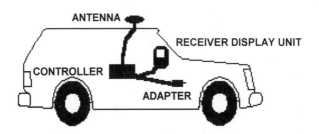

Truck and bus fleets are often equipped in stages. Typically, drivers and fleet managers start out with simple receivers, connecting them to other devices as needed and adding new features as experience with the devices is gained.

A cellular-phone connection may be added to auto and truck units. Audio features may also be added so that the driver needn't take his or her eyes off the road while the car is in motion.

Tests conducted in Europe indicate that private cars meant for city use may also require sensors designed for dead reckoning (DR) navigation. For many of the applications, the components may be run from a relatively small, inexpensive computer.

Chapter 4 contains more descriptions of vehicular systems and how they are being used in both private and public sectors around the world. Chapter 14 includes aspects of markets that are emerging for consumer products and services.

Marine-Vessel GPS Receivers

Marine-vessel use of navigational receivers is taken for granted. Traditionally, however, new designs have been only marginally more efficient at providing position information than their predecessors. After years of working around cumbersome systems, fleet navigators were ready for the breakthrough efficiency GPS provides.

Earlier technical breakthroughs prompted migration of marine navigators to the Navy's Transit system and combinations of systems. Not until today, however, have they had either the accuracy or ease of use that GPS receivers offer. Results from surveys conducted by the U.S. Navy after the installation of GPS-enhanced receivers in its fleet indicated that the new receivers obtained the most accurate locational information ever realized from any system. Implications of this to naval strategy and policy are expected to be far-reaching.

How marine-vessel receivers differ from receivers used for other purposes can probably be narrowed down to their databases and sea-worthiness. It may be mentioned, too, that calculation of the Geometric Dilution of Precision (GDOP) is of less consequence to users on the water than in the air. For mariners, calculating the Horizontal Dilution of Precision (HDOP) is of more relevance.

One of the largest international suppliers of GPS receivers, Trimble Navigation, was founded in 1978 to build systems for luxury yachts using Loran-C equipment. Today's products include differential-GPS devices that feed into marine autopilots and aviation flight directors.

Trimble 2101I/O Plus

Basic Aviation GPS Receivers

The typical portable aviation GPS receiver or panel-mounted unit consists of a multimode receiver, perhaps with ILS/MLS/GPS approach and landing capabilities. Multimode-receiver flight tests have been conducted by the Air Force and the Federal Aviation Administration since 1995 on Sikorsky S-76 helicopters and C-135C transport aircraft. Further testing is being funded by the GPS Joint Program Office.

Panel-Mounted Units

Panel-mounted GPS units for aviation can usually be installed as replacements for many old LORAN-C and other-type units, and some may even retain the same antenna footprints. Most are TSO-certified for en-route and terminal operations. They must, however, be installed and authorized by a licensed FAA representative or dealer. They can usually be repaired, however, by an approved dealer.

Northstar M3 Approach

Panel-mounted receivers usually have datacard slots. Cards with revised information can be purchased; so updating is easy.

Portable Aviation Units

Magellan

Portable aviation units usually must be shipped back to the factory for repairs or updates.

Reference-Station Configuration

Reference stations may be either permanent or temporary, and the setup required for each differs in a number of ways, depending on the degree and nature of monitoring to be done. A typical fixed-station configuration may consist of a multi-satellite GPS reference receiver, tracking options, a choke-ring antenna, processing facilities, operator interfaces and display units. Components include features for correcting ionospheric errors, handling C/A, P and codeless operations and logging data for as many as twelve GPS satellites.

Portable reference stations may be used by personnel in the field or set up for remote control. These units are used extensively for surveying, dredging, photogrammetry and/or flight-test projects. An all-purpose, lightweight (~10 pounds) model may combine a multi-channel GPS receiver with a radio and modem for transmission of data. These handle L1-band frequencies. Data link transmission systems can be used to send them differential corrections.

Satellite-Borne Receiver

A special class of dual-frequency receiver is designed for installation in low-orbiting, non-GPS satellites used by military and commercial organizations to augment their positioning and time-transfer services. These small, black-box units measure things such as atmospheric temperature, water-vapor content and delays — important to high-precision surveying, synchronization and geodetic applications.

GPS-Receiver Options & Add-ons

Vendor-advertised options for hand-held GPS receivers include:

- RS232 ports for connecting to a PC (good for updating)
- connection for hooking up to a full-size keyboard
- lighter-plug connections for vehicles
- gimbal holder for dashboard or control panel
- long-life batteries
- knobs for scrolling
- graphic or menu-driven interface (vs. command-driven)
- post-processing and mapping software, etc.

If a receiver can be upgraded to work with Differential GPS, it is said to be "DGPS-ready" or "differential-ready." "Ready" usually refers only to an extra connection slot or plug that can be used by a separately purchased differential beacon antenna and DGPS receiver.

> **"will upgrade to ..."**
> **+ special receiver**
> **+ antenna**
> **   = "will work with ..."**

Low-end aviation units carry tags such as "will upgrade to WAAS." The upgrade involves purchase of a separate component. A preferable (but more expensive) choice would be advertised as "Will work with WAAS." See Chapter 6 for more about Wide-Area and Local-Area Augmentation Systems (WAAS & LAAS).

Working with Other Devices

GPS receivers can be on the receiving end of data (input) from other devices, and they can transmit data (output) to other devices. They can also work interactively with other devices, receiving data from them and providing data to them or to others — i.e., one's output is another's input.

GPS-Receiver Cameras for the Outdoors

A professional gathering data in the field or a hiker who wants to remember details about a location cannot rely only on memory and a geographical fix, even if it is GPS-precise and entered as a waypoint in the receiver. That's why, to most people who work and explore outdoors, a notebook is essential. In it, a person records not only directions for getting to and from a site, but also anything unique about a place — whether related to availability of water, unusual arid patches, colorful sunsets or the view of geologic formations down the canyon. In forensic work, especially, such data are invaluable.

Photographs help uniquely identify a site, but efforts to marry digital photography with GPS locational features usually involve manually merging data from one file or system into another, a time- and labor-intensive task. Currently, for professionals, matching time-tags and positional coordinates with the photographs is something they must learn to do even though it is difficult. Most other picture takers would like to time- and position-tag their photos but can't.

The situation is changing. Cameras are now being built with GPS receiver capability so that images and positional fixes are gathered simultaneously. Some models are designed to capture as many as five images in two seconds.

Since the digital pictures are computer-compatible, they can accompany data as they are downloaded to databases for post-processing or examination. Data can be stored on computer disk drives or on removable PCMCIA cards.

Current camera models support specific GPS-receivers, but units can be custom-interfaced to work with others. In many cases, pre-GPS digital cameras may be retrofit to work with GPS. Some camera models support software that detects and identifies a receiver connected to it and includes that information with the image, as well.

An information panel alongside the produced image contains a log of both camera-specific details (e.g., exposure, lens and focus settings) and the latitude, longitude and altitude of the site photographed.

```
[28]
ISO:     400
Aperture:  F11
Shutter:  125
Lens (mm): 28
Exposure:  P
Program:  Po
Exp Comp:  0.0
Meter area: Mtrx
Flash sync: Norm
Drive mode: S
Focus mode: S
Focus area: Wide
SGPGLL
4311.451.N
07739.026.W
212914.A
```

Kodak Digital Science 420 GPS Camera

GPS to/from Other Devices

Examples of one-way input devices are electronic maps, compasses and waypoint editors. A waypoint editor allows a user to enter coordinates of points of interest into a computer for later transfer to a navigational device such as a GPS receiver.

In the comfort of a home or office, using maps or other sources of information, a person can enter the latitudes and longitudes of specific places into the program, perhaps typing them in via the keyboard. The computer can then be used to transfer these as waypoints to a receiver.

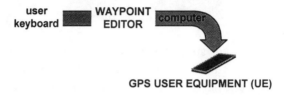

GPS USER EQUIPMENT (UE)

Electronic maps and mapping programs enable a person to use a mouse or pointer as an input device. With either, or with keyboard directional arrows, a spot is indicated on an electronic map. Coordinates are then electronically generated by the program and listed. If the user does not name the point, the computer program will assign a name or number to it. The lists can be edited and fed into the receiver (as input).

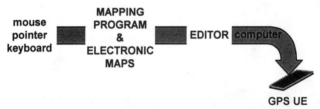

GPS UE

Electronic compasses may also be used as input devices. These are good as backup units if something goes wrong with the receiver but the batteries still work. They use very little power.

As illustrated in the previous section, the GPS receiver, itself, can be used to provide input. It can transfer its computations as data to other devices. The output of one connected device becomes the input of another.

For example, satellite signals feed into a receiver as input. After calculations are done, the results become output that can either be displayed (as a moving map, perhaps) or fed as input to another device such as a cellular phone, a chart plotter or fishfinder.

A receiver's output can also be used with a software program to run other equipment or other processes. If the results obtained from the external device are routed back through the receiver as new input, two-way communication is going on. This type of iteration usually goes on between receivers and computers.

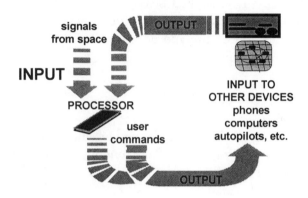

Depending on the application, a receiver may be used as a stand-alone unit, hooked up to one device, or it can perform as one component of a hybrid system with any number of devices. It is up to each user to configure the right system for his or her purposes. Since each device has so many features, however, assembling the right combination of electronics can be difficult.

This is compounded by a lack of standards for the many cables and clips and sockets that connect them or by devices that are physically connected but not able to communicate with each other because of software differences. With guidance, though, it is possible to configure many devices into one space-saving unit.

Capabilities of Different Receivers

Today, the various types of GPS receivers bear labels describing their capabilities or mode of operation — single-channel, double-channel, multichannel, multimode, sequencing or combined GPS/GLONASS. Their differences are described below. Most work well within their intended design and price ranges. Selection, therefore, depends more on the sophistication of use and degree of accuracy required by the user and his or her applications.

Sequencing Receivers

Sequencing receivers have simple wiring and share one or two channels with several satellites. They tune in, one at a time, to each of four satellites and have to sequence through all four before a position can be calculated.

Having to sequence through the satellites one at a time interrupts positioning and affects accuracy. In some models, however, the effects of sequencing are kept to a minimum by complex circuitry.

The advantage of sequencing receivers is that they require less power than other types to operate. They are also less expensive than continuous, multichannel devices, both features that make them attractive to casual users.

Single-Channel Sequencers

Among the many types of single-channel sequencing receivers are:

- starved-power, single-channel receivers that are battery-run and designed for portability;

- generic, single-channel receivers meant to be kept on continuously, using more power but providing more accuracy than portable, battery-operated receivers;

- fast-multiplexing, single-channel units with relatively sophisticated circuitry, work continuously, sequence very quickly between satellites and can make range measurements while monitoring satellite messages.

Double-Channel Sequencers

Adding a second channel to a receiver improves its performance in a number of ways. Most importantly, it doubles the signal-to-noise ratio, enabling it to detect signals under adverse conditions and to track signals coming from satellites close to the horizon. Also, with double channels, service is not interrupted because one channel monitors positioning data while the other contacts the next satellite.

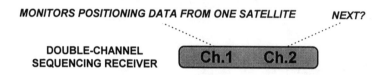

The drawbacks of two-channel receivers include their high cost of manufacture and higher power requirements. Many also feature more user controls and options than single-channel receivers, adding to the initial cost to a consumer.

Continuous, Multichannel Receivers

The receiver of choice among users demanding high accuracy is a continuous, multichannel receiver. These are the type used for technical and scientific applications like those conducted by surveyors and geologists.

Continuous, multichannel receivers are designed with a minimum of four channels but can have up to as many as 12. By monitoring four satellites simultaneously, continuous, multichannel receivers provide immediate position and velocity. Some multichannel receivers can track all satellites in view, not just the four best, and gathering signals from more satellites further increases the accuracy obtained (specified to ~1 centimeter per kilometer of baseline).

Regardless of the number of channels, the background noise remains constant; so, if the receiver is able to pick up more signals, the signal-to-background noise ratio increases, allowing the system to pick up and track signals too faint for others to detect.

For multichannel receivers, six channels appear to be the point at which performance and functionality are significantly improved. Five channels can be allotted to monitor four or more satellites, and one can be dedicated to gathering data messages.

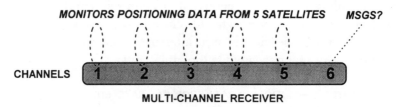

Multimode Receivers

The Instrument Landing System (ILS) has been used by commercial airlines around the world for decades for precision landings. In the 1970s, it was decided that ILS would be replaced by a Microwave Landing System (MLS), a ground-based system that supports aircraft landing operations for all types of landings. In the meantime, GPS was also being developed.

Since countries and states maintain the right to decide which of the three guidance systems (ILS, MLS and/or GPS) to install and use for precision approaches and landings, airlines will have to be equipped with receivers for all three types — costly and impractical if independent receiver units are employed.

The solution, one receiver that works in many modes, is called a multimode receiver (MMR). Basic types of MMRs are a 3-mode ILS/MLS/GPS and a hybrid LORAN-C/GPS receiver. More about these can be found in later sections on aviation and marine devices.

Combined GPS/GLONASS Receivers

GLONASS transmits data over a different set of frequencies than GPS. Most GPS receivers translate only GPS signals, and GLONASS receivers its signals, but devices or plug-in boards that work with both GPS and GLONASS signals are available. Unique receiver designs allow combinations of GPS and GLONASS measurements made across a wide range of frequencies. A single antenna picks up signals from whichever satellites of both systems are in view to obtain optimal positioning information.

By doubling the number of candidate satellites available at any time, the probability of sighting a suitable number for accurate readings is increased. A user tapping into both systems is likely to pick up signals from well over five satellites at any one time. This is especially important in dense, urban areas or in obstructed environments where only a relatively small portion of sky is visible. Levels of accuracy are better, too, for both positioning and velocity.

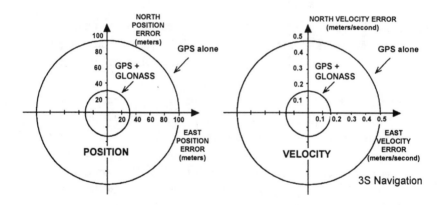

For aviation, in order to maintain system integrity, a GPS receiver must have a special channel supported from the ground — called the GPS Integrity Channel (GIC). Another unit, a Receiver Autonomous Integrity Monitor (RAIM), is installed in the aircraft to work with it. To use RAIM features with combined GPS/GLONASS, a special integrated receiver is necessary.

Software commands reconfigure the receiver to run different kinds of applications. Channels can be used for solely-GPS, solely-GLONASS or combined navigation, and they may also be used for calibrating ionospheric variations or determining vehicle orientation.

GPS/GLONASS receivers are still relatively expensive for the casual consumer, although they represent a good return on investment for professionals. Initial pricing for the most basic ones from Ashtech, Inc. was $6,000-$10,000. Other manufacturers are active in the market, as well, and 1997 prices range from about $6,000 to $50,000.

Waypoints

Waypoints are coordinates for predetermined positions (expressed in degrees, minutes and seconds of latitude and longitude). Their establishment and use are important for all types of navigation using GPS. Like football yardline markers or flags along ski trails, these virtual markers help people define and report progress along routes.

Marine and aviation waypoints have long been noted on charts and in logs, but waypoints being used with GPS receivers are registered electronically. They can be obtained from a number of sources:

- The receiver itself may hold a permanently stored database of essential waypoints, such as coordinates for airports, entrances to main highways, public buildings, U.S. Coast Guard stations, national parks, etc. Data in these differ according to the purposes or areas for which the receiver is intended. Prestored databases may need to be updated regularly. Some are easily done, but others may require that the receiver be returned to the vendor.

- Specialized databases or map datums provide coordinates for regions as small as neighborhoods or as large as the world. They can be purchased for most GPS receivers with options for updates or retrieved by computer from national or international databases and loaded into the receiver.

- A user can create his or her own database (file) of waypoints. Almost all receivers allow the entry of new groups of waypoints along routes.

Creating & Storing Waypoints

If the waypoints needed are not already provided, a person can create "user-defined" ones in a number of ways:

- Using the keyboard of a receiver or computer, a person can type in the exact numbers for longitude and latitude (if known) for a specific place and assign it a name.

- Someone wishing to establish the current location as a waypoint can simply assign a name and press a "load current position" button on the receiver. Its processor will then calculate and enter coordinates for the user's location.

Waypoints can be stored in a number of ways:

- A register of waypoints can be stored electronically in the permanent memory of a receiving device.

- Additional waypoint data may be stored in portable form such as on a compact disc (CD), on data cards or on disks.

When in use, a receiver "memorizes" positional coordinates (and, sometimes, names) for any location pinpointed by the user as a waypoint and stores them, usually in the order entered. Some receivers, however, allow sorting by alphabetical or numerical order.

GoTo & Routing via Waypoints

"GoTo" (or "To") is a simple but very important feature of a GPS receiver — and probably the most used. It accepts a user-defined waypoint as a destination and then methodically guides the user there.

A hiker, for example, first enables the GoTo function, enters a waypoint's name, code or coordinates to designate it as a destination and then follows directions as displayed by the GPS device. The same route can be used backwards for returning to a point of origin.

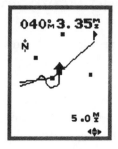

Magellan

A screen display generates progress reports, letting a user know how far away the waypoint is and how closely the path is being followed. Many receivers show steering maps with arrows pointing in the direction the user should move.

Magellan

Others display some sort of horizontal bar or ruler by which a user can also tell if he or she is off course and by how much.

The routing function of a GPS receiver is an even more powerful aid to navigation. A typical GPS route is a sequence of waypoints — perhaps 10 for the casual user. They are entered as a sequenced list into the receiver's memory.

As each specific waypoint is reached, the routing feature updates itself and automatically proceeds to guide the user over the next segment — over and over, until the final destination is reached.

Apollo

The order in which the program processes the waypoints is the exact order in which a user (or a program) has listed them. It does not optimize routing nor display anything but what is listed. Route efficiency, thus, is up to the user.

Retrieving a waypoint or route can be done in different ways, depending on the receiver and how it is used. The most common way to retrieve a waypoint or designate it as a new destination is by entering its assigned name or selecting it from a pull-down menu.

Receiver Susceptibility to Interference

GPS receivers are not immune to interference by persons who deliberately crowd the airwaves with noise to thwart others from obtaining clear signals. Such electronic attack from external sources is called jamming.

Equipment designers can incorporate different levels of jammer-to-signal (J/S) tolerances into the receiver and into the antenna systems so that they do not lose track of the satellites when jamming is directed at them. Performance testing and determination of the ability of a receiver/antenna system to withstand jamming efforts are especially important for GPS-guided military equipment.

Spoofed Receivers

In addition to being susceptible to jamming, a receiver can be "spoofed," in other words, technologically duped into processing fake signals and misrepresenting the results. Users being spoofed are unaware that the fixes they are obtaining are counterfeit and may wind up far off their intended course.

Receivers for standard positioning services (SPS) that access coarse acquisition (C/A) code are more vulnerable to counterfeit signals than military units for precise positioning services (PPS). Military P-code is less susceptible (but not impervious) to being spoofed.

Radio-Frequency Interference

Interference is not necessarily hostile; much of it is unintentional. Some commercial receivers exhibit low thresholds for interference from in-band continuous wave (CW) signals; some are susceptible to out-of-band signals.

Vehicle and hand-held receivers are highly vulnerable to errors caused by reflected signals and poor geometry in so-called "urban canyons," streets crisscrossing high-rise buildings. Users often learn ways of minimizing these errors, e.g., manipulating the antenna, obtaining differential corrections directly or from radio broadcasts or using a correction received from an area base station. Combining GPS with Dead-Reckoning (DR) also helps in such areas.

Very-high-frequency communications and instrument landing system (ILS) receivers have been vulnerable to interference by FM radio equipment — as evidenced by dire FAA warnings found on even household products that their use may cause interference. Studies are now being made to determine potential interference hazards to GPS receivers from such things as TV-station broadcasts. Hopefully, regulators will set realistic minimum performance standards for GPS receivers, especially for those installed in aircraft.

Atmospheric- & Sun-Induced Consequences

Atmospheric properties vary with latitude and the different seasons of the year. These conditions and others have consequent effects on GPS signals passing through from space and, thus, on the precision obtainable by receivers on earth.

Ions

The performance of a GPS receiver is especially influenced by what goes on 50-250 miles above the earth, in the ionosphere, where free electrons are generated by the sun's ultraviolet rays. Signals passing through this portion of the atmosphere are spread by the ionized gas molecules, causing a time delay before they are picked up by a receiver on earth. Also, the extent of the influence of the ionosphere on signal transmission varies both with the time of day or night and with latitude. For example, the depth of the layer changes from day to night, affecting the density of ions there.

Computer software in the receiver can measure the effect of the spread as a fix is being obtained. However, because the versions that do this use both L1 and L2 frequencies, a dual-frequency receiver is needed. Consumer SPS receivers that track only the L1 signal can compensate to some extent for ionospheric delay by using predicted values. These are included in navigation messages sent down with GPS signals as part of the satellite almanac.

Water Vapor

Air contains many substances other than gases — most importantly, water vapor, either liquid or solid. Wrapped around small, floating particles of sea salt and dust, it forms fog, clouds, rain, hail, sleet and snow. All of these affect signal transmission.

Concentrations of water vapor in the troposphere delay GPS signals. This "wet delay" causes major errors in accuracy along the path of satellite transmissions — up to 2.4 meters for a satellite directly overhead and up to 25 meters for a satellite near the horizon.

An instrument called a radiometer can be pointed at each satellite to measure how much water vapor exists along its line of sight. Its effects can then be calculated and corrections made.

Ice Clouds & Snowfall

During periods of ice-cloud and snowfall precipitation, there may be large discrepancies between readings from two receiver sites. Such disproportionate differences may be due to the localized nature of many snow storms or to a nonuniform distribution of ice clouds. Researchers are currently conducting tests to determine just how severe the ice-cloud or snow situation must get before accuracy is seriously compromised.

Rare Air

Also, under most conditions, air at lower altitudes is dense and may be considered a continuum. Air at higher altitudes may be so rare, however, that it does not obey the same dynamics of physics. Calculations for flight have to take these factors into consideration.

Sun-Induced Variations on Time

Converting the frequency of radio signals, particularly those involved in the transfer of time, is dependent on a clock-sun-earth orientation. So, sun-induced variations can affect the measurement and transfer of time as reported by satellites in orbit. Specific methods (with descriptive names such as Very-Long-Baseline-Interferometry) are used to compensate for them.

Choosing a Receiver

There are significant differences among GPS receivers and components, and there are many types of units available in every price range. For all but the very casual user, however, bargain purchases can turn into nightmares — the antenna may be shoddy, the internal timing mechanism may be maladjusted, or the unit may not work properly with other devices.

Before buying, a person should carefully decide how he or she wants to use the unit and what degree of accuracy or ease of use is necessary. It is also important to decide what a receiver will not be needed for — to eliminate the added costs and complexity extra features entail.

Assessing Requirements

If you intend to use the GPS receiver primarily for recreational or casual use, such as for trekking or hunting, the features you would look for would include portability, small size, light weight, low cost and low power requirements.

Because signal acquisition depends on a line of sight with the satellite, you should also ask how fast the unit can reacquire signals. Moving under tree cover or using GPS from blinds requires that a receiver pick up a new satellite as soon as possible after losing one so that there are always at least four. These features are important.

For outdoor hiking and casual use, however, you would not require a high-accuracy unit, nor would you need one that determined velocity accurately — unless you could maintain a speed almost as fast as Roger Bannister's 4-minute mile. The speed required to overcome errors introduced by Selective Availability is about 12 miles per hour. (There is also a speed above which receivers do not work.)

Likewise, for use with a car or truck, you would want a receiver that is small and relatively inexpensive. You would probably also want it to be differential-ready and able to determine velocity.

Marine users would require the above features, too, but in a sturdy, waterproof casing that would float and, perhaps, transmit a "man overboard" signal after being submerged. Boaters may also want their device to connect to others already installed; so, interfaces, both software and hardware, must be available.

Rugged casing and portability are also required for military field units. These receivers should, whenever possible, be capable of receiving P-code and, if security-cleared, encrypted Y-code. Military receivers may also require features for velocity and interfaces for varied output.

For pilots, aside from the obvious need for accuracy, the most important features are reliability and signal integrity. Aviators need to know that their equipment provides high precision all the time. GPS provides this availability — 99.98% of the time. Aviators' receivers must also be able to filter out erroneous signals or interruptions in signaling. This can happen when a receiver's "lock" on a satellite is lost or the power level fluctuates. Airborne receivers must be able to make use of aviation databases and determine velocity. If aviation units are not differential-ready, they should be upgradeable, at least.

GPS receivers used for surveying and mapping purposes have unique data-handling, accuracy and output requirements. Accuracy is more important for these applications than is the time required to get a position fix; so, if there is a choice, users opt for accuracy. Also, because field units take a beating, they may need replacing every few years; so, affordability is to be considered.

Troubleshooting

As you use your GPS equipment, you will become familiar with the limits and nature of its displays and output. Eventually, you will become astute in recognizing the signs of malfunction. You may be alerted by very large errors, absence of output or data that make no sense. Each of these may be caused by a number of conditions.

Very large errors may be caused by the space-based segment of GPS being "down" — unlikely, but possible — or by Selective Availability. They may also be caused by trouble in the ionosphere, a high HDOP or loss of signal (e.g., from tree cover on land or waves at sea).

Smaller errors may be attributed to atmospheric disturbances or, simply, the antenna being blocked or shadowed by an obstruction. Corrupt data are usually caused by signal interference, from a nearby source, perhaps, or by a faulty power supply.

If a device does not work at all or gives no output, an instinctive first look would be towards the GPS constellation itself (again, an unlikely culprit). The more probable cause would be the receiver antenna. It may have fallen, its view may be obstructed, or its cable may have been disconnected or damaged.

Checklist for Choosing a GPS Receiver

Everyone's way of using a device differs — consider how many two-finger typists you know. Some people prefer pushing buttons to spinning control knobs; some like to type. The display, controls, graphics and screen are the means by which you will be working with the device; so, check each one of them out.

No one receiver has all the options. Match what each offers to your needs for the best overall operation.

The wisest first investment in GPS, therefore, is that of your time. Think about how the receiver is going to be used, which features are required and which are not only "cool" but add real value to the purchase. A good idea when comparing receivers is to use a checklist like the one on the following pages.

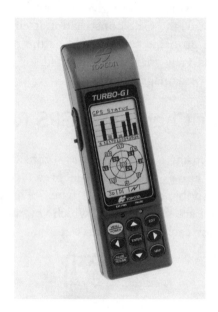

GPS RECEIVER CHECKLIST: THINGS TO CONSIDER

BASICS	
Price	→ your budget → intended use → added value of features
Upgradeability	→ "differential-ready" or "will work with WAAS" → if upgradeable, what must be purchased
# Satellites Tracked	→ the more the better
Measured Accuracy	→ horizontal and vertical → range limits (for velocity, altitude, pressure, etc.)
Measurement Units	→ statute, nautical or metric; interchangeable
Time-to-First Fix (TTFF)	→ receiver-dependent → application's need or personal tolerance
Rate of Updates	→ differing safety-threshold rates for marine, air, etc.
Memory Capacity	→ operability without batteries (minutes? hours?) → important if unit is to be stored or if owner is forgetful
Power Consumption, Battery Life	→ how long operable in continuous mode → how long operable in energy-saving mode → type and number of batteries needed → power plug, DC connection
Signal Reacquisition	→ ability to regain new fixes after interruption or loss → fast, moderate or slow
PHYSICAL	
Size & Weight	→ whether portable, pocketable or only luggable → fits on dashboard or with other instruments
Antenna	→ patch or quadrifilar → active or passive → remote or attached → mountability → sturdiness
Mounting Apparatus	→ antenna → unit itself (control panel, dashboard, etc.) → suction cup, fixed mount, Velcro
Physical Case	→ sturdiness → waterproof, water-resistant, flotable, etc. → carrying strap, accessories
Tolerance Levels	→ severe environments, pressure, temperature, humidity, shock, vibration, air content, salt

GPS RECEIVER CHECKLIST: THINGS TO CONSIDER

INTERFACES Display	→ how easily screen is read or output is delivered → for marine or aviation use, display readable in sunlight or glare → test with eyeglasses or goggles if usually worn → orientation — north-up, track-up, true north, magnetic north, bearing, etc.
Interface to Various Devices	→ availability of hardware (cables and slots) → availability of software for radio (VHF, CB), autopilot, fishfinder devices, etc.
Map Datum & Database Interfaces	→ conversion features if necessary → local datums optional or required → WGS-84 accepted
OPERATIONAL Waypoints	→ capacity and ease of manipulation → numbering, naming, adding, ordering and storing → route, segment and flight plan capacity
Dynamics (Speed & Velocity)	→ low, medium or high-velocity → effective accuracy range (e.g., 12 mph or 100?)
Distress Signals	→ man overboard, emergency rescue, SOS
Mode Switchability	→ hiking/survey, land/mobile/marine, air/land, etc.
Resistance to Radio Interference	→ reflected signals in urban canyons, for example → adjustability of antenna
Resistance to Accuracy Degradation	→ conditions (forest canopy, built-up areas, tunnels) → range limits
Unique Usage	→ changing regulations (for aviation, e.g.) → agency standards (cryptography, multifrequency, language, metrics, etc.) → need for acoustic or "heads-up" display
AFTER YOU BUY Documentation	→ complete, understandable instructions for use
Ease of Updating Databases	→ updates via data card, computer or dealer → conditions if unit must be sent to dealer or manufacturer for updating
Customer Support, Warranty	→ manufacturer's guarantee → dealer reputation → help contact numbers → response times

3

DIFFERENTIAL GPS
DGPS

People using nonmilitary receivers and Standard Positioning Service (SPS) can achieve accuracies equal to or even better than those offered by the military's Precise Positioning Service (PPS). The trick to this is a workabout called the Differential Global Positioning System, or DGPS, developed by the U.S. Coast Guard to augment Standard Positioning Service (SPS).

Essentially, Differential GPS is an accuracy booster to fixes derived from civilian signals. The "differentials" themselves are corrections broadcast via maritime radiobeacon that can be used to offset the imprecision of Coarse/Acquisition code. In order to pick up the signals, however, a receiver must have DGPS capability. This means that it must either be a DGPS unit from the start or be "differential-ready" and upgraded with a differential beacon receiver and antenna.

The current DGPS service is run by the Coast Guard Navigation Center (NAVCEN), which sends signals from two control centers and about 50 remote sites. There are no restrictions on establishing and running DGPS facilities; so, similar ones can be built locally and by others. DGPS will eventually become available worldwide.

Within range of a DGPS station, even nonmilitary users can determine their positions on earth to within a few meters or, in some cases, a few centimeters. Accuracy improves primarily with proximity to the station but also with better equipment.

Within 100 kilometers of a fixed reference station, conventional DGPS usually produces accuracies of 1-3 meters. Users within 1000 kilometers report accuracies from 2-10 meters. Surveyors and other professionals also employ a special technique called carrier-phase comparison to achieve results within centimeters.

All DGPS reference stations merely augment what already works. Neither Precise Positioning Service (PPS) nor Standard Positioning (SPS) Service requires a Differential GPS reference station.

How Differential GPS signals and services are denoted as compared to other types is as follows:

MILITARY				
PGPS	(PPS)	=	Precise (military) GPS signals	P-code
P+AS GPS	(P+AS)	=	Precise GPS + Anti-Spoofing	Y-code
CIVILIAN				
SGPS	(SPS)	=	Standard (civilian) GPS signals	C/A-code
DGPS	(DGPS)	=	Differential GPS signals	

How Differential GPS Works

Differential GPS uses a base (or "reference") station for which precise longitude, latitude and altitude have already been determined. Unless the actual plates of the earth beneath them shift, these numbers remain constant. So, any difference between these precise readings and those obtained from standard-service GPS constitutes the adjustment that must be made to make them more accurate.

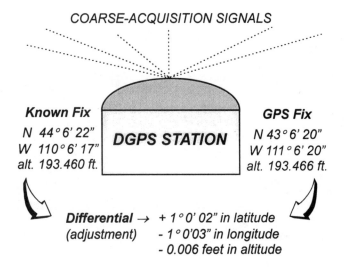

COARSE-ACQUISITION SIGNALS

Known Fix

N 44°6' 22"
W 110°6' 17"
alt. 193.460 ft.

DGPS STATION

GPS Fix

N 43°6' 20"
W 111°6' 20"
alt. 193.466 ft.

Differential → + 1°0' 02" in latitude
(adjustment)   - 1°0'03" in longitude
                 - 0.006 feet in altitude

Collective or Satellite-Specific Correction

Differentials can be obtained in either of two ways, collectively or specific to satellites in view. In the first way, the base station receives standard C/A code signals from a number of satellites in view. It compares the results to its known, precise coordinates. The signals are refined, after which the base station broadcasts a collective correction for each measurement to users. A user's receiver, which has already come to a conclusion regarding position, adjusts that accordingly to display more accurate positioning.

Results are optimal if the station and user are tuned in to the same set of satellites, but they needn't be to work. Improvements will just not be as precise with fewer shared satellites.

Distributing corrections can be done another way, too, via broadcasts of differentials for individual satellites. Instead of calculating and sending an overall correction, a DGPS station transmits a differential for each satellite in view. The satellite-specific corrections are picked up and stored in a user's DGPS receiver before any calculations are made — in effect, serving as an early-stage filter for signals arriving from each satellite. Thus, the receiver works with more accurate individual numbers to produce more accurate combined results.

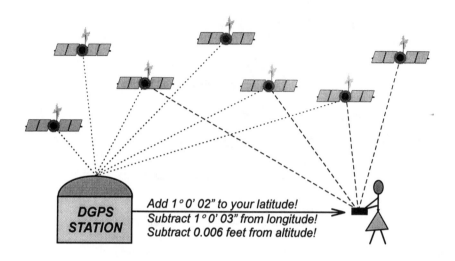

Instantaneous or Delayed Transmission

Differential corrections may be sent immediately (on an ongoing basis) to aircraft, vehicles or ships that need the information for "real-time" navigation. For users who need only one-time accurate positioning (surveyors and mapmakers, for example), corrections may be stored at a base station for later retrieval and what is called "post processing." Costs and equipment for each type of service differ; real-time transmissions are generally costlier.

Multi-Site or Networked Reference Stations

Results achieved through multi-site reference stations and networked reference facilities are superior to those achievable from ordinary, single-station DGPS. Just as accuracy improves with the number of visible satellites available for fixes, so does it improve when networked DGPS stations or internetted stations contribute integrity control to the process.

DGPS services to cover the continental U.S. would require more than 500 strategically placed monitoring stations. Depending on the types of communication links installed and applications used, costs for each may run from $10,000 to $200,000 plus yearly maintenance.

Government-Sponsored DGPS

Though owned by the U.S. Department of Defense, Precise GPS is not available to other government agencies. Like private citizens, civilian branches of the government must work around selective availability. They are turning to Differential GPS as a solution. Task forces have been set up to coordinate interagency efforts, specifically, to enable different nonmilitary agencies to share information, equipment and facilities — and to leverage the cost to taxpayers. A strong focus is on the development of standards so that different kinds of DGPS applications can use the same equipment.

The Coast Guard is developing its large-scale system, and the Forest Service began in 1988 to establish stations for management of forest resources. In 1991, the Federal Aviation Administration (FAA) started with a $500 million effort for improvements to aircraft navigation and landing technologies. The Department of Transportation (DOT) and the Environmental Protection Agency (EPA) are also actively pursuing DGPS as a solution to their need for improved accuracy. A table of permanent DGPS stations of various U.S. government agencies is presented below. Equipment and facilities installed in one place for six months or longer are considered permanent.

FAA Network & Augmented Systems

An augmentation network of 734 DGPS stations covering the mainland U.S. is being set up by the Federal Aviation Administration (FAA). Although primarily intended to cover aviation and marine agencies, other government agencies will be allowed to use them.

The FAA intends to distribute DGPS to these users through two systems, one for wide-area coverage and one for local-area coverage. They are referred to as either wide- and local-area augmentation systems (WAAS & LAAS) or wide- and local-area differential global positioning systems (WADGPS & LADGPS). Both mean the same.

PERMANENT DIFFERENTIAL-GPS STATIONS[*] U.S. GOVERNMENT AGENCIES		
Sponsoring Agency	**#**	**Principal Types of Applications**
Federal Aviation Administration	**734**	en-route flights; precision & nonprecision approaches; terminal activities
Coast Guard	**63**	marine navigation; harbor & harbor approaches
Army Corps of Engineers	**36**	buoy placement; dredging activities
Bureau of Land Management	**27**	surveying/mapping property; gathering geographic data; fire-fighting support
Forest Service	**26**	surveying property; mapping roads, trails & water
Environmental Protection Agency	**5**	environmental monitoring; pollution & contamination metrics; surveying & mapping wells, landfills
National Oceanic & Atmospheric Administration	**5**	surveying & mapping U.S. waters; gathering spatial data for geographic use
Geological Survey	**2**	detection of earthquake-fault movement
St. Lawrence Seaway Development Corporation	**1**	buoy placement

* adapted from U.S. government publication GAO/RCED-94-280

Eventually, wide-area and local-area augmentation systems will be used for all phases of flight throughout the United States. According to an FAA timeline, establishing GPS and wide-area augmentation as the primary and then sole-means navigation system (replacing all others) may take until 2010. Decommission of conventional systems will begin in earnest in 2005.

Since the FAA and the aviation industry have invested a lot in WAAS, a problem for both are potential losses in safety and costs if the DoD, citing security reasons, ever barred use of the system. Concerned European designers are developing separate augmentation and overlay systems. They are, however, expected to be compatible with U.S. GPS systems.

WAAS — Wide-Area Augmentation System

As its name implies, the Wide-Area Differential Augmentation System (WAAS or WADGPS) is meant to augment Standard Positioning Services over wide areas. It encompasses a $500-million network of stations to measure and transmit DGPS corrections via satellite. WAAS-distributed differentials reinforce the availability, accuracy and integrity of signals over a wide area.

Of the 734 permanent FAA stations, 33 are slated as wide-area DGPS stations. Each of these base stations consists of one main unit and two backups — seeming redundancies that are the key to WAAS reliability and its round-the-clock availability.

Differential corrections provided by WAAS increase the accuracy of Coarse/Acquisition signals. According to the FAA, WAAS will provide horizontal accuracies of about 3 meters and vertical accuracies of about 5 meters. These projected levels of accuracy for augmented systems are sufficient for most flights but not precise enough for Category-II and Category-III (and a few exceptional Category-I) precision approaches. The greater accuracies required by Categories II and III will be provided by local-area base stations. DGPS transmissions also reinforce system integrity by alerting users to possibly inaccurate signals from any of the satellites.

Each WAAS station (and back-up) collects positioning data from GPS satellites. The main station transmits these to 6 WAAS control stations (not to be confused with the military Master Control Station in Colorado). These control stations, in turn, transmit corrected signals to as many as nine geostationary satellites (not GPS ones). These satellites broadcast the corrected signals for use by aviators or mariners equipped with receivers that can pick them up.

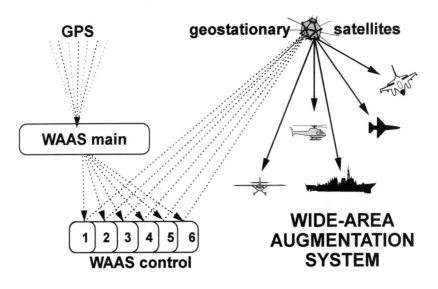

WAAS systems are still evolving, and testing is ongoing. Computer models of hypothetical, continent-wide WAAS configuration have produced anticipated results even better than FAA projections. Indications are that results obtained from a system of WAAS stations 400 kilometers apart approach those of Local-Area Augmentation Systems (LAAS) and do not depend on how close a user is to a reference station. (LAAS is described in later in this chapter.)

WAAS is expected to cover almost all Category-I precision approaches; so, monitoring requirements are stringent. Also, in order to be suitable for the wide service area, integrity monitoring must be done at each of several locations and combined — a bit more complicated process than that required by a single-station ILS.

Problems Implementing WAAS

WAAS is crucial to the Federal Aviation Administration's (FAA) goal of establishing GPS as the primary means of domestic navigation for civil aviation, but its implementation is subject to approval by the Department of Defense. Delays in getting this approval caused the FAA to postpone awarding early contracts, and milestones originally set for 1997 have had to be reset. In August 1995, an industry partnership of Wilcox, Hughes and TRW was named to supply a network of stations providing all en-route navigation and Category-I precision-approach systems for North America (and, possibly, other areas if regulatory agencies agree).

Indeed, WAAS may not be cleared for operational use before 1999. Once a contract is awarded, it is estimated that it will take 28 months for the contractor to develop and implement the system and for the FAA to approve and commission it. Also, it may require up to 28 months to develop the software alone. The task is complicated by several differential correction components in the WAAS message, each of which can be monitored separately, but for which integrity information must be correlated with an aircraft's position error.

Weapons Accuracy via WAAS

It seems that GPS reference points or reference stations, even if placed as far as 1000-2000 miles apart, can improve accuracies by as much as 15 feet, bringing it down to 25 feet. As few as two differential systems may even be effective.

The Department of Defense (DoD) is testing whether the accuracy of precision-guided weapons under development by the Joint Direct Attack Munitions (JDAM) program can be significantly improved with the use of portable WAAS reference stations. JDAM is a "tailkit" that can be attached to free-fall bombs, converting them to precision "smart" bombs. Because each costs about $33,000, and the armed services plan on buying almost 90,000 units, JDAM represents a significant investment for DoD in precision-guided munitions. Improving performance is a high-priority concern.

LAAS — Local-Area Augmentation System

The Local-Area Augmentation System (LAAS) is also referred to as Local-Area DGPS. Of the 734 FAA DGPS stations, 701 are slated as local-area base stations to provide closer-in corrected signals for precision landings in Categories I, II and III. LAAS stations are located at or very near airports since their signals can be picked up for only a few miles.

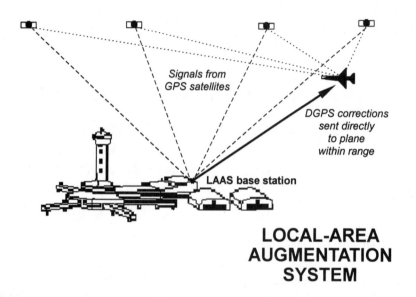

Signals from GPS satellites

DGPS corrections sent directly to plane within range

LAAS base station

LOCAL-AREA AUGMENTATION SYSTEM

Each local-area station requires about $1 million in equipment, a cost financed by local airport authorities. If national security allows WAAS stations to transmit more precise signals, fewer local-area base stations will be needed.

Users won't be able to migrate to the new LAAS system until both final determination is made of the local-area configurations and cost estimates are verified and defended. This is being done by the Federal Aviation Administration (FAA). One Local Differential Global Positioning System (LDGPS), however, has been used for precision navigation and cockpit display guidance in recent NASA testing of helicopter design, instrumentation and data acquisition.

U.S. Coast Guard DGPS Network

What the FAA is doing for air navigation, the U.S. Coast Guard is doing for marine and land navigation. Its network consists of 51 installed or planned base stations along the Atlantic, Pacific and Gulf of Mexico coasts of the U.S., around Alaska, along the shores of the Great Lakes and on the islands Puerto Rico and Hawaii. A joint Coast Guard/Army Corps of Engineers effort contributes 14 additional DGPS sites along the Mississippi and Ohio Rivers. Eventually, DGPS coverage will extend over most inland waterways.

Because work on the system has produced higher accuracies than the originally predicted 8-20 meters needed for harbor approach and navigation, the system is being put to use for other things, as well. The new applications include the use of GPS for positioning buoys, monitoring and controlling port traffic and conducting hydrographic surveys of the waters and currents of rivers and harbors.

Base-Station Sites

Each Coast Guard DGPS site has a main base station and a backup station. The base station receives signals from the GPS constellation via a special dual-frequency receiver. It then broadcasts corrected signals to marine users via radio beacons.

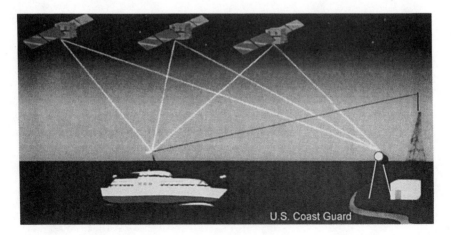

U.S. Coast Guard

Backup stations monitor system accuracy by running continuous integrity checks.   Logs of corrected signals are also stored in computers so that civilians and government personnel wanting the information at a later time have access to it.   Having the data available is particularly useful for mapping and surveying professionals who need the information for their work but don't need real-time fixes.

Regional Control Stations

In addition, each site is hooked up via communication links with one east-coast Regional Control Station (RCS) and one west-coast RCS and is remotely monitored by them 24 hours per day.   These regional stations also record and archive site data, assess a site's operational performance, detect system malfunctions or idiosyncrasies and provide operational status reports for all stations.   In the event of a national emergency, command and/or service changes will be put into effect through Regional Control Stations.

The anticipated working life span of the Coast Guard DGPS network is about 25 years, and its development cost has been estimated at $17.8 million.   Operations and maintenance of the system are expected to run about $5 million per year.

4

GPS ON THE ROAD & RAILS

Practical applications of the Global Positioning System for road and rail use are extensive. Very soon, travel on the four million miles of U.S. highways will be dramatically different from what we experience today. Indeed, with over 400 million cars and 130 million trucks worldwide, travel and commerce will change noticeably all around the world. GPS-provided precision and automatic mapping will provide motorists with increased options for arriving at their destinations quickly and safely.

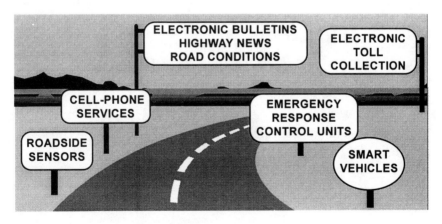

Control of railroad networks has become easier, too, by connecting GPS receivers and transmitters to sensors traditionally used along tracks to detect the presence of trains and conditions of the lines. Devices embedded in the railroad ties send locational data to train-based units. These, in turn, send the data to a central control station.

By increasing positional accuracy throughout the railroad network, the wide buffer leads that have always been required between trains can be minimized without increasing danger. More trains can be put into service when needed, freight cars can be filled to capacity, and track maintenance can be directed more effectively. The cost benefits of GPS-aided control and maintenance for a track system have been estimated at millions of dollars annually.

Vehicle Tracking & Navigating

Driver-controlled, in-vehicle navigation is one of the more visible ways that GPS is being incorporated into road transportation. The term "in-vehicle navigation" encompasses anything a driver does within the vehicle to get it from one place to another, including choosing a route, changing direction while in transit and responding to road and traffic conditions. Pre-GPS tools of in-vehicle navigation — maps, compasses, gyroscopes and back-seat drivers — remain as integral parts of GPS-aided navigation; so, drivers find it easy to migrate to the new technology.

A second approach using GPS is that of vehicle location and tracking, not by the driver but by an external control center. Fleet vehicles equipped with GPS receivers and a means of automatically transmitting the output to a central location provide management with the data for a dynamic moving map of their assets on the road.

The Department of Transportation is developing a master plan for an Intelligent Transportation System (ITS) based on GPS technology. Its aim is to raise the level of highway traffic management to that of air traffic. This and what is referred to as an Intelligent Vehicle Highway System (IVHS) are discussed later in this chapter.

A well-implemented tracking system incorporates all available technologies into soundly managed operations — vehicles equipped with locator systems (GPS receivers and externally mounted antennae), wireless radio communications systems (cellular phone) and sensors. Cellular phones may be hooked up to vehicle engine control systems, GPS transceivers (transmitter/receivers) and other data devices.

GPS receivers programmed for mobile applications provide almost immediate access to information on the position, speed and direction of travel of the vehicle. The information is analyzed, reconciled with a Geographic Information System (GIS) and displayed on moving maps. To complement these, monitoring equipment and control sensors will be installed along highways. More about these is presented later in "Intelligent Transportation Systems."

Smart Cars

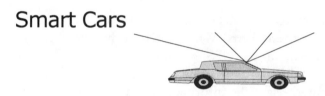

Change is happening smoothly and quietly as millions of travelers upgrade their present vehicles on individual bases. Affordable GPS car systems are now available, and many automobiles are factory-equipped with fancy-named satellite-aided navigation systems. One popular system uses GPS and a relay system to direct you to the nearest bank or allow you to unlock a car door if keys are left inside.

Many transportation and shipping companies have implemented locator technologies along their own routes for reasons of safety, cost effectiveness and time efficiency. As national highway systems are transformed — as planned — most cars and drivers will be ready.

A type of central monitoring feature incorporating GPS is being added to some vehicle-locating systems as a security measure against car theft and carjacking. Control centers track the vehicles and put drivers in voice contact via cellular phone with persons at response sites located around the country.

Vehicle-based sensors may include a logging feature that records data, tags them with exact GPS coordinates and feeds the information to stationary control units or collection devices along routes. Tracking vehicles in this way provides a more accurate snapshot of a vehicle's movement and relieves the operator of a vehicle from having to manually input data to a system. Thus, safety is heightened, stress is lessened and accuracy is improved.

Emergency-Response Features

Linking a car's GPS system with a cellular phone network allows both the reception of signals from the satellites and the subsequent transmission of location coordinates to a central location. Then, within minutes, local emergency-response services can be notified and dispatched to the site via a 911 call.

SOS buttons are mounted in vehicles so the driver can reach them but not accidentally activate them. When one is pushed in a cellular-phone area, the car-mounted GPS antenna receives the signals, pinpoints (and tracks) the location. A linked cell phone automatically calls the response unit, relays the information and puts the driver in voice contact with a person at the other end, who sees to it that local help is sent immediately to the scene.

Here and abroad, manufacturers are offering emergency-response features in many new models of cars. The marriage of GPS and cellular technologies is a logical, easy-to-achieve step to nationwide emergency coverage since about 90% of the populated areas in the U.S. have access to the cellular-phone network. Within the next few years, as parallel digital networks improve system capabilities, a subscriber base of 25 million customers is anticipated.

A typical vehicle tracking unit consists of a cellular transceiver, a modem, a multichannel GPS receiver and microprocessors. High-end models contain additional components. A typical SOS and/or tracking procedure is illustrated below.

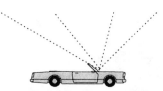

VEHICLE IN DISTRESS

- ACQUIRES GPS COORDINATES.
- SENDS SOS TO CONTROL CENTER.
- WAITS FOR HELP.

CONTROL CENTER

- RECEIVES SOS FROM VEHICLE.
- CALLS 911.
- RELAYS GPS COORDINATES OF VEHICLE.
- MAINTAINS VOICE COMMUNICATION WITH VEHICLE IF POSSIBLE.
- MONITORS RESPONSE.

911 or CAR SERVICER

- LOCATES NEAREST RESPONSE UNIT.
- ESTABLISHES COMMUNICATION.
- RELAYS COORDINATES OF VEHICLE.
- MONITORS RESPONSE.

RESPONSE UNIT

- RECEIVES INFO FROM CONTROL.
- PROCEEDS TO LOCATION.

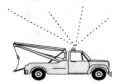

Typical Car Configuration for GPS

In-vehicle navigation systems can combine a number of advanced technologies to give a person more control over the driving experience. An effective in-vehicle navigation system includes GPS technology for precise locational coordinates, digital maps to track a vehicle's progress, digitized directories of information about and directions to local attractions or services and, perhaps, cell-phone connection and emergency-response features.

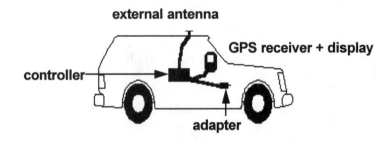

+ digital maps
+ digital information
+ cellphone
+ emergency SOS

Digital maps on plug-in cards or CD-ROMs are used to display roads, local regulations, exits on freeways, parks, airports, hotels, points of interest and local streets. Users may enter "waypoints" from which audible and visual directions can be produced.

Studies have indicated that the use of cell phones in cars increases the risk of accident four times for the duration of a call. It is presumable that other devices requiring manipulation are equally as risky. Thus, audio prompts are important so that a driver need not divert attention from the road en route. Set the volume low, initially, to avoid being startled the first time a booming computer-generated voice orders you around.

Rent-a-GPS-Aided-Car

Rental managers are now able to install GPS units in all types of vehicles — from golf carts to 18-wheelers — and monitor their fleet in real time without any voice communication. Each in-vehicle unit automatically sends its GPS-provided coordinates or locational data to a control center via 2-way radio or cellular network connection. An added advantage for fleet managers is that all information sent from a vehicle to the control center is logged and stored in the system's database, a valuable management tool since records can be retrieved for reference, analysis, cost assessment or, possibly, evidence in criminal or civil investigations.

On-board navigation systems with map displays are available in rental cars in many large U.S. cities for a few dollars extra ($6 in New York) per day. Their GPS locational coordinates and a gyroscopic dead-reckoning technology help direct customers to their destinations.

Mounted on the dashboard or on a flexible rod within arm's reach, the unit displays information and maps on a small LCD screen. Route-determination and mapping software are built into the system. (This author strongly advises drivers to go through the paces with instructions in hand before moving the car. Figuring it out "on the fly" is haphazard at best.)

Determining the Best Route

Hey, kid!
Let's make a right.
It'll be faster!.

The ability of a vehicle's navigation system to choose the best route from among many depends on its having a very detailed, precise geographic database and software that can match the pattern of the car's path with the road patterns stored in the system's computer.

The car's exact locational coordinates are available at all times via its GPS receiver, and these serve as a start point when a route-guidance feature is activated. A driver provides the destination, by either pointing to it on a map or typing in the name or coordinates. Based on current traffic patterns and road conditions, the system plots the most efficient route and displays directions on a screen map. Ideally, this is done while the car is stopped.

Infrared transmitters, placed along roadsides or at traffic signals, can be used as location designators. They can also be used to dispatch traffic information such as detours, construction, icing or accidents.

Gyroscope sensors are being tested for use in land-based passenger-car navigation, and results from tests conducted in France and the U.K. suggest that GPS be augmented with dead-reckoning (DR) capability for private cars used primarily in cities. Comparisons done with GPS alone vs. GPS with loosely- and tightly-coupled DR sensors, indicated that the most efficient and accurate results for close city driving would be obtained by the tightly-coupled system. The car's DR route-guidance software and map displays are integrated with a vehicle's GPS receiver unit and run by its computer.

Intelligent Transportation Systems

The U.S. Department of Transportation has plans to put highway traffic on a par with air traffic through the development of Intelligent Transportation Systems (ITS) based on GPS technology. The long-term project couples GPS navigation with both onboard and highway sensors, automatic mapping techniques and communication devices.

Also described as an Intelligent Vehicle Highway System (IVHS), the integrated system will make a significant contribution toward increasing highway safety and reducing the time it takes to respond to emergencies. Reduced congestion and reduced fuel consumption are among the benefits cited by proponents of the plan.

As a result of increasing DoT funding for IVHS, some technologies are already in place — for example, advanced traffic-management systems and electronic toll collection. Others are being developed and tested. Implementation would require vehicles with some features for autonomous operation — in other words, "smart cars."

Traffic Management & Control

Differential GPS (DGPS) is becoming one of the most practical ways of smoothing the flow of urban and rural traffic. With coordinates and timing established for routing controls and traffic signals within their districts, traffic engineers can evaluate areas of congestion or accident scenes and micromanage the flow of traffic around them.

Electronic tags that transmit the speed of commuter vehicles to a central station may be used to synchronize lights feeding into and following main arteries. Specially equipped probe vehicles can be put on the road to measure and transmit details of progress through traffic in real time to a central office. Data may also be routed for broadcast over highway advisory radio or display on electronic message signs over the highway.

Electronic Toll Collection

Methods previously intended to eliminate manual collection of tolls on highway systems have included infrared and radio-frequency systems and smart cards. Major highways are now being updated to electronic toll-collection systems (ETCs), and some cars are being fitted with gas-tank-mounted devices that work with the systems.

GPS is playing an increasingly important role in its implementation. Key components of an experimental toll-collection system in Germany are smart cards enhanced with GPS-receiver capabilities. These smarter cards will register the GPS coordinates of entry and exit points of a vehicle along a highway, along with fee schedules and payments that are already programmed into them. Like bank-debit cards, toll cards passing through (or passing over) a reading device would be debited according to the length and fee rates for the particular segment of highway traveled.

Initially, it may be more cost effective for public transportation and commercial vehicles to take advantage of electronic toll facilities than for passenger vehicles. The costs of fitting commercial fleets with the devices can be quickly leveraged since time, hassle and paperwork are drastically cut by any automation of the calculation and collection of fees and interstate tariffs.

Vehicle-Emission Control

One of the goals of the ITS is to help minimize the damage emissions from automobiles cause to the environment. Initial measurements of pollution can be made by coupling exhaust-emission sensors with roadside receivers. Locational and timing data can then be used with traffic patterns to provide alternate routing and to help identify offenders. Eventually, other types of sensors can be piggy-backed onto the highway network. These may be used to provide environmentalists, law enforcement or land managers with time- and position-tagged data as a public service or on a revenue-generating basis.

Vehicle-Location & Emergency Dispatch

Today's 911 emergency dispatch system is being extended through linkage with automatic vehicle location (AVL) technology to enable motorists to summon assistance to their exact location at the touch of a button. Because police, medical and roadside field units equipped with on-board GPS receivers can be tracked automatically, 911-dispatchers can know where all their emergency vehicles are located and in which direction they are heading.

After a target vehicle is located, route-guidance software can be used to provide best-route details for reaching the scene. Any car in distress, if equipped, can also be located and tracked.

The Federal Highway Administration (FHWA) sponsored tests to evaluate the effectiveness on safety and time of a combined GPS and two-way cell-phone system to help travelers in a 12,000-square-mile area of Colorado. Results may lead to the establishment of a commercial service center to provide roadside assistance.

Traveler Support

The planned ITS includes traveler information systems similar to services now provided by auto clubs. Trip and route planning, destination information retrieval and travel tips are to be accessible via computer or mobile-phone connection. These services are designed to complement on-the-road traffic advisories and emergency-response help described above. Travelers may also soon be receiving traffic reports and tips via receiver wristwatches, prototypes of which have been developed in Japan.

Advanced Public Transportation

An important segment of the overall plan deals with advanced public transportation systems. The goals of ITS in this area are to improve the efficiency and ability of buses, trains and cars-for-hire to respond to varying demands and to enhance safety.

Fleets can be monitored and directed around trouble spots, and backup vehicles quickly dispatched when passenger density increases. Moving map displays and digital databases help both supervisors and operators work efficiently. Riders benefit from quick response to their needs.

Problems Implementing an IVHS

The involvement of federal agencies and regulatory bodies as well as limitations on local and regional resources place administrative and financial burdens on those responsible for introducing IVHS technologies into their systems. Cooperation among private, public and governmental entities is essential. Liability questions arising from use of the technologies must be addressed, and levels of public acceptance must be ascertained.

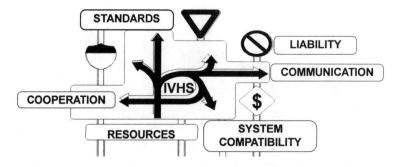

In addition, consensus must be reached on standards. An overall system architecture must be developed so that there is compatibility among the many IVHS technologies. This must be preceded by the establishment of a means for efficiently disseminating information about the benefits of such a system.

Trucking & Bussing

Tracking Truckloads & Cargo

Cellular communications for voice and data provide the trucking industry with a way of monitoring and communicating with vehicles and drivers. GPS receivers are now being added to these systems — Rockwell is equipping its on-board fleet computers with interfaces for holster-held GPS receivers.

Different kinds of companies are also joining forces to provide complete systems. Units built for the long-haul trucking industry integrate GPS receiver functions into cellular phones. These are hooked up to displays in central depots so that dispatchers can see all delivery vehicles positioned on maps on their screens.

Cargo containers in Singapore's ports are GPS-receiver-tagged. They are tracked by central monitors through the holding yards and beyond as they are moved, and the data logs of individual shipments do double duty as documentation for insurance and billing purposes.

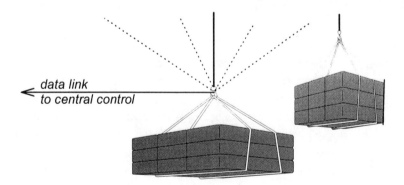

data link
to central control

Not only have shipping companies adopted tagging methods; the U.S. Pentagon's storage and assets are made "visible" to logistics engineers in the same way. Centrally situated managers keep track of all inventory using mapping software and graphic images.

Bus 2000, where are you?

Each of Scranton, Pennsylvania's 30+ Lackawanna County's buses has been upgraded with a GPS receiver, GPS antenna, mobile data terminal and radio transmitter. As each bus moves, its GPS data are automatically transmitted to the central terminal. Via moving map displays, fleet managers oversee movement of the entire fleet of busses at once. From a central vantage point, they can follow the progression of individual vehicles through the streets to assess various effects on particular routes.

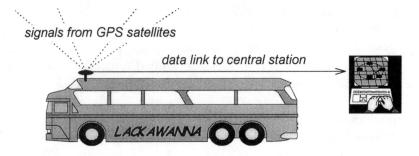

signals from GPS satellites

data link to central station

LACKAWANNA

Riding the Rails

Burlington Northern Railroad's GPS system is coupled with two-way communication devices that allow controllers to pinpoint the exact location of any of their locomotives and establish communication with the engineer. This real-time exchange allows a dispatcher to issue new instructions while the train is en route. Such interactive communication is particularly valuable for relaying to engineers the locations of potential problems such as track irregularities, damage or impact loads. It also allows detours for unscheduled pickups of freight or passengers so that cars can be run as close to full capacity as possible.

Signaling systems have always been used, and engineers have often combined these with detection systems for relatively good results. The early warning and accurate positioning possible with GPS widens the margin of safety and affords new ways to cut costs.

Old Way of Doing Things

The old way of detecting where trains are depended on energy sensors attached to circuits along the tracks. Train wheels passing over these would short the line, and the sensors would pick up the fall in energy.

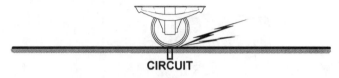

CIRCUIT

The system was good, but new rail designs and changing traffic patterns (e.g., almost nonexistent on some lines, heavily dense on others) warranted higher operational guarantees. Similar to the motivation for electronic toll collection, the track system required precise detection of the passage of a train through any segment.

Another method makes use of trackside transponders placed at specific locations. These respond to a passing train by transmitting a signal back to central control. Because of wheel slippage and other factors, however, this kind of setup is not exact and requires calibration on a regular basis.

GPS Determination of Location & Speed

GPS-equipped trains can now know their position and relate this to an accurate geographic reference (such as a Geographic Information System database or datum). The data can be transmitted back to a central control and to other trains.

Currently, portable systems of GPS receivers and accelerometers that sit on the floor of the car take frequent measurements of precise locations and the velocity of the car body at given intervals as it proceeds along the track. Slowly but surely, tracks and equipment are evolving from being isolated constructs into an integrated, interdependent system, the most important benefits of which are higher margins of safety.

How fast a train can be run safely over a stretch of track has long been determined by engineers through analysis, testing and experience. Now safety criteria for combined speed, track and car conditions can be GPS-tagged and programmed to alert engineers to potential line and car limits while en-route.

5

GPS OVER LAND

Personal Navigation

Lightweight, handheld GPS units, available for less than $200, are becoming standard backpack items for outdoor hikers and sports participants. The small, transistor-sized gadgets can be lifesaving, too. The Los Angeles County search-and-rescue teams use GPS to help locate lost non-GPS backpackers, accurately recording areas covered during search efforts.

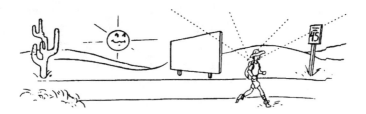

With combinations of GPS, virtual-reality acoustic displays and computerized databases, even visually-impaired persons can enjoy increasingly higher levels of navigational independence.

Walking, Hiking, Skiing

Jungle explorers, desert adventurers, rally drivers and hikers are among the more colorful beneficiaries of GPS technology. Although usually reluctant to forego the challenge of intuition, paper maps and a compass, they have welcomed GPS receivers and digital map displays. Combination devices offer the adventurer silent assurance he or she can stay on course, and they are fun to use.

Skiers equipped with GPS receivers can chart their own courses and, via cell phone or other type of transmitter, can communicate with others. One of the first publicized successes of GPS-aided tracking and self-location occurred in the early `90s, when a lone woman skied to the North Pole. Schoolchildren joined researchers in tracking her.

Swedish surveyors have collected three-dimensional GPS data in order to map out a 20-mile course for the Swedish National Cross-Country Championships. A reference station was set up at a known, exactly surveyed place in the vicinity, and a data link was established between it and the field equipment to transmit differentials. A telescoping antenna, which extended above the dense forest canopy that covered much of the trail, was mounted on a snowmobile.

What the field crew found out about the limitations of antenna software and hardware was interesting. Although their antenna could be raised to 9.4 meters (30+ feet), it did not work above 6.11 meters (~20 feet), nor did it work below 2.21 meters (~7.25 feet). It seems the antenna and receiver could be no more than 6.4 meters apart.

Six days' worth of data collection provided enough information about the course to draw up a topographic profile of the route. These helped entrants in the competition plan a strategy that would conserve their energy for difficult stretches. Before the race even started, each had not only a horizontal map of the course in mind but a vertical, topographical one, as well.

Aids for the Visually-Impaired

Sighted persons are not the only ones fortunate enough to benefit from GPS-provided time and locational signals. A sound-based navigational interface (such as the Personal Guidance System being built at Carnegie-Mellon University in Pittsburgh) can be utilized to give a visually impaired individual an acoustic view of his or her surroundings. The same data used to generate visual cues can generate high-quality, virtually-located sounds. GPS waypoints act as triggers, setting off the various sounds.

Acoustic displays are also becoming options for automobile systems so that drivers need not take their eyes off the road and are being introduced into control-tower operations to augment systems providing information to air-traffic controllers.

As the blind person carrying the GPS unit walks, the antenna picks up the signals from whichever satellites are available at the time. The receiver continually translates the signals into coordinates of latitude and longitude (corrected to within a few feet via local station), and the data are converted by a software program into sounds and words.

Surround-sound headphones deliver these cues so that they seem to come (thus, the "virtual" acoustic tag) from different directions. The headphones are fitted with an electronic compass that keeps track of how the person moves his or her head.

Specialized databases (GIS "infocards" or "infomaps") that voice-tag specific areas and neighborhood landmarks can be plugged into the receiver to work with the GPS signals. The satellite information is combined with local map information to determine, for instance, when a user is approaching an obstacle or specific building.

A user walking toward a bus stop, for example, may hear "Bus Stop M14" or "Express Bus Hamptons" grow louder as he or she nears and fade as he or she passes it by. It is important, however, that the user have ultimate control over how much and what kind of information is audible on any particular trip.

Destinations may be entered into some systems so that an optimal route can be dictated to the walker as he or she goes forth. Like the game giving "getting warmer" and "getting colder" hints to whoever is "it," the audio cues grow louder as a user approaches a marked location (a waypoint in navigational terms). Cues for the location of other waypoints may be fed into the background from other directions, as well — their faintness proportional to their distance from the user.

"M1 bus, 54th"

"library ... "

Customized units are available, but current models need to be made lighter and easier to use. An antenna, GPS receiver and a computer are carried by the blind person in a backpack, which is manageable but, weighing about 30 pounds (14 kilograms), still cumbersome. The total package presents a virtual acoustic display of the situation to the blind or visually impaired person.

Precision Farming

Drought and flooding are two of many variables with which farmers contend, and technologies that lessen the impact of the unpredictable are welcome within the farming community. In its move from military fields into the nation's agricultural fields, GPS has had such an impact. Precision farming — analyzing soil conditions and applying fertilizer as a function of location — now employs precision positioning provided by GPS.

Field Analysis & Distribution

GPS tools and techniques are used to collect extensive agricultural data. Factors such as soil acidity, contamination, infestation, drainage potential and density can now be pinpointed to exact locations. Exactly where and when certain conditions or infestations occur or change can be recorded and kept in a dynamically changing database.

Often not able to discern exactly which sections of land need custom attention, farmers may base land treatment on field averages or on the condition of less-productive sections. Without a means of microcontrolling, there is no recourse but to fertilize, spray or irrigate tracts of land as a whole. Consequently, many areas receive more fertilizer, insecticide or water than are needed to produce optimal growth — and the farmer pays for these. Likewise, under whole-tract farming, some areas do not receive enough to reach maximum growth — again costing the farmer in poorer harvests.

Today, however, increasing numbers of those who have traditionally relied on experienced "eyeballing" of fields and overall management strategies are reaping the benefits of GPS-aided precision farming. Being able to link up with satellite feeds to measure things such as crop yield and to collect data on soil content enables farmers to microcontrol the conditions of field sections as small as 1/100th of an acre. Collected data provide a meter-by-meter quantitative quilt of the fields, which then serves as a basis for intervention.

The learning curve may be steep for people just beginning to use site-specific techniques to measure and micromanage their acreage, but incentive is strong to stay on the farm, raise productivity and lower costs. Today's farmers are increasingly matching cash investments with investments in learning .

In order to pay off, however, a precision-farming system must be accurate within one meter and must be responsive to real-time commands. GPS technology satisfies these requirements. The GPS measurements are made and then matched to a standard Geographic Information System (GIS), which provides control points.

Fertilizing & Debugging: Functions of Location

Fertilizer can be applied as a function of location within a field. Soil variations are detected by sensor and mapped with GPS positions. The map is then stored electronically (via a computer program). Crop-yield data and field characteristics (soil type, salinity, etc.) are also given spatial coordinates and matched to field characteristics.

Based on these, a computer program can then generate a meter-by-meter working blueprint for adjusting variables that help the farmer optimize crop production and quality.   It can also generate a prescription map of fertilizer needs that guides a human- or robot-operated agrochemical applicator across the acreage, distributing fertilizers, bug sprays and/or water in paint-by-number fashion.

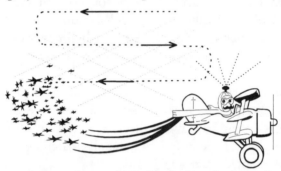

Yields increase as each section or individual plant bed receives exactly what it needs. Costs are decreased since the farmer doesn't overtreat large expanses of land on a par with the neediest.   Savings from distributed management of fertilizer have paid for an entire GPS system within two years of operation. By cutting down on the spread of chemical fertilizers such as phosphorous and potash, farmers also help the environment.

Yield Monitoring

This process — overlaying yield data with maps representing variable factors that affect crops — is called yield monitoring. As a combine moves across the acreage, an antenna picks up signals from the GPS satellites overhead and keeps track of the machine's precise locations.

As this is happening, the flow of harvested material is measured every few seconds as it passes through the combine.   Yield measurements can then be plotted on a simple graph or map, and contour maps showing growth patterns and variations in growth can be generated.

From all this information, a composite picture begins to form.   A farmer finds out exactly how much each parcel yields, which sections produce the highest amounts and which are losing money.   In addition, by correlating this information with data maps of soil conditions and other variables, the farmer has the tools to visualize exactly what is happening.

A lot more study has to be done in the area of yield monitoring.   For example, yield is affected by electromagnetic induction and a soil condition called water stress, but the correlation varies from year to year.   GPS coordinates provide the constants against which field technicians can match subsequent years' conditions.

Innovative measures are undertaken by soil engineers trying to harness the precision of GPS to their mapping projects.   Researchers at the University of Calgary in Canada time-synchronized a salinity meter to a GPS receiver via a personal computer.   They then dragged the whole system across their fields — at up to 25 miles per hour — on a nonmagnetic toboggan.   A computer tracked all data collected and assigned GPS coordinates to salinity measurements.

Customized Farm Equipment

Farming equipment is changing to accommodate new methods and technology.   Many new models come equipped with GPS receivers and accessories, and older models can be retrofit.   Costs will vary.

Field-installed options for combines may include sensors, a position receiver, a differential-correction signal, some sort of visual display and removable data-storage cards.   A mapping processor and software complete the package.

Within the decade, however, the cost of these options will fall, and many will be factory-installed. Top-of-the-line combines will have pre-mounted GPS equipment, soil-acidity sensors, mass-flow sensors, moisture sensors and planter population controllers.

Typical Ground & Aerial System Configurations

Many different components are available for assembling a system for ground and aerial measurement and disbursement of seeds and chemicals. Typical land and aerial systems consist of a computer with control and display units, a GPS receiver and antenna, a light bar to indicate if a machine or aircraft is veering off course and by how much, various cables and mountings, software and installation and operating instructions.

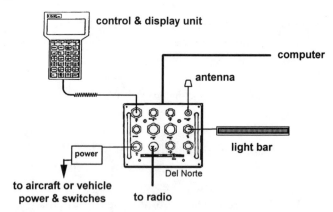

Other components can be added to the basic system to make it deliver more accurate measurements. The most important of these are a differential radio receiver and a differential antenna to receive and process differentials (corrections to overcome selective availability) broadcast via Coast Guard beacons or FM radio.

Robotic Field Hands

As mentioned before, robots needn't be anthropomorphic. They can be teleoperated farm machines programmed to navigate to precise, GPS-located sites to perform specific tasks.

Farm robots can be used to take soil samples, spread fertilizer or control irrigation valves. They can then be GPS-guided back to the barn or to another location.

An automatic air-drill planter can be microcontrolled to deliver material into the soil in amounts previously assigned to specific locations in a database. As the planting vehicle moves within the framework of GPS coordinates that constitute the area being planted, its GPS receiver tracks its whereabouts. A dashboard computer retrieves an application rate for the spot over which it is passing. This determines how fast the seeds are shot into the soil. Rate of flow commands can either be programmed in or be sent by a person controlling things from a central location.

Getting used to the medium is an important part of the investment a farmer must make in the shift to GPS-aided farming. The current inability of teleoperated systems to accurately relay degrees of resistance places a burden on users and programmers to adapt to how things get done in the new "environment." A trial-and-error approach is still necessary before unmanned machines can perform as effectively as farmer-driven equipment.

Software & Farmer-Support Services

A farmer must integrate all the information and new techniques with his or her personal management style and resources, and most are willing to retrain to stay in business. For some, though, the process may delay the realization of benefits from what is considered a substantial investment in the technology, discouraging many traditionally conservative farmers from opting in.

Thousands of Precise Measurements

Among the problems of GPS-aided farming is the great amount of time required to gather the thousands of observations needed for even a modestly sized (less than 100 acres) piece of property. Another is that occasional static or signals blocked by contours of the land may affect reception.

The market has responded, and farmer support services are becoming increasingly available, helping turn more farmers into enthusiastic GPS-ers. Data storage and information cards are available for use with most systems, and mapping software and services are relatively easy to obtain.

Mapping software contains data loggers, desktop data readers, cables, post-collection processing software and instruction manuals. Moving maps that can be viewed on a computer screen can also be acquired as options. Customized systems can be developed for specific pieces of land or for precise acreage measurements.

Mapping services include printed color maps illustrating rates of seed growth, the moisture content of the soil and the effectiveness of rotation or fertilization. Reports and spreadsheets can be generated from yield data, as well.

Pest Management Surveys

Of interest to agriculturists is certain parts of the world are surveys of swarms of insects that affect their crops. The 1985-86 infestation in the western states of the U.S. cost almost $23 million to control. Motivation is understandably high to generate maps of sufficient precision and quality for researchers to better their odds at predicting where the next swarms are likely to hit.

The Department of Agriculture and the Animal & Plant Health Inspection Service create and maintain grasshopper survey maps of areas vulnerable to the 400 known species of the pests. This has been done for many years (1944-1981 and 1985-present), and the cumulative picture has become a valuable tool for overall analysis of the effect the swarms have on a region over long periods of time.

Unfortunately, the data have not been accurate enough to help with predictions. Methods are now being upgraded with GPS tools and techniques. Part of the effort involves annual data-collection forays into the field for studying what is called "population dynamics."

At the University of Wyoming, reproduction of the insects and subsequent densities of infestation are observed and laboriously noted by hand on maps. Exact locations of high densities are defined as control waypoints. GPS was used to ensure the reliability of the data. Geographic Information System (GIS) software was used with a PC to process the data. Field maps and notes were then reconciled with templates of accurate state maps by comparing areas of vegetation, elevation or other observable features. Data gathered for a particular year were then superimposed on the templates.

Urban Patrol

The Los Angeles' Sheriff's Department uses helicopters equipped with computers, imaging systems, video and infrared cameras to patrol its jurisdiction of 3,200 square miles of varied terrain. A sophisticated moving-map display is connected to a GPS navigation receiver and reflects the locational information received.

A deputy in the cockpit's observer seat can access the system via keyboard and view the display (of video or graphics) on a backlit LCD screen. Objects and events sighted can be assigned coordinates as received by the GPS system and logged for Department purposes.

Car thief at waypoint 20! Roger!

In the Levee District of New Orleans (as in many large U.S. cities today), a display showing the exact GPS-derived locational coordinates for each independently moving vehicle in the police fleet are automatically updated in real time. The GPS-enhanced dispatch system not only provides more accurate positional data but is more time- and cost-effective than previous systems.

Rescue & Survival Systems

The U.S. military's laser terrain-profiling system has been enhanced with GPS to improve the precision of aerial photographs used with a survival radio system for locating personnel on the ground. In Tennessee, Erlanger Medical Center helicopters rely on GPS as a navigation aid to transport patients during bad weather. Other hospitals enlisting GPS for their helicopter ambulances include Minnesota's Mayo Clinic and the hospital and clinics of the University of Wisconsin at Madison.

Many automobile companies are offering packages for roadside help. Ford Motors' Roadside Emergency Satellite Cellular Unit (RESCU) includes GPS receiver and transmitter features that allow operators to turn it on by remote control. A stolen car or driver in distress can be tracked as it is driven or parked so that police can close in on it and attend to the emergency or make an arrest. (Also see "Vehicle Location & Emergency Dispatch" in Chapter 4.)

Drug Trafficking

One-third of the cocaine introduced into the U.S. comes through Caribbean nations, and drug traffickers' are increasingly using ships instead of planes for transporting the illegal goods. They are also adopting and using GPS and its related technologies to counter U.S. efforts to intercept shipments.

Unfortunately, this technology-abetted activity is happening at a time when the U.S. government's budget for enforcing the law has been cut and island nations are strapped for resources. As a result, the number and amounts of successful seizures of illegal drugs during the past few years has dropped.

Sending Machines on Missions

Teleoperation & Autonomous Navigation

When remote control or computer-programmed control is used with robot technology to get something done, it is called teleoperation or telemanipulation, i.e., driving or operating something by means of signals. Simply put, teleoperation is remote control without the box.

You, someone else or a computer program become the control, linked to the distant device by signals. The system is hooked up so that synchronized actions are made to happen in a remote location. Virtual-reality interfaces facilitate the use of some robot equipment, allowing a person at a distant end to feel "present" in the remote field if that is what is needed.

Autonomous operation is self-contained, independent of ground control, and digital flight-control systems are being integrated with GPS "engines" for UnManned Aircraft (UMA). Unmanned vehicles operating on test ranges throughout the U.S. use GPS as an adjunct to or replacement for radar, as well as a form of guidance.

Robots

Robots needn't be human-like; they can be any size, shape or material. As teleoperated machines, robots can be assigned to perform time-consuming or labor-intensive tasks and can be sent on dangerous missions.

Workaholics, robots can be programmed to navigate to precise, GPS-guided locations and do specific things on a time schedule, working, uncomplaining, until their gas runs out. GPS-guided machines can be harnessed into little armies sent to clear minefields, remove radioactive waste, gather things from the ocean floor or paint bridges. They can be programmed to navigate to a GPS-specific location and park themselves when done.

Because robot machines can be fitted with all kinds of sensors, receivers and measuring devices, they can also be used to monitor levels of light, noise, humidity and pressure. They can be used to measure liquid flows, from lava to raging rapids.

Armed with smoke detectors and heat sensors, robots can detect and investigate fires. If equipped with infrared and optical detectors, a robot machine can be used as a traffic monitor. Feedback devices and equipment-mounted cameras can alert real people of conditions that fall outside the parameters set by the computer program so that human intervention is possible.

A good deal of trial-and-error, however, is necessary before teleoperated machines can perform as effectively as directly-driven equipment. Current inability of robotic systems to accurately feed back degrees of resistance places a heavy burden on users to adapt to how things are accomplished in a remote "environment."

Getting used to the medium is an important part of the learning process for a user, and operators become better with practice. This is because responses by a mechanical robot can be disproportionate to (and usually more forceful than) responses delivered by a human-driven machine.

Teleoperated disproportion is why there is only one designated "driver" for critical-mission vehicles such as the Pathfinder on Mars, and it played a role in the little machine's trying to climb up Yogi Bear's side. A slight push on a lever by a remotely located human operator may be translated into a hefty shove at the remote site.

Random disturbances, too, such as magnetic effects from proximity to large metal objects often require that robot systems be recalibrated between tasks. So, people directing machines via GPS must anticipate a learning curve, especially when overseeing machines that operate in different positions (farm equipment, for example).

Robot Helicopter

Unmanned helicopters equipped with GPS receivers and connected by data link to a remote operator can be directed to fly to specific locations for surveillance or rescue. Since the robot's instrumentation always knows where it is, the GPS unit can interpret coordinates sent to it as a new destination and then be used to guide the vehicle there.

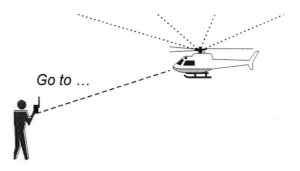

Go to ...

Earth-Moving Machines

GPS technology and computer-aided navigation systems are being applied to earth-moving machines (bulldozers) in the construction field. GPS is being used in all stages of construction, from initial surveys sites to accurate machine guidance and control. Drills can be positioned to drill holes with centimeter exactness, and shovels can be directly or remotely controlled to dig only so deep or so far.

The efficiency afforded by combining automation with GPS tools and techniques is translated quickly into higher levels of productivity and quality control. Field workers relieved of the labor-intensive stages of surveying are better able to concentrate on the actual construction process.

In a project called Computer-Aided Earth Moving (CAEM), the Department of Defense is cooperating with Caterpillar, Spectra-Physics Laserplane and Leica Corporations to develop a souped-up version of the old bulldozer.

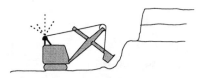

The goal of CAEM is an affordable, automatically controlled, GPS-guided piece of earth-moving machinery for the civilian sector. The model envisioned is expected to be faster and more accurate than manually-operated vehicles.

6

IN THE AIR

Over the past two decades, traffic-management technologies, satellite communication and advances in guidance equipment have brought about dramatic changes in how people fly. Communication and navigation now span oceans, and tracking and surveillance are more accurate. Windshear detection systems, high-speed data links for air-traffic control, virtual cockpit simulators and advanced landing systems have contributed significantly to air safety and efficiency.

GPS has prompted aviation's latest big change, making it possible to further raise the platform of aviation safety and deliver even better flight efficiency, capacity and cost advantage. Affordable GPS devices extend the benefits of the technology to everyone — private and corporate, military and civilian. Accurate GPS positioning is relevant not only to an aircraft's navigation but also as a safety feature to warn operators of potential collision. A pilot equipped with a GPS receiver and special type of radio can coordinate with other similarly-equipped aviators in the vicinity without have to rely on ground control. Each pilot ascertains the exact location (as determined by the GPS receiver) for his or her aircraft and broadcasts it (and its identity) to others nearby.

If there are many aircraft in one area, however, communications broadcast at regular intervals (every half-second, perhaps) may collide with one another, but an innovative technique developed at M.I.T. promises to minimize the confusion. Called "squittering," it involves sporadically timing very quick announcements over a particularly robust (and wide) radio channel. By broadcasting quick messages at random intervals, the chance of information getting through to the others is greater. More detail is given about this later in the chapter.

Flight Fundamentals

Promoting Safety

The Global Positioning System was first useful as an adjunct improvement to the safety factor of other navigation systems. Standard GPS is approved for nonprecision landings and is widely used as a backup to Omega and inertial systems. As differential facilities become more available and DGPS is approved as a sole means of navigation for precision landings, it will, ultimately, replace everything else.

Most existing types of ground equipment, expensive to build and maintain, will also be rendered obsolete. Thus, the existence, accuracy and reliability of GPS are opening up whole new venues for developing future air-navigation systems — and a unique window of opportunity to establish a worldwide standard for civil aviation.

Approach & Landing Areas

Approaches and landings are categorized by the International Civil Aviation Organization (ICAO) in ascending order of difficulty — Categories I, II and III (also denoted CAT I, II and III; Categories 1, 2 and 3 or Cat 1, 2 and 3). Increasingly higher levels of accuracy are required for each type of approach, and very specific guidelines apply for each. The objective of an accurate GPS navigational system is to enable precision approaches, missed approaches and departures for all three categories, with an overall aim of improving operational procedures and safety. How this is being accomplished is described later in this chapter.

Approach and landing areas include the length of the final approach segment plus its tolerance allowance. For nonprecision civilian use, the length does not usually exceed 10 nautical miles, and the ideal length is five nautical miles. The width of the approach area is usually one nautical mile each side of the course until the last stage, when it is narrowed down (sometimes to only as far as is visible).

Flight Rules

Visual Flight Rules (VFRs) apply to approaches and landings in which the pilot can see the runway. Almost all aviation receivers, including standard GPS, can be used for visual flight landings. No approval is necessary for their use. Instrumented Flight Rules (IFRs) are in effect for any landings not meeting VFR minimums. They require approval for all equipment used during the for approach and landing phases of flight. Thus, GPS receiver devices, too, must be installed according to specification and "IFR-Approved" before they can be used.

Instrument approaches can be even further enhanced by the emergence of vision systems designed to work with installed GPS devices. GPS-obtained positional data are combined with visual-sensor data to compensate for motion and correct radar images and image registration.

Other Classification Criteria

Other criteria also apply to the classification of landings. If conditions (such as terrain or runway configuration) dictate that an aircraft descend along a specific electronic slope, it is considered a precision approach, requiring communication with a ground-based system. Integrity — whether a system gives split-second warnings of failure — is especially important for precision landings.

If no slope requirements are in effect, the pilot is given directions to maneuver the aircraft into a safe "plate" position. From there, the aircraft is brought down according to standard instrument procedure — a nonprecision approach and landing.

The availability of a navigation system is another critical factor in aviation. This refers to the percentage of time that the navigation system is at the disposal of the user, and whether it is available on a continuous basis. Outages of even a few minutes are intolerable. GPS availability is assessed at a good 99.98%, with outages primarily limited to very high or very low latitudes. More factors determining Categories I, II and III are listed and described below.

Landing Categories

Category I & Category II (Cat-1 & Cat-2)

A Category-I landing is relatively easy, and most airline approaches today fall within this definition. Cat-I is an instrumented approach for heights above touchdown of at least 200 feet with a minimum runway visual range of 1800 feet.

At the time of printing, the expected conformance between a measured position and the actual position for a Cat-I landing must be within 7.6 meters (about 25 feet) vertically and horizontally. This is, however, considered an interim number subject to change.

Category-II landings are used for approaches in which the height above touchdown is at least 100 feet. The runway visual range must be at least 1200 feet. These are outlined in the table below.

ICAO FLIGHT LANDING PROCEDURE STANDARDS		
IF approach is:	*EASY*	*MODERATE*
AND height above touchdown is:	200 feet	100 feet
AND minimum runway visual range is:	1800 feet	1200 feet
THEN landing is classified as:	*CAT-I*	*CAT-II*

Standard (uncorrected) GPS is not considered accurate enough for the narrow range of altitudes involved; so, Differential-GPS is often used for Cat-I and Cat-II. Differential corrections are broadcast from reference stations, which may be Wide-Area or Local-Area Augmentation stations. Pseudolites — configurations of ground-based transmitters, monitoring and control units — can also be installed at the ends of runways to resolve signal ambiguities. Acting like substitute visible satellites, pseudolites enhance the levels of accuracy obtainable by aircraft in the vicinity of the airport.

Category-III (Cat-3)

Category III is, basically, a "Look-Ma-no-hands!" approach in which the aircraft is automatically guided and brought down onto the runway under quite stringent conditions. Cat-III procedures are required when, for example, the pilot cannot see the runway until the airplane actually touches down.

Category IIIa refers to landings with a minimum runway visual range of 700 feet but no height minimum. Category IIIb applies when there is a minimum runway visual range of 150 feet and no height minimum. Category IIIc applies to the most difficult of all approaches, and there are neither height nor runway visual range minimums or restrictions.

Various aviation agencies and private firms are investigating enhanced Differential-GPS for Cat-III instrument landings. An ongoing FAA program has been designed to find out if DGPS meets sensor-accuracy requirements for what is known in aviation circles as the tunnel-in-space concept.

ICAO FLIGHT LANDING PROCEDURE STANDARDS			
IF approach is:	**DIFFICULT**		
AND height above touchdown is:	anything	anything	anything
AND minimum runway visual range is:	700 feet	150 feet	anything
THEN landing is classified as:	**CAT-IIIa**	**CAT-IIIb**	**CAT-IIIc**

Other studies indicate that critical ICAO requirements for the automatic landing of aircraft and recoverable spacecraft (e.g., vertical positioning accuracy of 0.6 meters) are met by integrating an Inertial Navigation System (INS) with augmented (Differential) GPS.

COMPARATIVE ICAO CONFORMANCE LEEWAYS

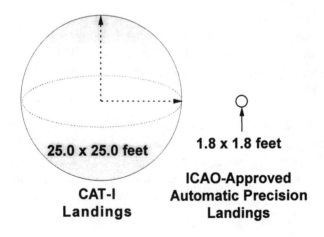

25.0 x 25.0 feet

1.8 x 1.8 feet

CAT-I
Landings

ICAO-Approved
Automatic Precision
Landings

Aviation Use of GPS

Aviation Waypoints

Most aspects of nonprecision approach and landing depend on the reliability and accuracy of aviation waypoints — spatial guideposts defined by very precise coordinates. By serving as progress markers along a route, different types of aviation waypoints help pilots maintain their bearing during flight and through the approach and landing phases.

Reference waypoints are specific control points from which the locations of other waypoints are computed. Waypoint segments are those sections of a flight track between two waypoints. GPS instrument-approach procedures, for example, include specific waypoints for initiating approach, determining intermediate positions and completing approach and touchdown.

Additional waypoints are often needed. Course-change waypoints must be calculated when the flight path changes, and turn-area adjustments are necessary for any changes exceeding 15 degrees.

When an approach fails, points must also be designated to indicate exactly where the approach "missed," at which point turns must be executed and into which holding pattern the craft must go.   Since current guidelines state that each waypoint's latitude and longitude be defined in degrees, minutes and seconds to an accuracy of one-hundredth of a second, it is easy to see why GPS is becoming an integral part of these procedures.

GPS Receivers & Databases for Aviation

GPS units for aviation may be portable or mounted on the aircraft's instrument panel. Some pilots of small planes began using GPS by taping handheld units onto steering devices or front panels. Today's panel-mounted sets have large screens (with good resolution), dials and push-button controls.

As described in Chapter 2, "GPS Receivers," the typical airborne GPS unit consists of a multimode receiver, with combined ILS/MLS/GPS approach and landing capabilities, perhaps. The differential receiver and processor may feed into a flight director or autopilot. Panel-mounted units must be authorized for use by the FAA and installed by someone licensed to do so.

Most GPS receivers come with some sort of preprogrammed database. In an aviation database, GPS-measured or GPS-verified coordinates are labeled as such. Instrument-approach procedures are identified by the prefix "GPS" followed by a runway number or letter — for example, GPS RWY 23 or GPS RWY D. A GPS-verified waypoint is prefixed by "GPS" and designated as GPS WP.

The table following this section lists what you might expect to find preprogrammed in an aviation database. Similar databases are available for marine and land use, as well.

Where GPS Accuracy Helps

The installation of precision-approach guidance at the ends of runways is only one of many ways to reduce risk to an aircraft and its passengers. The Global Positioning System is helping enhance safety by increasing precision in all phases of flight:

- maneuvering for take-off
- en-route navigation
- final approach and
- landing.

DGPS Waypoint, Altitude & Maneuvering Advantages

Flight distance (in nautical miles) is considered the amount of flight path between the aircraft and the next waypoint (which may coincide with the final destination). Use of DGPS lessens the potential for positioning errors of the waypoints themselves and for errors along the flight track.

FEATURES OF AN AVIATION DATABASE

Map Datums

for many predefined areas; usually a user-defined option, as well.

Latitude & Longitude for

most public airports	local, regional & national
most navigational aids	nondirectional beacons, FAA's VOR point-to-point system, including city/state identifiers, broadcast information, frequencies, etc.
intersections	identifier, country, location of nearest navaid (VOR, NDB)
airspace	where restricted, open or prohibited

General Information about

runway	coordinates, length, surface, lighting, etc.
navaids	city/state identifiers, broadcast information, frequencies, etc.
intersections	identifiers
communication frequencies	frequency requirements for different stages of approach and landing
airspace	whether restricted, open or prohibited
minimum requirements	safe altitudes for specified flight plan
pilot-controlled functions	pilot instructions for special approaches

Differential-GPS techniques also allow accurate altitude assessment and the lowering of minimum requirements without compromising safety. Maneuvering in the terminal area is safer with GPS-determined terminal-area waypoints. Precise waypoints are critical to an aircraft's ability to safely maneuver and position itself within the space, and more efficient use of holding areas is possible with GPS-provided accuracy.

In order to execute a turn at a particular waypoint, whether in the air or in the terminal area, pilots must be able to anticipate at which point before that to initiate the procedure. This requires exact determination of the position of the waypoint, as well as the position and velocity of the moving craft. GPS monitors all the factors, provides the capability of determining where a turn should be initiated and then relays this information to the pilot and/or to the aircraft's automatic systems.

For nonprecision approaches and landings, an obstacle-free turning area must be allotted. A secondary, triangular-shaped area, based on specific turn information, is also designated. Determination of the boundaries of both (for obstacle-clearance purposes) requires precise measurements — more achievable and reliable with GPS.

Tolerance of Fix Displacement

Alongtrack displacement tolerance is the allowance made for errors in craft positioning along a specified flight track. Crosstrack tolerance is the leeway to the left or right of the flight track.

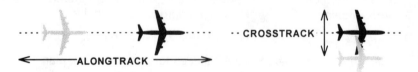

The ability to determine the limits of these tolerances and to reliably remain within them are crucial to the safety of an aircraft. GPS-determined coordinates help both the aircraft on the track and others in the vicinity to better define and respect the assigned boundaries.

The waypoint displacement area is a rectangular area formed around and centered on the predetermined geographical position (latitude, longitude and altitude) of a waypoint. Any aircraft within the area qualifies as being "at" the waypoint. Waypoint tolerance is the amount of error tolerated in flight for those predetermined positions. How large an area this is generally depends on the accompanying alongtrack and crosstrack tolerances.

Non-GPS Navigation & Landing

Non-GPS Nonprecision Approaches

Non-GPS navigational aids in widespread use today include those with acronyms you may have seen, such as VOR/DME, TACAN, RNAV, NDB and LORAN-C. Generally, these apply to nonprecision approaches, for which are outlined not only minimum standards for altitude, visibility and final approach but also requirements for operating under particular flight conditions.

VOR/DME

VOR stands for Very-high-frequency OmniRange, the Federal Aviation Administration's point-to-point navigational system that operates at very high frequencies. In use since the early 1950s, VOR transmitters provide locational readings to planes en route. Today's VOR, combined with distance-measuring equipment (VOR/DME), is the approved system for flight within the National Airspace System (NAS) — until 2010. By then, it will have been completely phased out and replaced by GPS.

TACAN

TACAN, which stands for TACtical Air Navigation, is the military's ultra-high-frequency VOR/DME. A short-range, land-based, line-of-sight system, TACAN provides positional accuracy of a few hundred meters but gives no velocity information.

Both VOR/DME and TACAN are currently used for en route navigation systems. Controlled migration to GPS (i.e., using GPS to augment the current system) is occurring. As soon as military aircraft are equipped for GPS and the Department of Defense determines that GPS satisfies the required navigation-performance standards for national and international airspace, TACAN, too, will be phased out, probably beginning by the year 2000.

RNAV — Area Navigation

RNAV stands for aRea NAVigation, a system that works either as a standalone aid to navigation or in computerized conjunction with a VORTAC (VOR/TACAN) system. It will be used as long as VOR/DME or VORTAC systems exist.

For locations that do not have their own VOR/DME or VORTAC transmissions but are within range of one, RNAV uses triangulation to program a phantom, surrogate waypoint, thus allowing a pilot to navigate as though there were a real waypoint.

NDB & LORAN-C

Nondirectional beacons (NDBs), stationary guideposts that transmit signals in all directions, have long been used as waypoints along shorelines for sailors and at airfields for pilots to help them get their bearings. They are still used in the U.S. during flight but usually only as part of instrumented approaches — as a compass locator, for example, during the initial stages of instrumented or nonprecision landing approaches in not-so-busy airports. Some NDBs provide pilots with indications of weather conditions. According to the 1994 Federal Radionavigation Plan (FRP) and other government reports, NDB phaseout is scheduled to begin in the year 2000.

LORAN-C, originally intended for use in U.S. coastal waters, is a non-FAA system operated by the U.S. Coast Guard. Based on the time-of-arrival concept, LORAN-C uses geometry on signals sent from both master and secondary stations.

A non-directional beacon (NDB) system transmits low-frequency signals from shore stations, providing positional data over a wide area, not just from specific points. It is approved for nonprecision flights at many airports and has been used by both private and military pilots for aviation. Twenty-four U.S. LORAN-C stations work in conjunction with Russian and Canadian stations to extend coverage to the Bering Strait and Canadian waters.

LORAN-C's equipment is expensive, but the 100 kHz radio signals parallel the earth's contours, unobstructed by topology; so, they can be picked up thousands of miles away. They may, however, be subject to skywave interference.

With LORAN-C, users can achieve relatively accurate locational fixes — 1519 feet or ¼ nautical mile. Users can usually return to previous locations to within 164 feet. Recreational boaters and professional fishermen know LORAN-C well and are increasingly transferring the experience and skills gained from its use to GPS-aided navigation. Combined GPS/LORAN receivers are available.

Non-GPS Precision Approaches

ILS — Instrument Landing System

The Instrument Landing System (ILS) is a passive, short-range system used with radar for precision-approach navigation. The trouble with ILS is that it is not easily modified to work with enhanced systems, its range is limited, and it often suffers signal interference — when it snows, for example. It can also happen when an approach is circuitous or in places where the terrain around the landing strip is either mountainous or obstacle-ridden.

Both the Department of Defense (DoD) and the commercial airline industry still use ILS for precision approaches, but rapid transition from ILS to GPS is expected. GPS can be used along convoluted flight paths and does not require straight, open approaches.

MLS — Microwave Landing System

The Microwave Landing System (MLS) is a system that measures azimuths to determine the elevation from the runway for landing. It is enough of an improvement over ILS that the Federal Aviation Administration had plans to upgrade all installed systems to MLS. However, as a result of GPS's high accuracy, reliability and economy in trials (and the very high costs of installing MLSs), those plans have been scrapped. The FAA is convinced that GPS is a better solution.

Migration to GPS as Primary System

There is already such momentum among pilots to adopt GPS as their navigational system of choice, it is certain that most non-GPS systems will be replaced. GPS provides not only all the surface and air-route capabilities of other systems at lower costs but also services runways within an airport. Also, since maintenance and operating costs for current, less-precise and less-reliable systems are high, the migration to free-access GPS is expected to proceed quickly.

In areas where there may be language difficulties between ground control and pilot, GPS-augmented navigation may circumvent disaster by serving as a reliable second opinion. A number of airline companies have installed GPS backups for flights over Russia and China. In addition, Persian Gulf nations are being encouraged by the U.S. to adopt a satellite-based air-navigation approach and to have augmented-GPS functional by the early 2000s.

Nonprecision Approaches with GPS

By augmenting traditional procedures with GPS, previously established criteria for nonprecision approaches are made more exact and reliable. Buffers required to compensate for inaccuracies of conventional positioning can be reduced without lowering standards of safety. More precise fixes also allow a lowering of the levels of tolerances previously allowed for displacement along flight paths.

Panel-mounted GPS navigation systems have been approved for nonprecision approaches, and the FAA has already approved a quick and inexpensive way for pilots to make the transition. A GPS "overlay" can be used with existing charts to give pilots of GPS-equipped planes a choice of landing either conventionally or with GPS. Eventually, over half the airports in the U.S. will qualify for GPS nonprecision landings.

Testing Precision Approaches with GPS

FAA-Sponsored Evaluations

The FAA is continuing tests evaluating the capability of Differential Global Positioning System (DGPS) to provide the accuracy and integrity required for all International Civil Aviation Organization (ICAO) Category-III precision approaches and landings. This is being done to demonstrate that GPS is a viable alternative to the microwave landing systems (MLS), developed by the FAA in the 1970s to replace the long-used ILS.

Flight tests are being conducted primarily to find out if particular DGPS systems meet sensor-accuracy and system error requirements for Category IIIb approaches. Other objectives include the assessment of system integrity and probable continuity of service.

In one such flight evaluation, a United Airlines Boeing 737-300 was equipped with DGPS receiving equipment and computing capability provided by Stanford University. Accuracies were evaluated for navigation sensor error and total system error based on the requirements outlined for the microwave landing system (MLS).

One hundred Stanford/United autolandings were evaluated. Of these, 90 were "touch and go;" 10 terminated with a full stop. The test system met the stringent requirements for successful approach and autolanding in 98 out of the 100 runs, reinforcing the FAA's insistence that GPS replace MLS.

In further attempts to hasten approved operational use of GPS for Category-III precision landings, the FAA has awarded contracts to a number of outside vendors. Deliverables were to demonstrate a DGPS system enhanced to provide the accuracies needed for Cat-III precision approach and landing and to demonstrate the feasibility of its becoming operational quickly. One of the vendors, E-Systems, tested their DGPS with an Israel Aircraft Industries Westwind business jet. Sensor-error requirements for FAA Cat-III Level 2 Flight Test Plans were met 98 out of 100 times, and integrity requirements were met in all runs.

Approved use of GPS-guided navigation for Category-III landings is of strategic business importance to shipping agencies such as United Parcel Service (UPS) and Federal Express since it would allow the carriers to operate in all types of weather. UPS has collaborated with the FAA in scores of Category-III tests of GPS-guided approaches and landings for their fleet.

Independent Testing & Evaluation

Independent testing is also done. After being turned down for an FAA research and development contract, the Boeing Corporation and four teams of avionics suppliers used their proposal as a basis for conducting their own testing program. Boeing's aim is to develop a computer simulation for Category-III GPS approach and landing validation like the one currently used to certify automatic landing with ILS systems. Four sets of DGPS equipment were used in more than 200 landings to provide data for the complex simulation.

GPS is being tested in France with wide-body transports, and German researchers are conducting studies on the feasibility of GPS meeting availability and integrity requirements for different aircraft. Airbus Industrie has been conducting trials of Cat-I DGPS on its aircraft since 1994, and they have demonstrated GPS-aided precision approaches in France, South Africa and China. Airbus' early evaluation of GPS as a primary means of navigation included integrity monitoring using signals from an additional satellite.

Much of the current precision-landing study has employed stand-alone GPS receiver techniques; however, certain multipath errors seem to persist that may be addressable through innovative integration of data from various system combinations. Researchers are exploring the possibilities of mathematically filtering and integrating data from GPS, an Inertial Navigation System, barometric and radar altimeters and a pseudolite to obtain better accuracy for at least Cat-I and -II approaches.

Special Cases

Helicopters

For a number of reasons, helicopter approaches and landings present unique challenges to pilots and controllers, not the least of which is the inherent instability of the aircraft. The high-accuracy, precision navigation and guidance needed can be obtained through the use of Differential GPS. Extensive testing has shown that positions based on DGPS guidance satisfy International Civil Aviation Organization Category-I accuracy requirements.

Typical use begins with the installation of an airborne DGPS receiver and related equipment in the helicopter. A ground-based DGPS reference receiver is then located at a site for which exact coordinates are known, and a very-high-frequency (VHF) data link is established between the receiver on the ground and the airborne receiver.

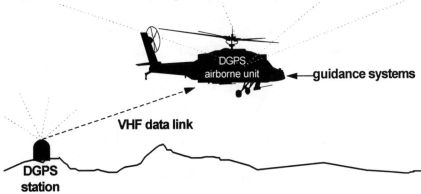

After that, a DGPS correction is transmitted from the station to the airborne DGPS unit (receiver). The corrected data, together with preset approach geometry, are used to calculate guidance commands. These are then sent to the aircraft's guidance instruments.

GPS and data-link technologies were used to provide surveillance for a low-altitude helicopter transportation system for the 1996 Olympic Games in Atlanta. The Atlanta Short-Haul Transportation System served as a free-flight "highway in the sky." to supplement ground transportation.

Many helicopter operations need to be carried out at low altitudes in order to ensure survivability in the face of threats and the constraints of time and fuel. Guidance systems for low-altitude flight incorporate algorithms that weigh knowledge of mission requirements and the aircraft's performance capability, then integrate these with a terrain map and precision navigation information to generate a route that minimizes danger.

Because such a trajectory (or route) may seek valleys and maneuver around obstacles to avoid collisions, there is little room for pilot hesitation or error. The mission may be flown at nighttime or in adverse weather. Therefore, most in-flight activities should be automated to minimize pilot load and made as visual as possible to maximize pilot awareness. Ideally, a graphic representation of the trajectory should be presented (as a "path in the sky") via a head-mounted display (HMD) to help a pilot visualize the scenario.

A passive terrain-following system with digital mapping and GPS is being developed in China. Of particular interest to the researchers are GPS' passivity and the benefits of receivers that obtain positional data without having to emit detectable electromagnetic waves.

For those readers familiar with laser tracking, one series of helicopter tests may be interesting. DGPS-derived guidance data were compared with laser-tracker data. Both standard (3 degrees) and steep (6 degrees and 9 degrees) glidescope, straight-in approaches were flown. Resultant accuracies were:

APPROACH & GLIDESCOPE	LATERAL ACCURACY	VERTICAL ACCURACY
straight-in		
standard (3°)	0.1 m (mean) +/- 1.8 m (2 σ)	-2.0 m (mean) +/- 3.5 m (2 σ)
steep (6°)	-0.1 m (mean) +/- 1.5 m (2 σ)	-1.1 m (mean) +/- 3.5 m (2 σ)
steep (9°)	0.2 m (mean) +/- 1.3 m (2 σ)	-1.0 m (mean) +/- 2.8 m (2 σ)
200-foot height		
standard (3°)	0.3 m (mean) +/- 1.5 m (2 σ)	-2.3 m (mean) +/- 1.6 m (2 σ)

A Hybrid: Future Air Navigation Suite (FANS-1)

The Future Air Navigation Suite (FANS-1) combines GPS-aided navigation with satellite data-link communications to Air Traffic Control (ATC) stations.   FANS-1 is meant to be an affordable, reliable worldwide system, and ATC ground stations and aircraft are already being certified in the Pacific regions. The Suite incorporates various techniques that can be used by station managers to alert pilots to communication problems or in-flight danger.   FANS-1 components include a full ATC data link and interfaces for sending messages into a flight-management computer. A flight-deck printer is also available for report generation.

The primary means of FANS-1 navigation is GPS positioning. An aircraft, equipped and FANS-certified, sends its GPS positions by satellite data link to an ATC station, which has also been equipped and certified. Station personnel are required to undergo training and be certified, as well.   Because establishing certified Air Traffic Control (ATC) stations does not involve large amounts of capital, some countries (Russia, in particular) look upon FANS-1 ATC ground stations as a means of opening up airspace to collect lucrative overflight tariffs.

Inadequate Support Systems

GPS won't work with some 30-40% of general aviation aircraft that lack the electrical systems to support the equipment. It also falls short for aircraft that may be operating without transponders (such as hospital emergency helicopters or planes in terminal areas). GPS does not solve all the problems of bird or aircraft intrusions, either.

Because these and other situations such as thunderstorms, wind gusts and wake vortices present unique problems not well resolved by GPS alone, a system complementary to GPS is being implemented by the FAA. Called TASS (for Terminal Area Surveillance System), this multifunction, ground-based radar system is being developed to replace all current wind, weather and surveillance radars by 2010.

Free Flight

One of the joys of private, small-plane pilots is freedom from ground control. Now, it is possible to have it in heightened safety. The reliability and accuracy assured by GPS allow pilots to collaborate and determine their own routes without the usual air-traffic control.

In free-flight, a pilot equipped with a GPS receiver and a special type of radio first ascertains the exact location of his or her aircraft (as determined by its on-board GPS receiver). Coordinates are then transmitted to all other similarly-equipped aviators in the vicinity.

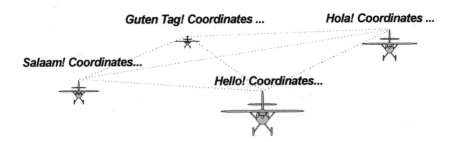

Each, then, is able to generate a composite of the traffic environment. Also, in a variation of airborne Automatic Dependent Surveillance (ADS), pilots can also transmit their coordinates to a controller or monitor on the ground — creating, in effect, a radarless control tower. The information can shore up a radar-based system if it does exist or be used for maneuvering aircraft on the ground.

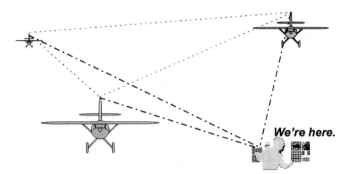

We're here.

Today, commercial routes are reviewed daily so that pilots flying east across the North Atlantic can take advantage of the best tailwinds. The same is done before heading back so that the plane encounters minimal headwinds.   In deference to the margin of navigational errors of current systems, planes are routed a safe 60 (nautical) miles apart.   This wide buffer zone is a necessary precaution, but one that limits the number of aircraft that can get boosts from the best winds.

When GPS navigation is adopted and approved for use, its precision coordinates will allow a reduction of this 60-mile buffer requirement. More flights will be able to safely fit in to exploit the best-wind zone, crossing times will be minimized, and less fuel will be consumed.

GPS Squitter

When there are many aircraft in one area, communications broadcast at regular intervals (at half-seconds, perhaps) may interfere with each other.   "Squittering" refers to MIT's Paul Drouilhet's innovation of sporadically timing very quick announcements over a particularly robust (and wide) radio channel as a means of minimizing collision among communications from flights.   Broadcasting quick messages at random intervals increases the odds of messages getting through.

Squittering uses the frequencies of other systems such as ADS and beacon radar; thus, it has the potential of seamlessly working in conjunction with them.   In some cases, though, this advantage may be of dubious merit.   For example, a lot of activity in the other systems may affect Squitter broadcasts.   There is also a potential for self-interference among Squitter users.

Squitter operations may also occupy the channels on the beacon frequencies to such an extent that users of the other systems are prevented from receiving a signal.

These problems do not preclude effective use of Squitter systems today, but they need to be resolved. Contractors are working with the team at MIT to manufacture devices that minimize problems. A trial conducted with surveillance helicopters over oil platforms in the Gulf of Mexico indicated that accurate, real-time free-flight control is possible today in the region with GPS/Squitter combinations.

FAA's Free-Flight Road Map

Our current Air Traffic Control system uses radar surveillance, and routes are defined by ground-based personnel and navigational aids. The trend in the FAA, however, is one of migration by the year 2010 from today's ground-based tower control system to a free-flight Air Traffic Management system. What is envisioned is a collaborative, predominantly air-based management system in which pilots, aided by GPS, chart their own courses and make the decisions. Expert ground controllers will still exist in parallel to help pilots prevent problems and intervene when necessary to solve them.

Data Links

The data links that carry the transmissions from pilot to pilot, pilot to ground and ground to pilot are probably the most critical element in the GPS free-flight scenario. Not only must they be dependable digital-message conduits, but their management must be within the capacity of persons involved with the system.

People are important parts of the data-link connection. Personnel must be retrained in the use of new devices and convinced to take ownership of new procedures. Supplying workers with user-friendly equipment and GPS training will be an area of fast growth within the avionics industry. (See Chapter 14 for further discussion of the opportunities opening up as a result of free access to GPS.)

New Airport Surveys

As pilot navigation becomes more precise and autonomous, less demand is made on the visual acumen of the pilot. That's the good news, but many maps have been drawn up by less precise methods than GPS surveys. Until airport and runway maps are re-surveyed, this can pose serious problems.

Hey! It's not where it's supposed to be!

A pilot using GPS will be able to aim precisely at coordinates listed on an aeronautical chart, but a runway assigned those coordinates by old methods may be hundreds of feet away or not visible at all.

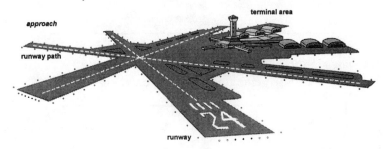

Among examples of this are Runway 13 at Las Salle County Airport in Cotula, Texas (off by 620 feet) and Runway 31 at Mid Valley Airport in Wesiaco, Texas (off by 186 feet). When GPS-surveyed, the Pago Pago International Airport in American Samoa was found to have been charted 1850 feet away from its true location. Luckily, most pilots today are aware of and anticipate the probable discrepancies. However, future total reliance on GPS dictates that airports (or, at least, the ends of their runways) be resurveyed soon and mapped to more precise coordinates.

FAA Resurvey Program

At the time of printing, 2,500 airports have been scheduled to be resurveyed in a five-year, $25 million program sponsored by the FAA. Cartographic technicians travel from airport to airport to plot 3-dimensional paths of their runways.

In order to accomplish this, personnel or contractors must set up a tripod tipped with an antenna at one end of each runway and take sub-inch readings (i.e., differentially corrected coordinates) via a connection to a truck-mounted receiver. The steps are repeated for the other end of the runway. Precise positions are thus obtained for both ends.

The antenna'ed tripod is then mounted on the truck platform, along with the receiver. A series of readings is then recorded as the truck travels the length of the runway.

In this way, a 3-dimensional map of the entire runway is plotted, and detailed charts can be generated from the data.

Standardizing

Another problem arises from the many differences among countries. Some countries consider cartologic information secret; others haven't acquired sophisticated mapping capability. Geodetic data gathering and organization also vary among countries.

Unfortunately, efforts by the United Nations' International Civil Aviation Organization (ICAO) have not yet succeeded in getting its member countries to conform to standardized mapping procedures. Addressing this problem involves having adequate databases of coordinates; an ability to transform local and national geodetic datums to the World Geodetic Survey (WGS-84). It also mandates the refinement of roughly established coordinates of other navigational aids to an accuracy comparable to GPS, itself dependent on the completion of many scaled pilot studies.

Agency Roles in Establishing Criteria

U.S. agencies involved with establishing and controlling flight standards and criteria are:

- Federal Aviation Administration (FAA),
- National Oceanic & Atmospheric Administration (NOAA),
- Office of Aviation Policy, Plans and Management Analysis,
- Office of Aviation System Standards, and
- Office of Airport Safety and Standards.

Others responsible for the implementation of flight criteria include:

- Service of Flight Standards and District Offices,
- Services of Air Traffic Rules and Procedures,
- Services of Research & Development and Systems Maintenance,
- Program Director for Navigation and Landing,
- Regional Offices for Standards, Air Traffic, Airways and Airports,
- Division of National Airway Systems Engineering,
- Division of Regulatory Standards and Compliance,
- International Flight Inspection Office and Area Offices, and
- Airway Facilities Sectors and Field Offices.

Federal Aviation Administration's Role

The Federal Aviation Administration (FAA) is the controlling interface for civil aviation in the United States. The Department of Defense (DoD) developed and controls GPS as a military system. Both operate under National Airspace System (NAS) rules. Before GPS technology and services could be transferred to the civilian sector, the two organizations had to agree on how it could be done without compromising military objectives. A 1992 memorandum outlined joint responsibilities and final plans for implementation. GPS signals, coverage, accuracy and facilities were then available to all civilian and military users within the National Airspace System.

Certification

Personnel at the FAA are responsible for certifying equipment for flight under FAA rules, which now includes GPS receiver units. Because safety is of primary concern, importance is given to how the design of the receiver's interface may affect pilot performance.

GPS and LORAN receivers get their signals from different sources but are basically alike in how they look and how they work — *if* they come from the same manufacturer. Although the configuration of buttons, displays and electronics is usually consistent among products from a single manufacturer, that design may differ considerably from those of another source. Such variations make it difficult to arrive at standards and, more importantly, may slow a pilot down. Thus, receivers have to be tested under actual flight conditions.

User-laboratory techniques are employed in conjunction with flight tests to further assess the interaction between the humans who use the machines and the devices themselves. Other characteristics of the GPS receivers (e.g., integrity and accuracy) are investigated, too.

Minimal Operational Performance Standards (MOPS) are published so that equipment manufacturers can understand and conform to the needs of the aviation community. Similar criteria for certification are being established under TERminal instrument ProcedureS (TERPS) and Technical Standard Order (TSO) procedures.

Monitoring

In a move to export safety standards to other countries, the FAA conducts inspections of navigation equipment on flights arriving in the U.S. Those failing to prove adequate safety standards and compliance face having their landing rights revoked. The stringency is resented by some countries, but lucrative U.S. landing rights enable the FAA to exercise its muscle.

Recently, in the course of its duties, the Agency witnessed a rather awkward attestation to the reliability of GPS-aided navigation. An inspection of an Aero Peru DC-8 landing at Miami revealed that none of the plane's navigation devices worked. A small, off-the-shelf GPS receiver was all that had been used for the 2,600-mile flight. When it happened a second time, the FAA revoked the airline's permission to land in the U.S.

Increasing Airport & Airspace Capacity

According to the FAA, demand for airport and airspace capacity will increase dramatically in the next 10-12 years. American air carrier operations are expected to reach 35 million per year by 2005, over one-third more than were reported in 1992. GPS is integral in plans to develop instrumented precision approaches and in airspace efficiency measures to accommodate the growth. Overall use of GPS to meet aviation goals is outlined in the FAA Satellite Navigation Program Master Plan. As described in the plan, the main advantages afforded by GPS are:

- consolidation of navigation functions into a single system;
- small buffers but heightened safety, increasing system capacity;
- flexibility through user-preferred flight paths;
- reduced costs as a result of efficient routing;
- uniform air traffic management (ATM);
- improved situational awareness on the ground and in the air;
- increased landing capacity for all aircraft types; and
- Category-II and -III precision-approach services.

National Oceanic & Atmospheric Administration

The National Oceanic & Atmospheric Administration (NOAA) creates and distributes assessments and predictions of weather and climate; the space environment; ocean and living marine resources; nautical, aeronautical and geodetic events and systems.

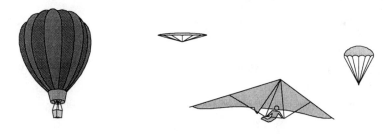

Key to accomplishing NOAA's mission in all of the above areas is the use of technologies that assure accuracy. GPS is poised to play a significant role in specific tasks that bear environmental impact. It and is becoming an underlying guarantee of precision for assessment of nautical, aeronautical and geodetic phenomena. GPS tools and techniques are being used increasingly by NOAA in its creation and distribution of reliable information regarding weather, climate, space environment, marine resources.

7

GPS ON THE WATER
Sailing & Boating

In the private sector, boaters join pilots in making up the most experienced civilian users of GPS and its most vocal champions. For years, their use of GPS-enhanced devices has exceeded that in most other sectors, and the pace at which commercial ships are upgrading to GPS is also increasing. Eventually, a good proportion of the half-billion vessels cruising and crossing the waters of the globe will add GPS to their panels of instruments.

GPS equipment for sailors and fishermen includes portable or permanently mounted receiver units and antennae. Interest in the technology has been boosted by easy linkage of GPS receivers to other devices such as fishfinders or maps.

How Mariners Know Where They Are

Charts for channels have been maintained to the highest standards throughout history, and all ships must carry hard copies of official hydrographic charts. Carefully unfurled onto ships' tables, these gave mariners reassuring glimpses of the terrain beneath and ahead of the waters they sailed. Today, however, sailors get added reassurance from oceanographic charts spread across electronic display screens. Many boaters don't even use paper charts anymore. Typically, they combine different pieces of electronic equipment to pinpoint locations and help them find their way. LORAN receivers, in particular, have been hooked up to fishfinders or chart plotters — becoming systems unique to their owners. Microwave positioning devices are also used.

Linking GPS to On-Board Systems

GPS, too, is becoming an integral part of more efficient and accurate hybrid systems. A GPS receiver hooked up to electronic chartplotters and trackplotters provides an important edge at sea — where a difference of only a few degrees in latitude or longitude can easily translate into many miles off course. Enticing customers to upgrade their on-board capabilities, vendors of products that can be used this way usually advertise them as "GPS-ready" or "differential-ready."

In the hands of experienced mariners, LORAN chartplotters provide relatively accurate fixes. GPS, however, provides extended means for self-location, routing and tagging significant objects with exact latitude and longitude coordinates.

With a pointer, a user indicates where he or she wants to go, and the system does some initial calculations and displays compass and distance information.

A trackball or button with directional arrows may also be used for moving the cursor around on the screen. After each entry of input by a user, the system updates the display. How quickly this is done depends on the receiver's processor speed.

Combined LORAN/GPS

For marine navigation, LORAN and GPS systems can complement each other. LORAN provides initialization and continuous coastal coverage when access to the GPS satellites is limited or precluded (e.g., under water or dense overhead coverage), and GPS surpasses LORAN for cycle selection, treating ambiguities and ASF-factor calibration. Combined systems seem to offer advantages superior to either system alone.

In light of the ease of use and accuracy offered by GPS, some manufacturers have already discontinued many lines of LORAN-C products. The system, however, will remain in use through 2000 or whenever there is a complete transition to GPS.

Evolution towards All-in-One Systems

What lies ahead is a type of system that combines everything possible — GPS, charts, radar and active sonar — to detect and avoid obstacles on and under the water. At any time, the boat's position is indicated by a crosshair or other type of pointer, and a user can zoom in on any area for more detail.

Information appearing on the screen (either LCD or CRT) includes symbols or icons for most things affecting the operation of that particular vessel, e.g., markers, buoys, lights, harbors, shoals or reefs. High-end GPS receivers give users the added options of customizing icons and how information is delivered via their screens. A user can name, describe and designate a place as a waypoint, then assign it an icon that will appear on the display. The types of icons available include those illustrated below.

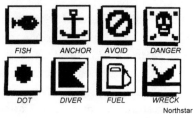

Northstar

Although multicolored displays are available, most marine charts have not been designed for color systems, and colors do not show up well in sunlight. Many sailors forego the option, preferring high-contrast black and either white, gray or green.

Electronic versions of paper sea charts are available, and most high-end systems work with electronic cartography. Area-specific databases are sold on microcartridges that slide into the receiver unit. These contain precise waypoints for reefs, depths, buoys, lighthouses, marinas and other items of importance for the area — anything that is on paper charts and more. Waypoints appear as part of the display.

Differential GPS has also been coupled with software in what are called electronic navigation systems (ENSs). ENSs are used not to replace published charts, however, but only to augment them.

Rivers, Lakes & Foggy Harbors

Marking Spots

Marking particularly rich fishing spots or scenic moorings is easy. With simple, one-button waypoint entry, a receiver automatically enters the GPS coordinates (and a code or name) for a spot into its database — as a retrievable waypoint. At a later date, the waypoint or its coordinates can be designated as a destination to guide you back. Fixes for favorite places can be published or shared among friends.

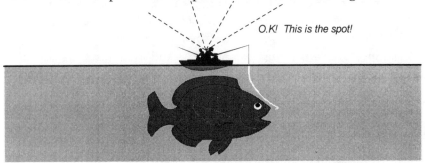

O.K! This is the spot!

Electronic Chart Display Information System — ECDIS

The most popular of electronic navigation systems — the Electronic Chart Display Information System (ECDIS) allows a navigator to retrieve and view specific information along a route. Standardized by the International Hydrographic Organization and the International Maritime Organization in 1984, ECDIS is a highly accurate aid in most ports and coastal waterways around the world, but it has been unsuitable for ports that have to be entered through long dredged channels. Its utility for dredging activity and blind navigation in confined areas is weak.

To address these shortcomings, ECDIS has been upgraded to work with Differential GPS to fix a ship's position to within 3 meters. It can now provide accurate measurements for water-channels, harbor approaches and entrances, platform positions and fisheries. It may be further enhanced to accept data files from other systems.

Dredging

The U.S. Army Corps of Engineers (ACE) oversees the maintenance of harbors, which includes dredging activities and buoy placement. In areas where dredging is planned, it is up to ACE to assess which plant beds may be in the path and to what extent the work could affect them. Projects employing GPS began in 1988. Since then, ACE engineers have developed an advanced-techniques GPS system and have established 36 permanent DGPS stations.

The current enhanced DGPS-system provides 3-D positioning in real time with accuracies of 1-3 centimeters in all three dimensions. Special monitoring systems are being developed, as well, for measuring and reporting water levels and quantities of material retained. Hopper dredges are fitted with instruments to automatically log in data and perform computations, much like the farm combines discussed earlier. Data obtained by these "silent inspectors" can then be displayed as graphics or in tables.

The Submersed Aquatic Vegetation Early Warning System (SAVEWS) has been built for more specific tasks of finding and mapping marine seagrasses. SAVEWS includes sensors, underwater sounding devices, a Geographic Information System (GIS), software and GPS. It delivers all the real-time data needed for engineers to make prudent decisions about how to get the job done in a way that is both cost-effective and environmentally sensitive.

Caveats for Boat Owners

Boating-supply catalogs are helpful in that they include descriptions and pictures of products for GPS, DGPS or linkage. Advice columns tell readers how to choose the right device, and customers can select from thousands of regional databases for sale. When reading product information, however, anyone intending to use a GPS receiver on a boat should be sensitive to the warning flags in the table below, most of which can prove dangerous on the water.

GPS RECEIVER EQUIPMENT FOR BOATS

WARNING SIGN:	*WHY YOU SHOULD CARE:*
slow updates or no mention of update rates	Among receivers, rates for updates range from many times per second to once every ten minutes. Single-channel receivers update about once every 10-15 seconds. For marine use, per-second updates are recommended.
small and/or patch-type antenna	Accuracy is compromised by an antenna that is too small, flimsy or of the wrong type for the application. Also, if the antenna is to be mounted away from the receiver itself, the range of a passive, patch-type antenna is short (a few yards, at best).
ground for antenna	Many antennae being sold and used aren't grounded. They should be.
inflexible antenna	If you have ever had the inclination to bend or shorten an antenna, make sure your GPS one is flexible enough. Many aren't.
no track-up display; north-up display only	Mariners do better with track-up or combined displays than with north-up displays only.
can plan only one route; little or no provision for waypoint information	Route and waypoint information is vital for all applications; low accommodation is a real drawback for most applications.
limited or no interfacing to other devices	Most mariners have already invested money and time in other devices such as chartplotters, LORAN-C, fishfinders, etc., which perform valuable functions and cannot simply be scrapped. In order to be cost-effective, any new technology should work with them. In addition, limited cabin space usually precludes setting up separate systems. Also, check the cables and sockets for compatibility.
limited conversion	Marine GPS units should be able to recognize and/or convert Time Differences (e.g., 5-digit LORAN TDs) into latitude and longitude.
no mounting brackets	Secure installation is important. Brackets may be fixed or on a swivel. To use a portable unit on a boat, a mount is necessary.

Safety for Oceangoing Vessels

Since the end of World War II, oceangoing vessels have generally doubled in length, width and draft. Seagoing commerce has more than tripled. This has resulted in high traffic and high-risk situations at ports around the world.

Between 1980 and 1988, in U.S. waters alone, tankers were involved in 468 incidents of grounding, 371 collisions, 97 rammings and 55 fires and explosions. Ninety-five related deaths were also reported for the period. In order to stop the escalation of such incidents, future marine and air navigation will have to rely on precise coordinate reference systems derived from GPS satellite information.

Modernization of Databases

The National Oceanic and Atmospheric Administration (NOAA) provides the nautical charting data that has traditionally served as the basis for U.S. nautical positioning. However, 60% of NOAA's data were collected before 1940 (and by-now-obsolete techniques). The majority of NOAA tidal prediction charts are so old and inaccurate that some have been withdrawn from use; 66% are over 40 years old. San Francisco and New York are among the ports affected.

Currently, there is a registration backlog, as well. Obstacles and obstructions are reported too often and too fast to be surveyed and recorded on charts in a timely way. GPS will provide the means for implementing NOAA's strategic plan for the year 2005, which focuses on modernizing its navigational tools and methods. Of particular interest is use of the technology for nautical charting and coastal-zone Geographic Information Systems (GISs).

Marine Identification Systems

GPS is providing the basis for a universal marine identification and tracking system. Aircraft fitted with off-the-shelf components can be used to notify a command carrier (or individual vessels) of the location and identities of vessels in their area or over the horizon. A satellite-data link provides the means by which accurate, real-time GPS coordinates for identified vessels can be transmitted.

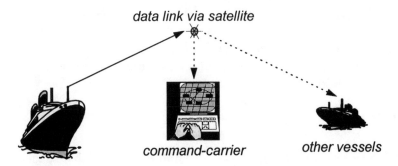

data link via satellite

command-carrier　　*other vessels*

Other methods, too, use GPS for marine identification and tracking. In one, locational information is provided in response to what is called "individual interrogation." One ship communicates with another and exchanges identification and GPS-derived locational coordinates with it.

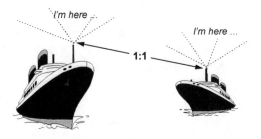

I'm here ...　　*I'm here ...*

1:1

The second approach is a broadcast approach. All ships transmit their identification and GPS-derived locations on a regular basis to all other ships within reception range. The margin of position errors for both of these methods, however, suggests that neither may prove adequate under high-density sea-traffic conditions.

1:all

A combined system is slated to become the legal replacement for other charting systems in the U.S. as soon as DGPS is available on all coasts This means that, as soon as standards for data formats are established, all oceangoing vessels in U.S. ports will have to be equipped with and use ECDIS/DGPS navigation. As other nations, including Australia, Canada, Finland, Norway, Sweden and the U.K., build stations, the overall effect on international marine identification and navigation will be dramatic.

U.S. Navy ECDIS

The Navy has developed its own version of ECDIS that is called the NAvigation Sensor System Interface (NAVSSI), and the Defense Mapping Agency is developing a digital nautical chart (DNC) database that will work with the new system. NAVSSI can use input from Omega, Transit (SATNAV) and inertial navigation systems, all of which are filtered to provide the best position, attitude and time. Data are then distributed via network to combat or weapon systems.

Efforts are under way to increase awareness of and reliance on NAVSSI and the global database so that it can replace all paper charts by 2000. In this, NAVSSI joins GPS as part of a trend extending previously classified military technology to the civilian sector. Other marine systems such as the Automated Vessel Alert (AVERT) sonar system and the Voyage Event Recorder are also being used in the private sector.

8

DEFENSE

Ultimately, technology is grounded in man.
Neither a weapon nor a strengthener of peace,
its task is to adapt itself to the power that determines war and peace.
It is subject to the ethics and justice of these states at the highest level.
translation from Ernst Junger, <u>Werke</u>

The usefulness of GPS to the military is reflected in the speed at which it is being incorporated into every aspect and branch of defense. In 1993, the U.S. Congress decreed that, by the year 2000, every major military vehicle and weapon design must incorporate GPS technology, or it will not be funded. This is significant since each modern combat division has between 3,000-4,000 vehicles.

GPS is considered not only as a better way to deliver weapons but also as a way to stem a runaway proliferation of different types of navigation systems among the branches of the armed forces. It is seen as a once-and-for-all chance to consolidate the many techniques and technology used by the military.

Also of concern to the Department of Defense and other agencies are the implications of worldwide proliferation of GPS-guided cruise missiles and weapons of mass destruction. 1995 candidates chosen for select Pentagon projects included navigation, nonproliferation and urban warfare, all of which rely heavily upon position-critical strategies and the use of the Global Positioning System.

GPS-Guided Missiles & Bombs

Cruise Missiles

Cruise missiles are small, ground-hugging, pilotless vehicles that can carry warheads over thousands of miles before releasing them. Positional precision is the key to the effectiveness of a cruise missile, which measures the altitude of the land over which it flies and matches it with a map stored in its computer memory.

GPS-aided navigation is now employed in Tomahawk cruise missiles and Standoff Land Attack Missiles (SLAMs), making the process of sending them along specific trajectories more accurate and easily accomplished. GPS is also being incorporated into the overall design of the Army Tactical Missile System (ATACMS). Current models of the ATACMS go as far as 240 kilometers (~149 miles) with precision. GPS guidance extends the rocket's range of accuracy by 60 kilometers, to 300 kilometers (~186 miles).

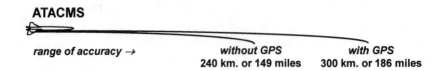

ATACMS

range of accuracy →   *without GPS*   *with GPS*
240 km. or 149 miles   **300 km. or 186 miles**

In missile flights using a trajectory reference system based on GPS, the ability to identify and estimate errors of inertial measurement units was superior to that of conventional radar, a feature that also makes it useful for performance evaluation of the units.

Integrating GPS and an inertial navigation system with synthetic aperture radar improves the accuracy of the synthetic-aperture radar that is used to deliver precision weapons. The combination provides absolute target positions of within 10 feet.

Bombs

Piggybacks

Rockwell's first GPS-aided bomb was piggy-backed onto a B-1B tactical munitions flight test, and a Northrop Grumman B-2 bomber carries the Air Force's GPS-Aided Munitions (GAM). A U.S. Joint Direct Attack Munitions (JDAM) program to upgrade general-purpose bombs with GPS-aided Inertial Navigation Systems (GPS/INS), should be operational around the turn of the century. Also slated to get GPS components are the Air Force's Mk. 80-series.

Glide Bombs

Some munitions-carrying missiles are simply released from planes to float or glide over the earth, scanning areas, looking for targets. Fold-out wings keep them afloat in silent mission until their laser radar equipment spots a target. The enemy tank or bunker is then hit with either the missile itself (diving like a bullet-rod of burning metal) or by munitions fired from the missile.

Other types of gliders are self-propelled, their trajectories guided by GPS Inertial Navigation Systems (GPS/INS) and receivers. A more formidable model is programmed to travel back and forth across about 100 miles, following a GPS-guided pattern, scanning for changes and targets of strategic importance. Its warhead is able to release its munitions in different ways, depending on the footprint of the target.

Combat Training

Land Combat Operations

GPS has changed things significantly for the foot soldier in land-combat operations. Its accuracy is of prime importance, but foot soldiers' field equipment must also be small, available, easy-to-use and reliable — making the hand-held GPS units that personnel are now issued ideal additions to their standard gear. Short-range field weapons can be more accurately initialized with GPS, and medium- and long-range weapons are being adapted to incorporate GPS in their navigation systems. Overall, ground forces benefit from GPS accuracy in:

- self, personnel & target location
- site surveys and navigation
- artillery placement
- tracking troop movements
- insertion & extraction missions
- minefield clearance.

Self-Location

Getting lost, one of wartime's most common mistakes, is less perilous than it used to be, thanks to GPS. Because GPS is a passive system in which a user merely picks up signals from the satellites and does not need to transmit anything, others cannot detect where it is located or when it is being used. A person in the field can, thus, determine his or her exact location, safe from enemy detection.

Soldiers positioned in waypoint-deficient desert environments (as was the case in the Persian Gulf War) are able to affirm their location via handheld receivers and, when necessary, relay the coordinates to others. If help or rescue is needed, locational coordinates are transmitted to rescuers or headquarters randomly and/or encrypted so detection by an enemy remains improbable. Back at headquarters, commanders can simulate accurate computer displays of what's happening by reconciling actual data with maps of the combat arena.

In both the Persian Gulf and Bosnian arenas, GPS receivers proved themselves essential to a foot soldier's and airman's equipment. Using a simple GPS device, a U.S. pilot downed and hiding in Bosnia was able to determine his exact location and later communicate it to a rescue helicopter in the area, minimizing the time and exposure of the rescue effort.

Projectile-type weapons also have to know where they are. Since they are programmed to travel a specific distance, any uncertainty of position at the launch site or in flight displaces the ultimate target location by the same amount.

Friend or Foe?

When communications facilitate precise location of self and friends in the field, there is an increase in confidence and what is called situational awareness among the troops. This is especially important when the identity of a person is unknown; a soldier must be able to send an unmistakable "Don't shoot! I'm one of you" signal to those around. Lack of such situational awareness has resulted in "friendly" tragedies during combat, underscoring the problem. Subsequently, development efforts for better equipment were stepped up. Now, a device called SABER (for Situational Awareness Beacon with Reply) combines four vital components — receiver, identification beacon, radio and computer — into one small survival unit.

Radio   IFF Beacon

GPS Receiver   Computer

SABER's GPS receiver is used for self location. The Identification as Friend or Foe (IFF) beacon is used to transmit identity. The radio receives replies and communications. The computer compiles all relevant data and generates visual displays or reports of what everyone in the field is doing.

Accurate Location of Targets

 A semiautomatic howitzer has been made more effective by coupling it with a U.S. Army Research Laboratory's (ARL) computer program and GPS. It provides a field artillery unit with the capability of attacking a moving target with indirect artillery fire, providing tactical advantages not only for major military conflicts but for small-unit, low-intensity confrontations, as well.

The M1O9 howitzer configuration consists of an on-board ballistic computer and a forward observer (FO) equipped with a laser rangefinder and laptop computer. Observer locations are determined from GPS signals fed into the computer as input.

The computer program enables the observer to enter a target path, update the position of the moving target as it follows the path and predict where the shot will fall. It also allows a change of target path during the mission.

Navigation in Hostile Environments

One of the most valuable features of GPS equipment in the field is that it delivers positional and timing information to troops with no danger of their location being detected from the signals. Search time is cut dramatically when foot soldiers know exactly where they are and can navigate quickly to where they must meet. When their positions are known to themselves and to "friends," troops can be deployed into hostile territory with more confidence, and evacuation missions can be carried out with more precision. Waypoints can be set for deployment or used for backtracking to previous positions.

Clearing Minefields

The wake of recently published data on the alarming numbers of land mines left strewn around the world from warfare and skirmishes has heightened the urgency by world organizations to clear as many minefields as possible from populated areas. Millions of civilians have been killed as results of leftover munitions. Most of these devices are undetectable, and many have gradually moved over time as a result of natural forces. Delineating areas within which people and livestock are in danger is often imprecise and hazardous.

Operation Clean Sweep, implemented after the Persian Gulf War, helped bring the problem of this dangerous war trash to public attention. Kuwait's territory was divided into seven areas, each assigned for mine and vehicle cleanup to one of the multinational forces. Responsibility for an area of 3,126 square kilometers fell to the United States. Within it was a 146-square-kilometer (57-square-mile) minefield. A U.S. company, Conventional Munitions Systems, was contracted to deal with clearing the munitions and other war leftovers. An estimated 1.25 million bombs and 500,000 land mines were strewn about the target area.

The cleanup squad first had to determine the exact positions of unexploded bombs (duds); then move and/or destroy them; locate and recover abandoned vehicles and demolish bunkers. GPS was used to exactly position and describe each lot of munitions as it was found. Crews went on foot or by truck across the desert, entering data on what was found, who found it and how many pieces were there so that recovery or destruction could be carried out.

Spatial databases are used to list exact GPS coordinates for areas that are dangerous. This unique set of waypoints can be loaded into the receivers of persons liable to be working in the area. When the position (latitude and longitude) of a user is determined by his or her GPS receiver to match any of the coordinates flagged in the database, an alarm can be triggered.

> **IF:** database danger waypoint = GPS-receiver position
> **THEN:** sound alarm

New field devices are constantly being developed and tested. With a handheld digital communicator, military personnel clearing mines are able to establish exact boundaries for areas of concern. With such precise definition, teams responsible for detonating the live mines can be assured they are working in the right areas.

One device, called a tactical automated situation receiver, contains a portable processor, a GPS receiver and a paging device, combined into a small, sturdy, field-worthy unit. The unit (and the person carrying it) are tracked via GPS coordinates transmitted by the field device. Concurrently, a constantly updated database containing all known mine locations for a specific area is matched with these coordinates. If field workers do not have the database and alarm feature loaded into their GPS receivers, a paging channel can be used instead to warn them when they are approaching dangerous territory.

Defense Training & Testing

Range Tracking

A GPS-based range-tracking system is being developed by the Range Applications Joint Program Office (RAJPO). RAJPO's mission is to develop a line of GPS-aided range equipment for the U.S. Army, Navy and Air Force. In collaboration with the U.S. Air Defense Artillery Test Directorate, RAJPO is also investigating the use and accuracy of GPS-derived time, space and position information in operational testing environments.

Air Combat Training Ranges

The Global Positioning System is playing a role in advanced air-combat training ranges. Because GPS satellites are visible from all but the lowest elevation angles in almost all types of terrain, tracking for air combat purposes can be now achieved to ground level without having to use radar altimeters and terrain models usually necessary for determining the Vertical Dilution Of Precision (VDOP). If the stations and aircraft share the same spatial plane, as they do when GPS is used, the VDOP is constant and need not be calculated.

Also, because portable GPS receiver systems can be deployed as personnel-held gear, coverage can be expanded without having to establish permanent ground sites. High-capacity data links are used to transfer of tracking information among large numbers of trainees.

NATO's COMTESS

COMTESS stands for NATO's Combat Mission Training Evaluation and Simulation System, a training tool that combines live air missions with very complex simulated flying. By accurately reconstructing real missions and using them as bases for expected combat scenarios, the system reduces the number of actual flights necessary for a pilot to achieve combat readiness.

COMTESS allows pilots to simulate air-to-air and ground-attack missions under varying conditions. Playback is used for debriefing purposes and to evaluate responses. The system fits into the aircraft or simulator and uses GPS components to maintain continuous position determination.

PC Mission Planner

The GPS Mission Planner (GMP) is a computer program that runs on an IBM PC. Operational units use it for mission planning and for conducting survivability and navigation assessments based on realistic scenarios. Features of the GMP include:

- a trajectory generator,
- satellite-almanac data defining the GPS satellite orbits,
- broadband jammer specifications and
- digitized terrain-elevation data.

The GPS Mission Planner supports trajectory generation for air, land or sea vehicles and has "sanity" checks for altitude acceleration, terrain slope and velocity limits. A survivability measure is computed based on exposure time to various threat types, and results are graphically displayed.

Potential Threats to the GPS Itself

Deliberate Attacks

The Global Positioning System is not terror-proof. Each of the three segments — space, control and user — is vulnerable to particular threats from hostile sources, accidents or human error. Unintentional radio interference has occurred, suggesting the real possibility of intentional "spoofing," e.g., transmitting counterfeit signals to lure an aircraft into danger.

Among potential threats to the GPS, some are more serious than others. These may include:

- direct laser or particle-beam firing upon satellites in space;
- attacks on master control centers and satellite facilities;
- sabotage from within facilities or the military;
- spoofing of systems by terrorists;
- bursts of electromagnetic pulses (EMPs).

Hackers, extortionists or terrorists bent on disruption will find, though, that most potential threats (and some they may not even have considered) have been anticipated. The obvious kinds of built-in or outlined countermeasures for targeted segments include nuclear and laser hardening of satellite casings, backup monitor stations, backup antennae, EMP shielding and encryption of command and communication links.

Combinations of wide- and local-area DGPS systems will also provide a means by which aviation signals are spoof-proofed. In addition, the next generation of security devices will include tamper-resistant modules of chips that incorporate all anti-spoofing, cryptographic and encrypted-key functions.

Nondeliberate Causes of Failure

Anomalies may occur that affect the performance of the Global Positioning System. A whole class of problems exists relating to satellite transmission, in general, and to satellite position, code generation, upload capacity and degradation of the space environment. For example,

- Blocking or masking of signals may occur when the direct line of sight between a receiver antenna and a satellite being used is broken, e.g., if the receiver is located under trees or water, in a tunnel or in densely fabricated buildings.

- Very high electromagnetic conditions such as thunderstorms may interfere with the signals from space.

- Hardware or software may fail. Power supplies may be lost, or actual physical damage may occur to equipment. Software may be riddled with bugs.

- Operator error may jeopardize the accuracy and integrity of a system. Poor training, typographical errors in data entry, faulty installation and setup, as well as cavalier attitudes toward use, contribute to the causes of failure.

- Also, as is the case for most complex systems, successfully integrating the many interfaces, peripheral equipment, embedded systems and software that comprise GPS requires resolution of numerous discrepancies and incompatibilities — one of the system's biggest challenges.

- Orbiting debris, ranging in size from melons to pickup trucks, will occasionally threaten to hit a satellite. In such a case, the satellite would have to be moved temporarily out of the way — to a higher orbit, perhaps. This type of maneuver had to be used recently when a piece of space trash was tracked on a collision course with the Hubble telescope.

Adversarial Use of GPS

Overall Threat to the U.S.

In discussing the prospect of GPS being used against the U.S., the most encouraging aspect may be that GPS allows performance to be enhanced but does not offer radically new offensive power to a user. Also, in order to take maximum advantage of the promise of GPS, it is necessary to integrate its capabilities with many other systems and to educate and organize military personnel to use them effectively.

For a while, at least, most countries are not in the position to fully implement these conditions; those able to do so are traditional allies of the U.S. Still, long-term, defensive measures must be based on an assumption that precision locational power will be available worldwide. A short-term concern may be that the political effect of even limited action may be greater than the physical effect if strikes are delivered precisely on target. A more remote concern is that the focus of research and development may be influenced. Resources everywhere may be siphoned from nondefense into defense efforts to ward off potential adversarial strikes.

Proliferation of Accurately-Guided Missiles

Of particular concern to the U.S. military is the proliferation in non-allied countries of missiles capable of carrying weapons of mass destruction very quickly to their targets. In the past, danger has been somewhat limited by missiles that were dependably inaccurate and decidedly low-tech.

The situation can change. Statements eschewing the possibility of non-major powers acquiring ballistic missiles sophisticated enough to threaten the U.S. are strongly challenged by the National Security and International Affairs Division and other segments of the intelligence community. Their objections are based primarily on intelligence shortcomings and a failure by many to consider "alternate futures" that can easily change the scenario.

GPS will have a significant role in such alternate scenarios. A little knowledge, work and use of GPS may be all that are needed for anyone's missiles to reach their goals with a much higher degree of success. In an evaluation of the effectiveness of augmenting short- and medium-range (300- to 1,000-kilometer) missiles with GPS capability, there was an assessed improvement in accuracy of 20-25% — with Selective Availability having almost no effect.

Assessing the Threat

Since GPS technology is so widespread, and applications using GPS for both offense and defense purposes are proliferating faster than government policies can be implemented, the use of common tools and well-defined terminology for early assessment of threat to U.S. security is necessary. Inter-agency and inter-service tools for the quick and early screening of potential threats are crucial if preventive measures and countermeasures are to be effective.

In 1995, Rand Critical Technologies Institute published The Global Positioning System, Assessing National Policies, a report prepared for the Executive Office of the President. In it, researchers summarized their assessment of a GPS-based threat to U.S. security. It stressed the importance of placing any particular challenge to security in the context of military objectives, national assets, regional influences and actual survival of the nation.

A by-product of their analysis is an example of the type of easy-to-use assessment tool described above. Magnitudes of seriousness were assigned on a scale of 1 (no threat) to 5 (threat to survival):

LEVEL	ASSESSMENT OF GPS-BASED THREATS TO U.S. SECURITY
1	The least vulnerable (i.e., not threatened) was the actual survival of the U.S.
2	The possibility of preventing the U.S. from winning a major regional contingency was considered slight.
3	GPS in adversaries' hands may pose a moderate threat to critical national assets such as military facilities or civilian infrastructure.
4	The threat to U.S. security from an adversary's improved ability to attack military targets such as ships or fixed plants was deemed formidable.
5	GPS in the hands of terrorist or special-operations perpetrators posed the greatest threat when U.S. population centers and strategic sites are targeted.

9

MAPPING & SURVEYING

The user segment of the Global Positioning System owes a hearty round of thanks to the surveyors, geophysicists and cartographers. Their insistence on quality tools is the secret behind the sophistication of much of today's GPS equipment.

As early as 1983, when survey-quality GPS receivers became available, the surveying and geophysical communities eagerly adopted their use. Although the GPS constellation was not yet fully operational, these practitioners were patient — and they had an advantage. Their work involved static measurements, which meant they could "make do" with fewer satellites, scheduling their data collection around those times enough would be visible. Among the very first authoritative, practical texts on the use of GPS in the civilian arena was Leick's GPS Satellite Surveying.

The favor is now being returned as GPS systems and techniques revolutionize the way cartographers and surveyors do their jobs, delivering to them previously unattainable levels of accuracy. Their cumulative activity will translate into the development of consistent Geographical Information Systems (GISs) worldwide.

Field workers quickly realized the benefits of the handy new tool. It increased the precision, speed and distances over which necessary baselines could be measured. Fewer people are needed now for field projects. Data collection and the ability to post-process the data have made life easier for all involved. The old tools of the trade, described below, are lovingly but inevitably being put aside.

Conventional Tools of the Trade

Surveyors have traditionally relied on a number of instruments to help them determine the size and shape of segments of the earth's surface. With these tools, angular and linear measurements are taken of anything from small, family plots to whole continents. Results of such surveys are usually put into pictures or graphics

Links, Levels, Transits & Sextants

Early point-to-point (linear) measurements were made with tapes or chains. These were usually made up of either 100 1-foot-long links for standard measurements or 100 shorter (0.66-foot-long) links for measuring in acres. (This latter length squared equals one acre.) Link measurements are not accurate enough for today's purposes.

Levels were also used. A surveyor's level is, essentially, a crosshaired telescope mounted on a tripod. It is adjusted to a true horizontal line with cross bars and plumb lines. These, combined with a measuring stick (a leveling rod), are used to measure elevations in the land.

The most commonly used surveyor's instrument is the transit. A transit is, basically, a level mounted so that it can be angled at varying degrees and with which precise measurements can be taken.

For example, to find the angle between two intersecting lines, a transit would be set up where the lines cross. Readings would be taken along each of the lines separately, and angles would then be calculated from their differences.

Mariners measured latitude and longitude with an instrument called a sextant, which measures the angles of stars above the horizon by means of a moveable arc calibrated in degrees. The sextant held an advantage over the transit and other instruments in that it did not have to be kept in one position.

Using mirrors (one fixed and one movable), a person could sight two objects, such as a star and a point on the horizon, at once. By adjusting the movable mirror to the extent that the images seemed to coincide and by noting how much of a calibrated gauge was traversed, a navigator could calculate the angle between them from his or her location. From these, latitude and longitude can be found.

Triangulation & Map Making

The properties of triangles are important in mapping objects or land features. The relationship among angles of a triangle and the sides that contain them is fundamental to GPS positioning and is used by GPS in mapping a unique land feature — a person with a receiver.

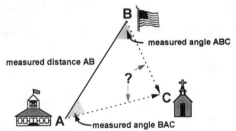

A simple example of how surveyors position objects using this concept is provided in Appendix B, "Triangulation." The difference with GPS is that most of the action takes place above ground, in space. Each satellite knows its distance from the others, and relevant angles can be found.

Surveying with GPS

Surveyors used GPS long before many other professions, primarily because their tasks were area-defined and focused and because they didn't need continuous coverage to realize significant gains from use of the technology. Today, with the help of GPS techniques and devices, labor-intensive surveys are being carried out with higher accuracy, lower cost per earth-feature identified and fewer persons needed in the field.

Increases in productivity are impressive. Project managers have reported that one person armed with GPS equipment can usually perform jobs that ordinarily required two or three.

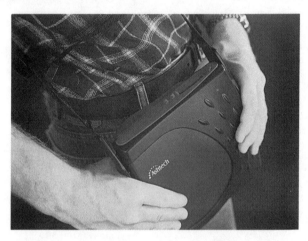

Even in cases in which localized, conventional surveys usually suffice, e.g., in easily-accessed places, much better and more cost-effective results are achieved by augmenting older methods with simple GPS techniques. Recently, by linking GPS satellite navigation technology to software developed at the University of Melbourne, researchers were able to map more than 250 miles in one day.

Most surveying jobs will eventually incorporate the use of GPS technology, but three particular types of work are positioned to benefit the most from advanced GPS techniques and equipment — topographic, cadastral and geodetic.

Topographic Surveys

Topography is the art of representing the features of the earth's surface. Topographic surveys include the heights and contours of particular regions or places, and topographic maps show mountains and valleys in relative elevations. More detailed topographic surveys also determine and log the locations of buildings, roads, sewers, wells, water lines and power lines. GPS is being used increasingly by municipalities to update local records and maintenance logs.

GPS helps researchers and field workers obtain more accurate positional information for many of the natural and manmade features shown on topographic maps. One existing application involves instruments mounted on a high-altitude aircraft, the three-dimensional position (to within a meter) of which is monitored by Differential GPS receivers. The times-of-flight of repetitively transmitted pulses of laser beams are then used to calculate surface-elevation profiles.

The U.S. Geological Survey usually conducts topographic surveys and publishes thousands of maps on a standard scale of 1:24,000. These maps are currently being digitized to form a repository of detailed, descriptive geographic and locational information (called a Datum) for use in both government and public domains.

Because such repositories serve researchers and scientists worldwide, they must be as accurate and comprehensive as possible. The Environmental Protection Agency (EPA), for example, uses GPS-accurate data for conducting environmental analyses and for assigning responsibility for damages in legal disputes.

Cadastral Surveys

Surveys done for the specific purpose of establishing legal and political boundaries (for ownership, representation or taxation, for example) are called cadastral surveys. A cadastral survey limited to one piece of property is called a boundary survey.

The U.S. Bureau of Land Management (BLM) relies on cadastral surveys to determine the legal boundaries of public lands. GPS is being used to increase the accuracy of boundary-map measurements.

In the private sector, stakes may be involved when boundaries differentiate between zones allocated for different purposes. For example, commercial property in some areas may sell for multiples of what an owner could sell residential property, and disputed property lines often foster costly litigation. Verifying coordinates with GPS techniques can play a role in determining the outcome of many of these legal battles. The availability of land maps that reflect GPS accuracy should discourage court cases.

Geodetic Surveys

Geodetic surveys attempt to define the exact coordinates of points on the earth's surface, the lengths and directions of lines on its surface and particular effects of gravity. Slight variations in the time of the earth's rotation, for example, have been measured and attributed to tidal forces.

The stations that monitor these changes (and determine the position of the earth's axis with respect to its crust) are attached to moving tectonic plates, and are consequently moving, as well. Thus, exact locational information must be recalculated regularly — and is where Differential GPS is used very effectively. (See Chapter 11 for the implications of GPS technology in the field of geodesy.)

Cartography

Over the centuries, different means and methods have evolved for recording views of the world, from alignment with constellations to gridlines on a piece of paper. Traditionally, each perspective rendering (or map) has been stored independently, and the number has grown, especially since the arrival of Geographic Information Systems (GIS).

Distortion factors and scales of these renderings (or maps) vary greatly with purpose. Some maps are hand-drawn; some are digital transfers from source maps. Digitized versions may have to be combined, or information from hand-drawn maps may have to be manually entered into a database for subsequent merging. Combining their information is a non-trivial task.

Map Reconciliation

Often, either for specific projects or in efforts to standardize, composite maps emerge from a number of different sources. Proportions representing data collected in the field, however, vary greatly from data derived from aerial photographs. Almost all maps, too, have been subject to a certain amount of human intervention — fine tuning deemed necessary to make them "right" (e.g., avenues not crossing buildings, aligning boundaries with streets, etc.).

All these adjustments must be considered. Before maps can be used together, their data must be reconciled. Reconciliation may be done by direct comparison, or it may require mathematical solutions. Again, work for which a single map is being used won't ordinarily be jeopardized by adjustments of this type, but they do detract from the credibility of analyses based on the map.

Today, GPS is greatly facilitating the task of reconciling existing documentation. It is the affordable, easy-to-use way of exercising quality control over future reference material.

Map Scales & Projections

A map scale is a defined, proportionate relationship between a real measurement on the earth's surface and its representation on paper, electronically or mentally. Generally, the same proportion holds true for all things represented. In large-scale maps, small details are blown up. In small-scale ones, large areas and features are miniaturized — a map of the world, for example.

Ratio

There is always a clue somewhere on a scaled map to help a person attain perspective. The relationship may be stated in words (e.g., One inch on the map equals 500 feet.) or an equation (1"= 500'). Map scale may also be shown as a ratio (1:500), a fraction (1/500) or a graphic illustration (perhaps of a ruler) showing relative distances.

Distortion

The many ways our spherical earth can be projected onto a flat surface also complicate the job of reconciling maps. Each type of projection arranges the parallels of latitude and the meridians of longitude differently.

On the globe, the meridians of longitude converge at the poles; they may be spread out to various degrees in flattened renditions.

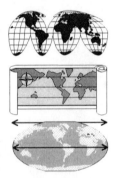

Also, even in a single flat map, the extent to which areas are distorted varies. Certain areas (near the equator, for example) may be truer proportionately than those as higher latitudes.

Reference Grids

Because of the difficulties of reconciling maps, position fixes are often assigned coordinates specific to any one of a number of reference grids. These serve as bridges to other coordinate systems in a slow march towards universal standards.

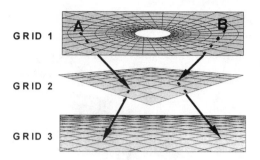

Universal Mercator

One type of chart, the Universal Mercator projection, is particularly convenient for navigation. Devised by Gerardus Mercator, a 14th century Flemish cartographer, the Universal Mercator simplifies navigation by flattening out the spherical surface of the earth into straight, equidistant lines representing latitude and longitude.

On a Mercator map, distances between lines are not constant. However, because each gridline indicates a constant north-south or east-west compass direction, staying on course is easy.

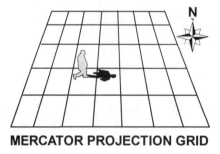

MERCATOR PROJECTION GRID

Datums

The type of mapping system used with the Global Positioning System is called a datum, which is a compilation of data, information and knowledge useful for a specific purpose such as navigation. This word is different from the singular form of data and is pluralized as datums. A datum used with a GPS receiver is a source of maps, numbers, coordinates, landmarks, waypoints and hints for users.

Each datum has a name and is usually tagged with the year of its last revision. If you purchase a GPS receiver, you will probably be given a choice to buy datums specific to your area and expected use. Datums come packaged as books, CD-ROMs and data cartridges.

A reliable datum (or mapping system) includes a configuration of collection and control facilities and a proven method of compiling data. Many datums are available to the public, but since they are gathered, published or provided independently by both official and unofficial entities, there are often discrepancies among them. Maps are not usually reconciled; so, errors of hundreds of miles may occur if coordinates of one are simply substituted for those of another.

Below are listed some of the general terms associated with datums.

GENERAL DATUM TERMS	
vertical datum	a register of heights
horizontal datum	a register of distances
geodetic datum	a source of geoidal data; representations of local or global ellipsoids
sea-level datum	theoretic level of the geoid; in practical terms, the mean sea level derived from the average of tidal cycles over 1 year
regional datum	a geoid-shaped ellipsoid in a particular region and related to a particular point in that region
global datum	refers to an ellipsoid approximating the shape of the entire geoid (total earth area)

World Geodetic Survey Datum — WGS 84

GPS features are providing the foundation and tools for a dynamic, worldwide grid that can be easily converted to other datums. The current reference for GPS positioning is the grid established for the World Geodetic Survey datum (WGS-84).

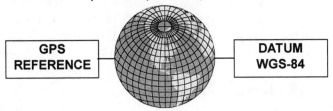

Other Datums

Around the world, other datums are considered reliable and detailed enough to become de-facto standards for particular uses. Very often, ties are established (e.g., between Tokyo/North American datums and North American/European datums) to provide even more extensive and consistent references.

Some examples of datums in use today around the world are:

- North American Datums of 1927 (NAD 27) & 1983 (NAD 83)
- National Geodetic Vertical Datum of 1988 (NGVD 88)
- NGS Horizontal Datum
- Australia Geodetic 1984
- European 1950 & 1979
- Military Grid Reference Systems (MGRS)
- Ordnance Survey of Great Britain 1936
- Bermuda 1957
- Provisional South Chilean 1963

Some datums carry names descriptive of local or regional focus. If you purchase a GPS receiver, you will probably be given an option to buy datums specific to its expected use or to an area, e.g., "Bahamas." These are available on microcartridges, computer diskettes or CDs.

Consistency & Quality Control

Optical-Lens Distortion in Photogrammetry

Using photography to make maps or scaled drawings is called photogrammetry. Cartographers use aerial photography extensively, but because images taken through an optical lens are subject to distortion, adjustments such as camera calibration, focal length and radial distortion have to be made to render measurements more precise. Tests conducted in the U.S. and in Europe indicate that the use of GPS for large-scale photogrammetry can significantly reduce the number of control points needed. If the problems of calibration, offset and drift are addressed, precision of terrain points is maintained with many fewer waypoints.

Database Integrity

Maintaining quality control of the database when map sources of varying scales and resolutions are combined is of overriding concern to anyone using the information in them. Engineering-level quality control has to be established to align measurements and waypoints, and map-accuracy tests must be conducted.

To do this, GPS surveys are used to pinpoint specific locations on the ground, which are then designated as control points. The Environmental Protection Agency uses GPS-surveyed control points to recompile EPA base maps and conduct accuracy tests on other maps used in remediation. Airports construct what are called waypoint monuments as control points.

Various Data-Collection Methods

The ways data are collected vary as widely as the people and tasks involved. The process may be as simple as a field worker walking the land, entering waypoints as he or she goes, or it may involve aircraft, aerial cameras and pre-processing or post-processing facilities.

Enlisting GPS technology with conventional methods allows exact determination of the location and orientation of the carrying vehicle, affording higher degrees of accuracy at lower cost. Electronic equipment mounted on moving land vehicles or in aircraft may even process data on board as soon as it is collected.

Helicopter-borne geophysical surveys have used GPS to pinpoint electromagnetic levels in the Voisey's Bay and Harp Lake areas of Labrador, Canada. A 12-channel Differential GPS navigational system was connected to magnetometers. GPS provided the precise locational coordinates that must accompany each piece of information. Results using this approach were so good that the range of flights was extended throughout Labrador.

Geography-Based Management

Looking at things where they are and questioning why they are there comprise the science and art of geography. Traditionally a discipline of images, geography is now emerging into arenas of economics, politics and sociology.

With the help of technology, the spread of information is making the world "smaller," and people want to know more about it. World atlases are being published more frequently as the number of nations on earth nears record level. New countries and thousands of associated names are being added or changed. Things are changing so quickly that, in 1992, the National Geographic Society went from yearly to monthly updates of its atlas.

Demand is increasing for up-to-date geographic references for commercial, academic, recreational and public purposes. GPS tools and techniques provide the fast, inexpensive collection of reliable, accurate measurements that can satisfy this demand. A description of one such type of database, a Geographic Information System (GIS), is given later in this chapter.

Repositories of Digitized Data

Many ways exist to store geographical coordinates for features, boundaries, altitudes and places on and near the earth. Collections of these that are organized so that people can easily find and use what is there are referred to as geographic, spatial or real-space databases.

Depending on its focus, a database may be global, national or local. The collection of geographic data can be very small, restricted to a local area or set of attributes, or it can be quite large, encompassing information about whole nations or the entire globe.

People "mine" databases for raw material and repackage it in unique ways. An example of this is a digitized version of the National Geographic Society's world atlas that has been released on CD-ROM. Its features invite children to virtually visit places, hear the languages spoken there, peruse photo albums or review statistics.

Spatial information can become part of a central repository of information available to everyone. If what is presented in an information package depends on real-world specifics, their context, altitude, latitude and longitude are included in a spatial database.

In spatial databases, images catalogued and registered along with exact coordinates can be triggered to appear when a device registers those coordinates. Thus, images and information are rendered interdependent; one always refers to or display the other. A GPS receiver can be used to trigger the display of a virtual image or directional sound.

"fossil digs"

GPS also helps people build spatial databases. The actual collection of coordinates for new locations is made easy, and its very precise measurements form the bases for reconciling other databases and maps. Coordinates gathered by old methods can be corrected, and resources using those data can be updated.

Geographic Information System (GIS)

Accessed via computer, databases called Geographical Information Systems (GISs) are revolutionizing the way agencies and businesses make land-related decisions and how people learn about the world. A GIS is specialized software that uses the principles of geography to maintain and present a variety of data and information types. It provides ways and makes it easy for users to draw relationships among them.

A GIS is also an inventory-management toolkit, helping people locate and keep track of almost anything. With a handheld GPS receiver, data can be easily collected and assigned in the field, and data can be easily revised, as well. Things that are moved often, for example, can be electronically "tagged" with GPS-receiver components, and their constantly updated fixes (coordinates) transmitted via data link to a central inventory control.

Since each GIS is designed as a dynamically changing database, data entered into it become part of the system as a whole. The computer processes new and changing data according to the relationships defined for them in the overall program. Data from other systems or gathered for other purposes may be imported directly into a GIS if they are formatted properly. If not, they can be converted to GIS format and then added to the GIS database.

Information is displayed in a GIS as text, a map, a 3-D picture or a combination of these. Each new entry to the database is checked in context with information already there, and the impact each new entry has on resident data is reflected throughout. The advantages of using a GIS are greatly increased with good database and conceptual management and involvement of persons familiar with project goals.

Sometimes, query-language software is used as an adjunct to a GIS to allow a user to ask the system questions. For example:

- An ecologist investigating the feasibility of conservation efforts may need to know how many bodies of water in a particular area are large enough to support wildlife.

- A pathologist may wonder about the effect topological features of an area may have in the spread of specific infectious diseases.

- A warehouse manager of goods that require regular rotation (such as steel or lumber that may warp if left in one position for long periods of time) or a freight handler on a dock, who must ensure a smooth flow of shipments to their right destinations, may request information on queueing. They may need to know of traffic-management constraints that may affect their shipments under various conditions.

- A city planner may inquire about possible detours around traffic congestion or need to manage evacuation routes in case of disaster.

- On the battlefield, too, strategic advantage often lies simply in knowing the terrain and its features better than an adversary and in the confidence gained from a heightened sense of situational awareness.

GPS & GIS

GPS techniques and GIS databases work well together, saving their users money and time. The wealth and accuracy of data obtainable from GPS enriches GIS databases and increases their reliability.

Utilization of GIS databases helps planners prevent and correct errors in the earliest stages of GPS projects. In targeted surveys, GIS tools reduced GPS-project planning time by 25-50%.

Running a Simple Application

Implementation of a GIS is straightforward. It is relatively easy for surveyors, city planners and land-management officers to acquire and use a set of GIS "tools." A core, generic setup might contain a personal computer, software, maps and a program designed to convert or reconcile mapping scales. Once the hardware (which can be a desktop unit) is acquired and installed, database software is needed to create a digital database for the project area.

GIS software is then used to access a base map of the area — which contains a registered National Geodetic Survey (NGS) dataset. Each control point in the NGS data set that corresponds to a project area is converted and used to create a GIS graphic point in the new database. Analysis determines if and where new points are needed and how they should be entered into the program.

GPS comes into the picture as the tool by which accurate positional data are obtained for objects, boundaries and places within the targeted area — landmarks, fire hydrants, access to gas lines, street lights, zones, etc.

Collecting the local data involves going to individual locations of things and entering their coordinates into a file. This can be done simply by cruising the streets in a car at a moderate rate of speed with a GPS receiver on board or walking the area with a manpack GPS unit. As each feature is passed, a waypoint-entry button is pressed to record the site, its coordinates and a brief description.

Ashtech

Entries can be annotated either then or later with details such as maintenance alerts, inventory tags, schedules or even specific locations for street lamps that require amber replacement bulbs. Collectors must be aware of errors that can be introduced by tree cover, high buildings or natural obstructions, but most receivers on the market are suitable for this type of application.

Back at the office, these data are entered into the digital database. Selections can then be extracted at any time, and graphic points can then be created in the GIS.

Baltimore County, Maryland, based a 1995 GIS project on a collection of 869 wide-angle aerial photographs. Using airborne GPS-determined camera positions to precisely pinpoint features in the photos (particularly conditions along coastlines), workers "georeferenced" the county's computerized information system.

The aim of the Baltimore project — to lay the foundation for a high-precision, high-resolution all-county GIS — required the integration of the new findings with local and other data. The approach was effective and economical.

Rural areas may link GPS/GIS services with local 911 emergency calls so that exact geographic locations can be automatically recorded. Digital display maps of the immediate areas can then be used to route rescuers or emergency vehicles to the scene.

Growing Demand

In the GIS area, the potential of GPS technology is just beginning to be realized. A major application of GIS has been the mapping of the locations of features specific to asset management.

McDonald's uses the GIS to select sites for new restaurants, the oil industry taps into the database to survey oil-well sites, and the U.S. Forest Service uses GIS and GPS measurements to delineate old- and new-growth areas. The added integrity of the data in a GIS that is derived from use of GPS is invaluable to applications such as these.

The oil industry has been using GPS and GIS systems for geodetic control networks, for controlling scale on ground photos and for precise locational fixes in field work.

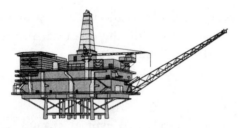

Oil-industry applications are now being enhanced by the addition of a special type of map. Geodetically-correct digital mosaics are created from GPS positional data and Geographic Information System data and used as a background grid for computer-screens or light-tables. Called digital orthophotographic maps, the new tool helps planners analyze, control and correct surveying data.

Commercial demand is growing to extend and update present spatial databases and reconcile their reference points with GIS. Before different systems can be combined or used together, however, the control points of each must be checked for accuracy and the various reference points reconciled — a task for which GPS is particularly well-suited.

Geodesy

Geodesy is the study of the size and shape of the earth and of the gravitational forces that influence them. The word is derived from the Greek word "geodaisia," meaning "division of earth." No one knows exactly when people started studying geodesy, but it seems that mankind has always wondered about the nature and extent of his domain, and the evolution of geodesy as a science was inevitable. Geodesy may be approached either geometrically, with focus on the size and shape of the planet, or physically, in which case attention is given to the dynamics of the force of gravity and its effect on the earth. The two disciplines, however, greatly influence each other.

Size & Shape

Geometrical geodesy uses observation and measurement in order to determine the size and shape of the earth. It involves determining both the figures and areas (and the relative positions) of portions of the earth's surfaces and the figure of the earth as a whole.

Among the most curious, innovative geodesists was Eratosthenes, a Greek Keeper of the Scrolls in Egypt at around 220 B.C. Also a mathematician, he took it upon himself to find out how big the earth was. Despite the fact that his research tools consisted of only a tower, a water well and a calibrated camel, he managed to come up with a pretty close estimate. (See Appendix B for how he did it.) Today, Eratosthenes' counterparts are able to achieve more accurate measurements than ever before — with a lot less trouble. GPS tools and techniques are instrumental in facilitating the study of geodesy and furthering our knowledge of this near-sphere on which we live.

Many of us are familiar with the term "geodesic" from those vaulted structures of lightweight polygons known as geodesic domes. This type of structure was of particular interest to Richard Buckminster Fuller, an American architect and inventor who saw, through the study of geodesy, a way he could combine geometric stability with ease of construction.

By dividing up the surface of a structure into sections that all evened out to a dome, Fuller was following on a small scale what geometrists have been doing mathematically on the scale of our planet — the space-frame principle.

By dividing up the earth into a framework of small spaces and using mathematics on precise measurements within each of the framed spaces, geometrists have been able to derive a "normal" level of the earth's surface structure (which also determines sea level).

Movement & Gravity

Physical geodesy focuses on the rotation of the earth around its axis and the movement on its surface of large plates of land mass. It may be thought of as a dynamic version of the old term "geo-metry," or earth-measurement.

In addition to its concern with size and shape, physical geodesy involves the earth's gravitational field — in other words, the dynamics of the force of gravity that link the earth to objects on its surface and in the space surrounding it.

The solid, outer layer of the earth's surface is divided into about 20 plates. Each seems to move independently, slowly responding to changes in the earth's interior. Learning more about the nature and extent of even the most minute of these motions adds to our understanding of earthquakes and other natural phenomena.

Geoids

A short explanation may be helpful in understanding an important basis for geometric and physical measurements of our earth — a virtual surface or "earth-dome" called the geoid.

Imagine that all points on the earth's surface were equally distant from its center and that the force of gravity didn't vary from place to place — as if all land and sea ran together and were level. The spherical image that comes to mind is a convenient way (for most general purposes) to think about the earth's surface and gravity.

As if all points on surface were level and gravity equal ...

This "normal," which can be calculated mathematically, assumes an earth that is smooth and made up of homogenous material. The mathematical normal (or reference spheroid) is the convenient constant upon which many scientific measurements and calculations are based.

This geoid, however, is only an approximation of the true terrestrial gravity field of the earth. The true gravity field is based on both the distances from the center of the earth to the points on its surface and the densities of the materials found along the path between them.

The forces of gravity in any area vary according to the varying densities of the materials found there. To get the geoid measurement close to the real assessment, it must be derived from as many exact measurements possible of the real terrestrial gravity field of points on earth.

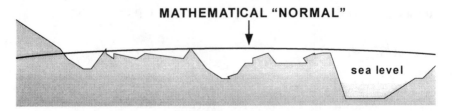

When, in reality, varying forces of gravity are in play.

The differing mass distributions have little consequence in an averaged-out model of the geoid but cause significant dips and rises in true geoid measurements for real areas. Because the effect on measurement in even a small area may amount vertically to tens of meters or yards, measurements must be made independently for small sections of the geoid around the earth. This is critical if altitude is to be determined accurately.

There are many methods to determine the true geoid heights for individual sections of the "earth-dome," and computer models have been used extensively. Now, GPS is being used, too. In continental domains, leveling data is compared with GPS positioning. Modeling can still be used then to compute, for example, the extent of crust under sea margins or the depth of crustal root under mountains.

Good results have been obtained from the use of GPS in measuring the geoid. A 900-kilometer-long line around the Great Slave Lake area, Northwest Territories, Canada, defined an area used to compare geoid predictions from known methods and models and those from 88 GPS stations. Accuracies achieved from GPS were significantly true to those obtained from field work and complex models.

In Australia, the geoid is defined by the Australian Gravity Anomaly Data Bank, and the integration of GPS-determined heights into the Australian Height Datum (AHD) is being considered. An extensive GPS network provides data to the South Australian Department of Lands and the Royal Australian Survey Corps, which is evaluating the feasibility of combining GPS with AHD values.

In these and many other ways, GPS is benefiting both theoreticians and practitioners alike in the sciences. Theoreticians benefit by acquiring from field workers the amounts of quality data needed to study the dynamics of gravity and the deformation of the earth's crust and to make projections. Hands-on practitioners consider the easy-to-use and highly accurate differential-GPS techniques and equipment essential to their work.

Geodetic Networks

Persons measuring the subtle and not-so-subtle movements of crustal plates via GPS collect the data they need from either an entire network of stations, from a subset of a network or from a combination of stations from different networks. Each subset's measurements has a unique, inherent, composite error. Positional coordinates determined by data from one subset may differ from those obtained from another subset, even for the same position.

For networks covering distances of tens of miles, some errors can be attributed to less-than-perfect satellite orbits, but some errors occur because different subsets of the geodetic network are used. Researchers must assess the extent of the latter. This is done primarily through the establishment of a number of fixed points called fiducial stations that serve as a reference frame for crustal deformation measurements.

Geodetic surveys and networks help cartographers establish the control points or networks of reference that serve as bases for accurate land mapping. In the U.S., the National Geodetic Survey (NGS) establishes the network and gathers and corrects data on physical landmarks or specific points on the earth's surface. From these data, national registries of vertical and horizontal measurements are compiled — the NGS Vertical Datum and the NGS Horizontal Datum. This type of geodetic datum is the basis for surveys that account for the curvature of the earth. Ultimately, there will be global control networks.

Changes in any measurements over time can reflect changes in the plates upon which the landmarks rest. If the datum is to be both accurate and detailed, however, numerous, well-placed control points are necessary. The Hekla volcano in Iceland is surrounded by a distant array of control points, first measured with GPS in 1989. Remeasuring after an eruption in 1991, scientists hoped to determine the exact extent of change, but because the control points were not close enough to the volcano, all they were able to confirm was a deflation of the surface.

Earth's Orientation & Its Geocenter

An early (1991) study enlisted a worldwide network of GPS receivers to record daily estimates of the earth's pole position over a three-week period. Easily collected GPS coordinates compared favorably to results obtained by conventional, labor-intensive geodetic techniques. In later studies, GPS measurements appeared to compete extremely well with those of other techniques, generating nearly continuous centimeter-level earth-orientation information.

Compared to data obtained from very-long-baseline interferometry (VLBI), GPS-gathered data provide results of sufficient quality to replace VLBI for estimating most pole positions. GPS also provides a viable alternative technique to satellite laser ranging for monitoring variations in the position of the earth's rotation axis.

Today, the use of GPS and a globally distributed network of highly precise receivers is becoming the means of choice for monitoring and measuring variations in the earth's orientation. The extent of these variations is important to the study of high-frequency earth-orientation-related processes and to spacecraft navigation. In addition, the efficiency and cost-effectiveness of GPS-based positioning techniques are not limited to the long term. Studies of rapid determination of fluctuations over a short term indicate the same economy.

GPS is helping in another area of study. The location of our earth's center of mass, its geocenter, is constantly shifting — up to four centimeters on one axis and 30 centimeters on another. Because of the influence that this dynamically changing location and orientation of the earth have on orbiting bodies, for example, scientists measure them both.

It is also important to track and measure variations of the earth's rotation. Because the ocean's tides are a big part of the dynamics, tidal computer models have been used extensively. Up until recently, these and satellite lasers were used to estimate shifts and predict the effect these will have on other calculations.

Today, GPS measurements are also being collected from stations on the ground and from low-orbiting satellites (not the GPS ones). For earth orientation, ground-based control points produce better-than-centimeter measurements. For the location of the geocenter, GPS techniques agree within 7-13 centimeters with traditional satellite laser techniques.

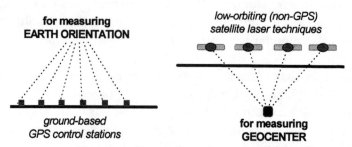

Results from a worldwide geodetic experiment indicate that collecting and combining data from both ground sites and satellites produce significantly better levels of accuracy than can be obtained from either source alone. All measurements, too, are being accomplished more easily, cheaply and quickly today with the help of GPS.

Measuring Gravitational Fields

GPS is helping us add to our knowledge of the earth's gravitational field, especially over vast areas of ocean. By coupling a GPS receiver with a gradiometer mounted on a low-orbiting platform, a geodesist can map the field with a higher degree of accuracy than ever before.

GPS data are gathered by an on-board receiver and a worldwide network of ground receivers. Results of some early experiments show that the combination of both GPS and gradiometer produce accuracies better than those obtained from GPS-only or gradiometer-only techniques.

10

GEOLOGY

Geology is the study of our earth as a part-rock, part-metal body. In addition to earth history, geology includes its layering, paleontology, mineralogy and petrology.

Traditionally, geologists have been occupied with that part of the earth's crust accessible to human observation. They investigate the composition, structure and physical changes that occur on and in the earth, such as mountains wearing away, plains flooding or coastal areas building up or changing. They study the deposition and distribution of metals and minerals and how strata reflect physical influences on the earth's crust.

Geologists may approach their work with a focus either on the physical geology of the earth or on geology as history. Physical geology looks at the earth as we find it around us, what it is made of and how it changes. Historical geology places the development of the planet in the context of the different life forms it supports. Both approaches require exact measurements, and GPS is helping geologists obtain them. A GPS receiving device is an integral part of a professional's toolkit.

U.S. Geological Survey Role

The U.S. Geological Survey (USGS) develops and implements plans for the collection of data on the elevations of the earth's surface. These highly accurate topology measurements are the basis of a national database and modeling tool called the Natural Systems Model. It is used for calculating water surface slope, depth, velocity and direction of flow — all major issues facing ecosystem restoration and management.

Access to Global Positioning System technology has led to many improvements in geophysical equipment. It has led to advances in techniques for many applications, dramatically upgrading the process of collecting new data and providing a cost-effective means for refreshing the old.

The USGS establishes guidelines and determines the levels of accuracy required from the equipment and methods used. In many cases, however, data collection is thwarted by environmental conditions and the costs of working around natural forces. In dangerous environments, such as in the Everglades, traditional methods (requiring a specialist's presence in the field) don't work.

Plate Tectonics & Crustal Deformation

Currently, geologists' interest in GPS focuses on measuring the extent of change in the physical makeup of the earth's surface. Causes of measurable change include dramatic events such as earthquakes and volcanic eruptions, as well as the slower processes of weathering and erosion. The ranges and accuracies of these measurements are being extended with GPS-aided techniques.

Rafts on the Planet's Surface

Plate tectonics is the part of geology that focuses on the ever-shifting layered plates that form earth's rocky-metallic crust. It is the study and precise measurement of structural deformation of the crust and its underlying causes.

According to a 1980 National Academy of Sciences report, our realization that continents are moving like rafts on the planet's surface, driven by immense forces within the crust, has brought about a "revolution in scientists' concept of the planet." Today, GPS is giving that revolution a booster shot, and the excitement continues. The ease of use and accuracy of the new technology have allowed scientists to measure subtle shifts of only a few millimeters over great portions of the earth's crust. For example, GPS provided the first practical technique for measuring deformation in the offshore regions of southern California. More than five years of geodetic measurements of subcentimeter precision have been gathered from GPS satellites via a geodetic network established along the coastline.

Converging Plates

Plate dynamics and locations of earthquake-prone areas are being studied with new vigor, providing a powerful framework for detecting deformation along complex continental-plate boundaries. GPS facilitates more precise measurement of relative plate motion at convergent boundaries and, especially, in places not suited to global-model techniques.

Problems such as kinematic descriptions of crustal deformation and the measurement of plate motion at convergent boundaries, however, are not easily modeled. New equipment and techniques are constantly being sought, and thresholds are being established by the U.S. Geological Survey for achieving precision of short-range, kinematic-type GPS measurements to the level of millimeters.

In order to study the convergence of the Eurasian, Pacific, Philippine Sea and North American plates, Japanese researchers have established a fixed-point network in the Kanto and Tokai districts. The Global Positioning System and the 10-station grid are being used to detect crustal deformation and monitor the cycles of frequent earthquakes among the plates.

Strain Accumulation

Geologic applications include the operation of GPS receivers as strainmeters, and networks provide the frameworks for monitoring strain accumulation along faults in earthquake-prone areas. GPS measurements can be taken from all or a subset of the grid on a regular basis and analyzed for signs of potential earthquake activity and displacement.

Tests have been conducted to compare the performance of GPS units to that of high-quality strainmeters in monitoring local crustal deformation. Results indicate that the use of GPS may be preferable for short-term measurements (those taken for 6 months or less).

Strain accumulation was measured with GPS across the Imperial Valley in California, from 29 stations for three years and 11 stations for another two years. While considerable, the GPS-obtained rates of accumulation (first 5.9 cm/yr. right-lateral; then 5.2 cm/yr. valley-crossing deformation) were lower compared to rates calculated from 15 years of terrestrial geodetic measurements. This suggests less earthquake potential than previously had been assumed.

The Superstition Hills earthquake series in 1987 was the first time a large earthquake occurred within a GPS-networked area and for which pre-earthquake measurements were available. Thirty stations from among 42 set up in 1986 were revisited after the quake (from 1988-1990), and large earthquake-attributed displacements were observed — nearly 50 centimeters within 3 kilometers of the rupture and at least 10 centimeters within 20 kilometers of the seismic zone.

Geological Histories

The capability provided by GPS technology to detect and track very small displacements provides analysts with a more detailed history of movement than has been possible in the past. Experiments using a fixed-point GPS network to measure deformation off the coast of Japan's Izu Peninsula in 1989 provided researchers with a continuous, evolutionary timeline for underwater volcanic activity. Through the data, they got a peek at some seismic events rarely capturable in pre-GPS days, underscoring GPS's effectiveness as a research tool for physical and historical geology. GPS is also being used to extend historical logs of triangulation and astronomic azimuth data that have been collected since 1875. Trilateration data obtained since 1970 are also being added to and kept up-to-date with GPS measurements.

Some notable results obtained by researchers around the world from GPS-enhanced geodetic-measurement projects include the following:

- Satellite data from GPS indicate strongly that Australia and Antarctica are pulling apart. A study conducted by plate tectonic researcher Kristine Larson puts the rate of Australia's north-northeast creep at two to three inches per year.

- The south flank of Hawaii's Kilauea volcano is being displaced seaward at rates up to 10 centimeters (~4 inches) per year. Dilation within the volcano and slip on a fault beneath it were each measured at rates of 15 centimeters per year.

- In Northwest Anatolia (near the Sea of Marmara), GPS was used with a dense 45-site monitoring network to precisely measure the field of movement within active earthquake belts. Average westward movement of Anatolia toward Eurasia was 2.4 centimeters (~1 inch) per year, and a general strike-slip motion in a WSW-ENE direction was observed.

- A 1989 GPS-aided survey done in Loma Prieta, California was compared with one done in 1990, after an earthquake. The coseismic displacements there measured 410 mm horizontal and 341 mm vertical.

- The same approach allowed a determination of the motion between the North American and Pacific plates. Experiments in Mexico's Gulf of California indicated motion of 47 (+ or -7) mm per year of Cabo San Lucas relative to the North American plate. The use of GPS provided the precision.

11

GPS & THE ENVIRONMENT

The nitty-gritty field aspects of protecting the environment and its ecological balance are becoming easier as professionals arm themselves with GPS receiving devices. Their use in this and other fields in which precise locational coordinates must accompany on-the-spot data collection and measurements is more common than most people realize. An integral part of today's field worker kit is either a handheld GPS receiver or a heavier-duty field device with standing antenna. With either, the on-site portion of a field worker's job is significantly easier.

Personnel are not only able to obtain more accurate results, but they are able to complete more projects in less time than with traditional equipment. Time and money are saved, too, as maps and reference databases are reconciled and upgraded to reflect the precision and abundance of data now possible with GPS.

Applications in which GPS is used range from tracking endangered species and logging seasonal movements to mapping underwater grasses to predicting weather patterns. Descriptions of how some of these are being done differently with GPS follow.

Habitat Inventory

When experts in habitats visit an area, they make note of the type of ground underlying the habitat, the vegetation in and around it and the site's orientation to the study area, recording it all on field sheets. Digital cameras that interface with GPS receivers will relieve the field worker of much of this burden by electronically tagging pictures with GPS-precise locational data. Specially-adapted camcorders are also used to take infrared videos of the areas from the air. The multispectral, digitized images are then correlated to field sheets.

When experts in marine and estuarine near-shore habitats visit an area, however, there is a problem. Because most near-shore habitats do not have dramatic natural or cultural features, they do not stand out enough to serve as reference points on images scanned from aircraft. To even trained eyes, they usually look rather nondescript, making it difficult for analysts to pinpoint exactly where certain site measurements and characteristics were obtained.

The collection of ground verification data is a particularly effective use of GPS technology, and GPS was used in this way in a project to inventory the near-shore habitats of Puget Sound in Washington State. Using a portable GPS receiver, field experts collected GPS data along with the habitat data at each field site. What was noted at the site was tagged with exact coordinates, and image analysts were then able to correlate image data to field data with precision.

In order to study the use by sea turtles of an estuarine habitat in North Carolina, two positioning systems and a directional sonic telemetry system were evaluated. Differential Global Positioning System results proved superior, and DGPS has been recommended as the system of choice for future studies.

Endangered & Migrating Species

Ninety species of animals and plants were lost during the 3,000 years of the Pleistocene Ice Age. In the 375 years since the Mayflower landed (1/8th the time), however, over 500 species have disappeared — a 45-fold increase in the rate of extinction.

Despite heightened awareness of the problem within private and public sectors, the threat to animals and plants remains considerable. In the U.S., according to data analyzed by the Nature Conservancy, California and Alabama alone account for 49 extinctions and 95 possible extinctions.

With many more species on their way out, the National Oceanic & Atmospheric Administration (NOAA) is using GPS extensively to measure and monitor the chemistry and biology of the environment and to understand the dynamics of ecosystems — an important step in slowing the rate of extinction.

Independent conservationists and survey firms are equipping themselves with GPS attribute-collection systems to gather more information in shorter tours of duty. In Tanzania, Africa, researcher Sharon Pochron mapped in detail the habits and range of specific troops of yellow baboons over a 15-month period. In Florida, after Hurricane Opal in 1995, shoreline damage and its effects on communities had to be evaluated. Using a similar system, one surveyor, Kathi Martin, was able to remap the drastically changed shoreline quickly so that reconstruction could begin.

Animals

Among a growing number of projects, the National Park Service is reconciling its maps with GPS-based coordinates and using GPS to locate and track animals threatened by encroachment on their habitats. GPS-tagged data are being collected on Gambel's quail in southwest Utah, and rare desert tortoises in Joshua Tree National Monument in California.

Elk are being collared with small transceivers and tracked via GPS as they move about Montana, and GPS keeps tabs on grizzly bears there, as well. Armed with portable equipment, field researchers also study bear habits and log any track changes in foraging patterns.

Field workers also GPS-tag and follow disease patterns in plants that are essential to the bears' survival. Adventurous personnel locate and map waterways, boundaries and establish GPS-coordinate logs of the exact locations of food sources within the animals' habitats.

The Environmental Protection Agency is also using GPS to trace migration and study animal habitats — particularly those of endangered species. With GPS, exact locations of surfacing whales can now be documented, and their migrations and breeding patterns can be followed with more accuracy.

Plants

The EPA is also busy mapping rare plants and those that are noxious to wildlife. Observed boundaries of endangered (or endangering) species are being GPS-tagged so that patterns of growth and changes in conditions within their areas can be viewed regularly over long periods of time. Analysts can use the data to justify action if intervention is necessary to preserve the ecological balance.

Underwater Meadows

Underwater meadows of grass provide sanctuary and food for small fish, and the plants' root system is a deterrent to erosion. Because the plants cannot survive without light, waterfront construction and shore traffic often stifle growth or destroy them. So does dredging.

Now, developers can make allowance for existing meadows or compensate for those that cannot be preserved. To be able to do so, maps of threatened plants must be drawn with great precision and superimposed on construction blueprints. This was done for eelgrass meadows in Washington State's Puget Sound when docklands were being converted for commercial use.

GPS receivers deliver the precision needed, but since they do not work below the surface of the water, engineers devised a system of floating platforms, receiver/antenna units and underwater video cameras connected to an above-surface television monitor.

In this type of setup, the GPS unit feeds the date, time, latitude and longitude into a personal-computer database. The towfish line from which the camera is suspended is weighted to fall straight down, ensuring that the camera is always vertically below the GPS unit. The imaging system supplies the video signal and, perhaps, gridlines to help a user pinpoint things on its display screen.

Each field of view captured by the camera covers about one square meter. A permanent visual image is time-tagged and stored with its exact coordinates every two seconds.

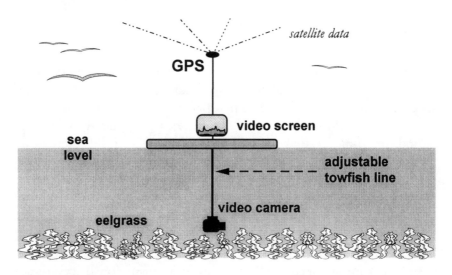

An operator is assigned to manage the length of towline, raising or lowering the camera to follow the contours of the seabed from just above the eelgrass. The "altitude" part of the measurement is derived from this. Another operator regulates how fast the towline is moved over the area (about one meter per second) so that estimates of the coordinates of an image are possible to derive even in the absence of GPS coordinates.

Another system, the Submersed Aquatic Vegetation Early Warning System (SAVEWS), has been developed by the Army Corps of Engineers to assess the potential for damage to underwater plants from dredging in their vicinity. It was designed primarily so that ACE engineers could quickly detect and map individual seagrass beds before any dredging actually starts. Using a combination of sensors, software, underwater sound equipment, Geographic Information System components and GPS, SAVEWS provides near-real-time feedback of the lay of the underwater terrain and its meadows.

Differentiating Species

GPS is also being used in conjunction with airborne video systems to differentiate among plant species' coverage in rangelands. The "remote sensing device" used to take the videos is a standard color camcorder adapted to acquire infrared images.

The digitized images reflect differences among plants and between plants and the surrounding soil. Merging the data with a Geographic Information System and GPS coordinates for the area, researchers obtain images on which precise locations are imprinted. These become a basis for evaluating changes and/or infestation.

The same basic approach is used to study how developers infringe upon areas of essential sources of food for animals. Building projects have the potential of severely upsetting the ecological balance of an area and threaten the survivability of many forms of wildlife. Combined GPS and GIS techniques help researchers map and classify very small differences in the habitats, e.g., the fragile food sources of grizzlies in Montana.

Natural Resources

Delineation

In addition to its increasing use for outlining transportation routes or mapping land to be developed, GPS and its allied technologies have become invaluable tools for delineating natural resources such as wetlands or forests. Equipped with a GPS receiver to collect locational data and a connection to a GIS database, an environmental professional can map an area quickly and accurately. Aerial surveys can also be conducted.

Forest Delineation using Standard GPS

In northern Sweden, helicopters flew along forest lines with known positions, obtaining standard GPS coordinates as they went. Researchers wanted to know how readings obtained from nondifferential techniques would match known positions. Results did not match positional data exactly but were considered satisfactory for fertilization and liming projects. A second study determined that standard-GPS measurements of plots in forested terrain were sufficient for maps on the scale of 1:20000.

Natural-Resource Management

The U.S. Bureau of Land Management has established a number of differential base stations (DGPS) to help its engineers in surveying and mapping property corners, gathering geographic data, and monitoring levels of groundwater and the effects its withdrawal has on land surfaces. Regularly scheduled measurements are also taken to monitor erosion along seashores and changes in the levels of rivers and reservoirs.

As of 1994, 26 permanent base stations were being used for these purposes. Other facilities and equipment will be made available as multi-agency collaboration is expanded.

Fire Detection & Assessment

Sokkia

In addition to the above, the U.S. Forest Service has integrated DGPS with navigation systems installed in many of the service's surveillance aircraft, especially in aircraft used in the detection, assessment and suppression of forest fires. For these jobs, because of hazardous conditions and the need to fly missions at low altitude (2000 feet) and relatively slow speed (120 knots), it is important to keep position uncertainty to a minimum. Small aircraft and helicopters are often employed, and justification is growing for increasing the role of robot helicopters.

An aircraft flies over a fire zone, logging GPS fixes every fraction of a second of the perimeter and of hot spots. This stream of fire data is relayed to ground teams on an ongoing basis.

A system called Firefly makes use of 2 twin-engine Forest Service aircraft fitted with infrared sensors and GPS navigation receivers. Surveillance planes locate fires, sampling signals at 10-millisecond intervals. They integrate them with the GPS-enhanced navigation system, then waypoint perimeters and hot spots. The final step is to communicate and send near-real-time fire maps to ground personnel.

Land Subsidence

Over time, a large tract of land may sink, usually due to a withdrawal of groundwater beneath it. Certain geographical areas are more prone to this land "subsidence." For example, Sacramento, California, has an observed history of decreasing surface elevations recorded at intervals since the early 1900s, and Mexico City suffers from subsidence because it was built on a drying lake bed. Since the 1990s, however, traditional monitoring has given way to the ease of use of GPS devices and methods. Comparative annual measurements are important in order to understand the nature and extent of subsidence. GPS is providing the means for easily establishing benchmarks and monitoring ellipsoidal changes over time with 1- to 2-centimeter (less than 1-inch) accuracy.

GPS-Aided Weather Prediction

Nature's dynamics, often dramatically beautiful on a grand scale, can wreak social and economic havoc on individuals' daily lives and property. To be effective, emergency measures must be based on the accurate observation, prediction and assessment of damages and on the swift delivery of information.

A main goal of the U.S. National Oceanic and Atmospheric Administration (NOAA) is a comprehensive system for anticipating, monitoring and dealing with environmental events. GPS is a significant component of its technical toolkit. It is used for gathering reliable data regarding weather, climate, space and marine resources and for studying of nautical, aeronautical and geodetic phenomena.

Predictions of climate variations such as drought, flooding or ocean warming are based on observations over extended periods (e.g., seasonal, annual, 10 years or 100 years), and computer models can re-create scenarios of the past for extension into the future. Also, because the accuracy of data determines the quality of the outcome, GPS-based data upgrade the validity of results from models of natural phenomena such as hurricanes. Studies of human-caused problems such as pollution and a thinning of the ozone layer, which also involve scientific details, exploit the strength of accuracy of GPS-collected data to gain credibility and reinforce calls for action.

Tracking Hurricanes & Weather-Balloons

Inaccuracy in predicting where a hurricane will hit ground is expensive and dangerous — from efforts to needlessly evacuate and protect areas not in a hurricane's path to losses and damage suffered by people and property in areas not accurately pinpointed. Estimated costs for prediction errors is $1 million per mile-off-target.

Meteorological balloons, which provide information about the speed and direction of the wind at certain heights, have traditionally been tracked by Omega, a radar system used by the U.S. Meteorological Office. The possibility of continuing with Omega for meteorological experiments after its announced phase-out date of 1997 has been dropped because the Meteorological Office intends to use GPS.

The National Weather Service has contracted the U.S. Air Force to track hurricanes. Pilots fly over a hurricane, dropping radiosondes (sensors) into it. As these are tracked (until now by Omega), they measure specific characteristics of the area through which they fall and relay the information back to a receiver. Wind direction and speed are determined from changes in the tracked position over time.

Crews of the Air Force Reserve's 53rd Weather Reconnaissance squadron use GPS data to pinpoint the location of a storm. Carrying commercial, hand-held GPS sets on their missions to check the position of the eye of a hurricane, crews penetrate a storm and fly inside it.

The ease with which accurate readings can be obtained with GPS encourages more vigorous collection of hurricane data than traditional methods even though radiosondes for use with GPS are more expensive and may be more prone to "swing" than those for Omega. In 1995, with accurate readings made easy with GPS, crews increased the pace of their tracking and got 71 position fixes on the location and progress of the eye of one storm alone, Hurricane Felix. With traditional methods, the average number of penetrations for other storms that year was only 20.

Sensing Climate Changes

GPS is being enlisted to augment the ways experts detect global and regional climate change. In turn, what is detected adds to our knowledge of the same atmospheric variables that affect GPS signal propagation. In Switzerland, for example, Differential GPS is being used in conjunction with laser altimetry to detect minute fluctuations in the heights of glaciers, often harbingers of climactic changes.

Another area of study focuses on the very sensitive interplay among concentrations of carbon dioxide and high water vapor content in some areas of the globe. Since these affect wet delay and refractivity of signals from GPS satellites, they must be measured precisely. GPS, itself, is helping researchers do this. Ground-based receivers and sensors estimate amounts of precipitable water, and computer models simulate GPS signal delays under varying conditions. Reversing the process, i.e., monitoring real measurements of signal delays, may prove a practical way to anticipate climate change.

Lightning Storms

Meteorologists in the United Kingdom use the time-of-arrival (TOA) concept to locate severe thunderstorms over Europe. Electronic "snapshots" of lightning strokes are time-tagged and sent to control stations, where scientists measure the TOA of a waveform generated by the strokes. In its capacity as a time-transfer utility, GPS serves as the time reference, ensuring system accuracy and extending its range.

Hydrologic Studies

The U.S. Geological Survey (USGS) designs, develops and implements plans for measuring elevations on the earth's surface. Such surface topology data are essential for calculating water surface slope, depth, velocity and direction of flow — all major issues facing ecosystem restoration and management.

Most of the data collected feed into a resource database and analysis tool called the Natural Systems Model. In many cases, however, data collection is thwarted by the costs of working around poor conditions, including the environment. In dangerous environments such as in the Everglades, traditional methods don't work — especially if they require a specialist's presence in the field.

Hydrologists may need to factor in even slight elevations (as small as 3 centimeters) to properly assess the effect of water flow on surrounding areas, a level of precision so stringent that standard measuring techniques don't suffice. Helicopters are sometimes used, but the vertical accuracy attainable by them may not be precise enough for some purposes. GPS techniques provide an alternate that is not only cost-effective but provides more accurate elevation data.

Everglades Ecosystem Project

Problems of managing and restoring ecosystems in south Florida center around the availability of clean, fresh water and its distribution. The terrain in south Florida is expansive and very flat — "low relief" in cartographers' terms. Surface waters move in sheet flows through the Everglades, from Lake Okeechobee to Florida Bay and the Gulf of Mexico.

In 1995, three agencies (the U.S. Geological Survey, U.S. Army Topographic Engineering Center and National Oceanic and Atmospheric Administration) pooled their human and equipment resources to use GPS techniques to collect high-accuracy elevation data for a large expanse in the Everglades area.

A dozen scientists and engineers used dual-frequency GPS receivers, computers, air boats and other means to perform field work and process the data collected. They also developed a methodology for others to follow.

GPS Solution to a Difficult Problem

The results obtained from the Everglades project through GPS varied from known control points by an average of only 1.4 centimeters. These findings substantiated the premise of the project, which was that GPS techniques are an easy, cost-effective solution to what has been a difficult problem — measuring the sheet flow through expansive, low-relief terrain. An extension of the project includes data collection for the generation of elevation maps with a vertical accuracy of only six inches (15 centimeters). GPS locational coordinates will be collected every 400 meters for over 8,000 square miles of difficult terrain. Forty-eight resultant maps will include GPS surveys of features such as levies or roads that may affect water sheet flows through the area.

Natural Systems & Economic Prosperity

Necessary adjuncts to government's goals of economic prosperity and the strengthening of U.S. trade are improvements in the quality of life and an increased protection for lives and property. Access to GPS and its devices has revolutionized the way we acquire space-time data, monitor the environment and manage our natural assets.

Conservation of Coastal & Marine Resources

As conservator of the nation's coastal and marine resources, the National Oceanic and Atmospheric Administration is responsible for describing and predicting changes in the earth's environment. It also assumes responsibility for determining how societal and economic decisions affect it. Oil spills rank high among the problems it faces.

When oil spills occur, the distribution and dispersion of the oil must be tracked and time-tagged. To help in this task, NOAA has designed a device coupling a laptop computer with a GPS-receiver. Laplogger, as it is called, can be carried and/or used by trackers on aircraft. Sightings of spilled oil can be positioned, time-tagged and logged automatically (on a predetermined schedule), or a person can enter the data via keyboard at will. Field trials of spills along the Mississippi River Delta and in Tampa Bay, Florida, uncovered some minor problems with implementation of the system, but overall performance was good, and its continued use is planned.

DGPS within the EPA

Differential-GPS is being used increasingly in environmental applications. The U.S. Environmental Protection Agency (EPA) has been building expertise in the use of differential techniques for years, investing a great deal of time, money and effort into training EPA personnel in understanding the technology and in establishing operational procedures and methodologies for its use. GPS is supported as the way to achieve accurate, consistent locational coordinates. It is also being used to detect and correct pre-existing errors in EPA databases.

Principal EPA Applications of GPS

Principal applications of DGPS within EPA include environmental monitoring such as surveying and mapping landfills, wells, outfalls and other facilities. Personnel are being trained in the technology and its potential relevance to Agency applications.

Overall, EPA uses GPS for quantifying the spatial accuracy of various GIS databases and maintaining quality control of the databases when map sources of varying scales and resolutions are used and combined. Researchers and field workers also test and evaluate various pieces of equipment for portability and for easy conversion of data to GIS format.

Of overriding concern is the second item — maintaining quality control of the database. Map scales used in the past for representing data collected in the field often vary greatly from scales derived from aerial photography. As a result, quality control had to be established to engineering-level precision.

The first part of exercising control required that a map-accuracy test be conducted. GPS surveys were used to pinpoint specific locations on the ground, which were used as control points to recompile EPA base maps and conduct accuracy tests on other maps used in remediation projects.

Remedial Investigation of Superfund Sites

The Environmental Protection Agency is responsible for restoring the ecological balance of endangered, contaminated or destroyed sites. There is a "Superfund" from which the Agency grants contract money to get the work done. Project proposals are investigated and prioritized; only those ranked high on the National Priorities List qualify for Superfund money. Described below are a number of EPA efforts designed to show how Geographic Information System (GIS), remote-sensing technologies and GPS control data are being used by professionals to facilitate the remedial investigation process.

Old Southington Landfill

One such project was conducted at the Old Southington Landfill in Connecticut. A database for the landfill was developed from data layers derived from large-scale and small-scale map sources. Little of the material was in digital form.

There were many spatial-relationship problems when the information from the different sources was combined. Their solution came from a combination of techniques and technologies, including digital cartography and photogrammetry. New and old aerial photographs were converted to digital (computer-readable) maps of roads, cultural features and water resources. Thematic overlays of other factors (e.g., previous activity at the landfill, etc.) were also added to the maps. Nine GPS-located control points were established for the landfill and used to update (and correct) maps of the area.

San Gabriel Basin

In 1986, it was determined that the groundwater in the San Gabriel Basin in southern California was heavily contaminated with organic solvents. The site was put on the National Priorities List (NPL) for remediation. The ultimate goal of the project is to identify those parties responsible for contaminating the ground water and to recover costs of remediation through litigation.

Other agencies are watching the project with interest. Surveys such as this provide specialists both within and outside the EPA with the accuracy and confidence necessary for them to pursue enforcement of regulations and legislation.

In this case, however, it was difficult to identify the source of the contaminants since a number of smaller sites within the study area were being investigated for other reasons. In order to delineate the extent of contamination and monitor its movement, and to narrow down the number of possible sources, an extensive network of GPS-located monitoring and water-supply wells was used.

Previously, wells were often assigned coordinates based on how close they were to particular facilities (used as control points because they would show up in aerial photos). In the EPA project, the GPS survey team first established each wellhead's exact coordinates, then sampled groundwater and recorded data for each wellhead continuously for five minutes.

The descriptive information was entered into the project database via the GPS receiver. Well locations that had been previously designated and stored in the GIS database were corrected.

The streets and intersections of San Gabriel were also surveyed to align data already in the GIS database so that future work would be spatially accurate. This was done simply by driving an antennaed truck up and down the roads, plugging in GPS waypoints along the way and logging each bit of information into the database.

GPSEE Waste Sites

GPS techniques are being used to establish locations and times for information gathered about radioactive, hazardous or mixed-waste sites. An automated system, dubbed the Global Positioning Site Environment Evaluator (GPSEE), has been developed for surveying contaminated sites and monitoring them after remediation to ensure that environmental recovery is complete. GPSEE is designed for use by both the Department of Energy and the Department of Defense, as well as a number of private industrial facilities.

GPSEE consists of a base station and a number of field stations in different locations. Data collection and recording into a database are done by field operators. Using chemical and radiological sensors, field operators survey the site directly, collect the soil and water information needed for analysis, then record the exact location for each entry as determined by a GPS receiver.

Sokkia Spectrum

They then send the data back electronically to the base station. In this way, by testing on site, field personnel eliminate the need to cart samples around with them.

12

UTILITIES

Timing & Synchronization

Improvements in protection, monitoring and control of power and telecommunications systems depend very much on how well the entire system is synchronized. In order to accomplish this and hone the system for optimal performance, data must be captured by different kinds of recorders along the line.

If "tagged" according to a common time standard, these line data become more valuable. After-the-fact analysis of a line disturbance, for example, requires a log of very precise timing in order to determine the sequence of events that led up to the problem.

The atomic clocks in GPS satellites provide the utilities industry with the reliable, precise time standard needed to log line disturbances and synchronize events. By standardizing (to microseconds) the time between substations of interconnected nodes, engineers can maintain closer control over a network, whether it is used for the transmission of electrical power or for communications.

Traditionally, disturbance recorders and sequence-of-events recorders have used designated "master" clocks at individual sites. These common time standards have been local — at industrial centers or at power-generating stations or substations. Efforts at synchronizing sites by transmitting time-code signals among them are limited by the sensitivity of such signals to different kinds of interference (from high-voltage, for example).

The problem is formidable and costly. Settlement of liability disputes arising in the industry often depend on the ability to differentiate the cause and effect of transmission-line disturbances. Up to now, the 100-millisecond time code available from the Geostationary Operational Environmental Satellite System helped, but the time code provided by GPS is even more accurate.

Basic GPS equipment for time and frequency synchronization includes a GPS receiver with a down converter, a choke-ring antenna, modem and/or printer interfaces, a power supply and cables if necessary. The receiver should have an internal crystal oscillator to maintain operation if an external reference source is not available.

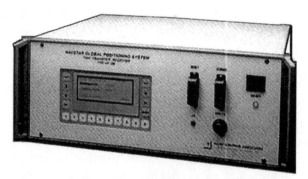

Allen Osborne Associates, Inc.

Some units have display panels; others are designed to function as remotely-controlled black boxes. High-end time-transfer receivers may also have an internal rubidium oscillator, track more satellites, calibrate for ionospheric distortions, remove errors from selective availability or process Y-code.

Power Systems

Access to GPS has led to improvements in the protection, control and monitoring of interconnected power systems. Systems using GPS allow the detection of lightning and the post-disturbance analysis of faults. They also provide greater time-of-arrival and direction-finding accuracies.

GPS-aided applications within the power industry focus on control, fault location, synchronization and phasor measurement. How they fit in is explained below.

Control

Voltage control and signal leakage along power lines are recurring problems for the whole cable industry. Access to DGPS techniques is helping power-systems engineers resolve these problems by locating sites of signal leakage or voltage variances with greater precision than ever before.

For years, LORAN has been used to help locate cable leakage; however, most LORAN transmitters are along coastal areas, limiting its usefulness. GPS receivers and sensor equipment, which can be installed along any lines and coupled into a central control station, allow coverage worldwide and provide accuracy better than a width of a street. Also, tested systems work equally well on or above land.

Location & Analysis of Line Faults

Faults are detected on overhead lines by the observation of traveling waves propagated in both directions from the fault. Faults are also the cause of interruptions in the line, in which case, traveling waves are transmitted along the line from the terminations.

Detection and analysis of these high-frequency pulses have always been a problem. Generally, tests are staged along lines at various locations — an expensive and potentially dangerous undertaking. The effective use of GPS positioning and timing for synchronization can, at least, lessen (and perhaps eliminate) the need for this practice.

A number of innovative techniques have proven excellent tools for the sampling and analysis of power-line anomalies. One shown to be fast, selective and accurate employs synchronized samples from two ends of a line. In another, satellite-synchronized simulations of actual events along power lines are played back through remotely located systems.

Strategically placed digital fault recorders with GPS satellite receivers are the key to solving the problem. Small, inexpensive GPS receivers placed at substations along lines provide the locational coordinates of fault transmission in the context of a uniform, accurate time base.

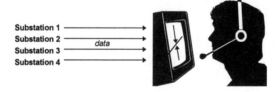

Phasor Measurement

The ability to follow the dynamics of a power system is vital to effectively monitor, protect and control the system, but estimating its state at any point in time is an imprecise art, at best. A new technique called synchronized phasor measurement is proving not only precise but time- and cost-effective, too.

GPS-coupled devices called synchronized phasor measurement units are placed at strategic points throughout the system. Phasor measurement units gather GPS-time-tagged data directly, providing management at a control center with sufficient information to confidently visualize the state of the system. Standards for interfacing them with large power systems are being established by the Institute of Electrical and Electronic Engineers (IEEE).

Telecommunication Networks

In order to provide quality transmission to users of their high-speed circuits, telecommunications companies like AT&T, MCI and US Sprint must continually upgrade and monitor the synchronization of their networks. The need has escalated with increasing demand for new types of data lines, synchronous optical networks and more stringent international standards for transmissions and data formats.

Many serious network problems don't noticeably affect the quality of voice communications going over the lines but could, if left unfixed, halt altogether the transmission of anything.. To preclude such a scenario, a lot of effort goes into preventive maintenance and control, far from customer scrutiny.

Over the years, a variety of methods have been used to keep the circuits and services going, and these have included the use of LORAN and microwave technologies. With GPS, it is possible to monitor and verify the performance of national telecommunications network with levels of precision at least 100 times better than current international (CCITT) standards.

One such system combines long-term GPS timing accuracy with short-term oscillators placed along the network. Each node contains a master clock that synchronizes other clocks in the node and distributes its signal to neighboring nodes. Monitoring equipment at each node is used to verify performance of the clocks and align them with the GPS time base. Some systems use clock-validation techniques that also align system time with Universal Time Coordinated (UTC).

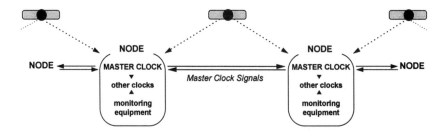

Pipelines

GPS measurements can be used to detect minute changes over time in the position of any three-dimensional objects, and these include oil and gas pipelines, on which any type of structural stress is a cause for concern. GPS detection of deformation in the structure of a pipeline allows engineers to precisely monitor any changes in pipe positions to subcentimeter levels.

Precise locational fixes are transmitted regularly or on demand from control points along the lines. Differences over time provide statistics for assessing the extent and gravity of deformation, giving experts one basis for determining if intervention is necessary.

13

EXPLORATION

The curiosity of pioneer mariners delved more deeply than the cut of the bow through the waters they sailed. It was their original wonder about what lay below the sea's surface that sparked, and has since influenced, serious exploration of the ocean's floor and environment.

Exploring the Oceans

Knowing that waves could either help them or hinder them in reaching their destinations, these early navigators were also aware of the correlation between the phases of the moon and patterns of the tides. Searching for more information and relationships, they were the first to study oceanography as a form of science.

Oceanography did not become a precise science, however, until the 18th century. Then, within a few really productive decades, Benjamin Franklin published his chart of the Gulf Stream, Marsigli and Donati built the first scientific dredge, and the British explorer, "Captain" (James) Cook, sailed the Pacific seas in his ship, *Endeavor*.

Practical concerns rather than romantic adventure drove later progress in the study of oceanography when it became feasible to string telegraph cable along the ocean floor between continents. Wear and tear on the cables and their retrieval, if necessary, for repairs were problematic. There was also danger to the cables from the residents of the underwater neighborhoods.

By learning everything they could about the sea bed and its idiosyncrasies in order to solve these problems, engineers were laying the groundwork for major advances in the field. Today's environmental science of oceanography continues to be conducted for scientific, economic and social purposes, and GPS is fast becoming a part of it.

GPS tools and techniques are used primarily for geological oceanography, the study of the ocean's structure and its bottom sediments. They are also used in the study of the currents and circulation of the seas (physical oceanography), and in the strategic use of the ocean for navigation, communication and military advantage (marine technology). Although GPS receivers do not work under water, they can be made part of a combined system of sonar data links and radio telemetry. They can also be placed on platforms called drifter buoys

Sea-Surface Positioning

Traditional geometric leveling across large water surfaces has always posed problems because of refraction. Now, however, GPS can be used to accurately calculate sea level and measure ocean-waves, study and track currents and temperatures and measure seafloor geodesy.

Drifter-Buoys

Accurate sea-level measurements are obtained with the use of GPS drifter buoys. GPS-obtained fixes can then be used to calibrate and control the sea-level components of satellite altimeters. Because GPS buoys are lightweight and practical in design, they are more easily handled than traditional LORAN drifters.

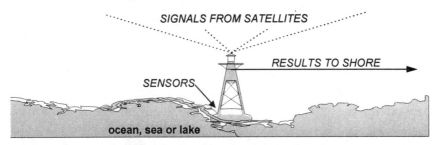

A generic type of drifter buoy is illustrated here, but there are many design types. Researchers at the Scripps Institute of Oceanography at La Jolla ran experiments to see if the type of platform influenced results to any significant degree. Testing both waverider and spar designs, they concluded that GPS produces high accuracies on all types of platforms. A stronger determinant on accuracy seemed to be the height of the GPS antenna phase center above water level.

In another test of the accuracy and cost-effectiveness of GPS buoys, eleven were built on Lake Huron. Each was also equipped with a sensor to obtain temperature profiles immediately below the surface. Results indicate that the spatial and temporal resolution provided by GPS drifters is superior to that of Argos drifters. Utilizing differential techniques (DGPS), researchers achieved accuracies within 15 meters.

Kinematic GPS

"Kinematic" software is being developed to help in the task of sea-surface measurement. A kinematic approach is one that assumes "pure" motion," eliminating any influences by mass or force. Differential GPS in a kinematic mode better verifies satellite altimeter readings and determines a radar altimeter bias than other methods.

Coupling kinematic methods with differential techniques is the focus of much sea-surface-measurement research. Of particular interest is the transmission of corrections in real time and the effect that moving antennae might have on accuracy.

When used with readings from a GPS receiver placed on a free-floating buoy with an antenna on top, the kinematic software removes motion-induced ambiguities that may affect the accuracy of measurements. More reliable wave heights can then be determined, as well as velocities and directions of ocean currents.

Conducting this type of kinematic-mode study involves the complex synchronization of photogrammetric cameras, survey vessels, ground-effect vehicles and other instrument carriers. However, results are positive. It seems that, as such GPS-supported aerial triangulation becomes routine, fewer ground control points will be needed for kinematic mode use than were required for traditional, non-GPS methods.

GPS-Aided Control in Space

The demand for high precision has also been extended to space, but the use of the use of GPS in space is more about control than about exploration. GPS positioning is used mainly for guidance in the autonomous retrieval of spacecraft (e.g., the Shuttle), especially for the final stages of entry — when it descends from an altitude of about 10,000 feet to a precision landing. GPS is used in addition to the vehicle's standard navigational aids of flight control computer, electronic compass, yaw gyroscope and data recorder.

Integrating a space vehicle's Inertial Navigation System with Differential Global Positioning System capabilities (INS/DGPS) allows a capsule to autonomously de-orbit and make a precision touchdown. Tests have demonstrated that safe runway landings are possible even without expensive navigational aids such as TACAN, DME or MLS. This may eventually release NASA from the need to maintain costly ground tracking stations.

Precise control systems are being developed around the world, and different types of services will become available. The German Space Agency has supported development of a High-Precision Permanent Positioning Service (HPPS) offering accuracies of +/- 1 centimeter.

Returns, Retrievals & Rendezvous

Freedom, the international space station being developed, will be home to revolving crews with heavy work loads. Easy access and immediate, safe returns must be "givens" as evidenced by a number of close calls caused by systems breaking down on MIR. Also, a return vehicle can not be dependent on its passengers being able to run it, especially during or after emergencies.

Only Differential GPS and high-precision altimeters can provide the positional and velocity accuracies needed. Several manned space projects other than *Freedom* already incorporate GPS in their control systems, and the ease of use of GPS devices and precision of results ensure their incorporation into all future systems. These include units for assuring shuttle availability, precision in launching and various aerospace planes.

HOPE (H2 Orbiting Plane) is an unmanned, winged space vehicle developed by Japanese scientists. Designed to deorbit and reenter the atmosphere after only one revolution, HOPE will provide an opportunity to gather data and test precision and control driven by its vital component — a five-channel GPS receiver.

The homing in, rendezvous and subsequent docking of space capsules in orbit present very complex problems. Their orbits must be precisely measurable. GPS receivers on board are being used to reduce any ranges of error in position and velocity to a minimum. Researchers working on this have learned that optimal results are obtained by using only those GPS satellites visible to both vehicles rather than by observations from all satellites possible. Other teams are using data from the MIR space station. They are investigating how the distribution of ground reference GPS reference stations affects positioning results.

Attitude, Orbit & Antenna Adjustment

GPS satellites' signals can be used to help other satellites maintain their orbits and keep their antenna pointed at the earth. Results have demonstrated the effectiveness of GPS in supporting orbit and trajectory determination for low, high and interplanetary applications. Because GPS receivers are small and light, mission planners hope to incorporate them as on-board stationkeepers for determination of the ephemeris for many types of orbits.

One compact system called GPS Tensor controls space vehicles from launch time through orbit by issuing all the necessary navigation and attitude information — e.g., roll, pitch, and yaw angles, exact position, velocity, time and orbit specifications. Using standard C/A code, it promises to replace conventional attitude (orientation) aids such as earth sensors, sun sensors and gyros.

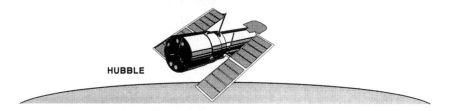

HUBBLE

GPS is also used to accurately position and deploy the antenna of a spacecraft so that attitude determination can be maintained. A small influence on where an antenna is placed and how it is deployed can produce disproportionately erroneous results.

Some of these can be anticipated and resolved (by geometrically calculating the deployment angle errors of the fixture on which the antenna is mounted, followed by a mathematical procedure called Kalman filtering). Accurate GPS coordinates minimize the potential range of error.

14

MARKETS & OPPORTUNITIES

As a worldwide utility, the Global Positioning System has opened up opportunities for marketing and innovation that transcend borders. Indeed, one of the goals of open-access is to provide opportunities for American businesses to supply the world with GPS-related products and services. Many old businesses will adapt their standard lines and services to incorporate GPS-related features, and new businesses will be formed to provide GPS-specific products or services around the world.

Exact figures are unknown, but wide ranges of numbers are quoted by analysts for the potential growth and profit from GPS-related products and activity. These are discussed later in this chapter.

What is known, however, is that the technologies associated with satellite navigation and time transfer are quickly moving from the domain of engineers and technicians into the domain of public commodities. The U.S. Department of Defense's investment of taxpayers' money in GPS has not only provided its promised return of military advantage, but the promise of its by-products has encouraged entrepreneurs around the world.

Civilian Industries from Military R&D

An Entrepreneurial Hierarchy

The main participants in the growing commercial GPS industry are original manufacturers of equipment, manufacturers of peripheral equipment and service providers. Together, they comprise what has been described in Pace et al. as a GPS-engendered "food chain."

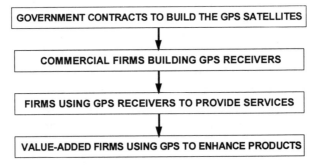

Commercial Markets

According to a 1995 report prepared for Congress by the National Academy of Public Administration and National Research Council, the commercial market for GPS services has been doubling every two years and was currently generating $2 billion per year in business. As early as 1991, Colwell-Kirtland International sold more that $100 million worth of GPS receivers to nonmilitary users, and two-thirds of its 1992 sales (~$600 million) were for civilian use.

Around the world, companies ranging from construction-vehicle manufacturers to airlines are adapting GPS for civilian use. The fastest-growing part of Trimble Navigation's business is tracking and communications, and much of that is due to civilian access to GPS.

The transportation industry will be changed. The U.S. Department of Transportation's Intelligent Transportation System (ITS) aims to raise highway traffic to the level of control and safety of air traffic. GPS will increasingly be integrated into vehicles and highway systems across the nation. Other nonmilitary government agencies and corporations are similarly upgrading their own transportation systems, adding "intelligence," the main components of which are tracking and GPS navigational equipment.

Airports large and small are reassessing their requirements for approach and landing, many opting away from previous decisions to install microwave systems in favor of GPS, DGPS or GLONASS systems. In a move promoting GPS as the primary means of navigation, the International Civil Aviation Organization dropped its mandate requiring international airports to possess a microwave landing system by 1998.

All of these projects have been nurtured by the investment in GPS made over so many years by the military. It is an example of a multibillion-dollar defense project providing almost immediate benefit to civilian industry and individual citizens.

Subcontracting

World Bank Projects

The U.S. Trade and Development Agency promotes the participation of U.S. firms in exporting GPS equipment and technical expertise via World Bank-financed projects. The Agency provides assistance and export trade information regarding potential opportunities abroad. Current interest in GPS technology focuses primarily on Geographic Information System applications.

Government Subcontracting

The General Services Administration (GSA) is a U.S. agency that entertains proposals for Global Positioning Systems support. Contracts are awarded to facilitate FAA and other-agency requests that cannot be met efficiently in-house — for example, activities and products needed for special long-term research and development. One such project is the contract for the Wide-Area Augmentation System (WAAS) to measure and transmit Differential-GPS corrections over vast areas via satellite.

Contractors wishing to provide systems (to the FAA, for example) usually provide complete testing facilities, as well. These may include ground-reference and signal-monitor equipment, a ground-to-air data link and an aircraft fitted with a DGPS receiver/processor that feeds into a flight director/autopilot. The Aerospace Corporation, which was instrumental in the creation of GPS in its early days under Ivan Getting, continues in its role to provide scientific and engineering support for the U.S. military. In 1993, the nonprofit organization received $15.5 million from the Air Force to operate a research and development center.

Consumerisms

Among civilian users of GPS, aviation and marine aficionados lead the way in numbers, enthusiasm, experience and knowledge of available products, but other groups are quickly catching up. These include users in business and academia.

As prices of equipment come down, and sales of GPS receivers and optional equipment to casual and recreational users grow faster than manufacturers planned, numerous business opportunities will open up for people providing the services and products below. New players may not be able to share the academic or professional distinction associated with the development of the system, but many will gain notice from having made money as suppliers of GPS services or products.

The wish list of customers of GPS equipment and components starts with products that are functional, reliable and easy to use. Ideally, products should be modular and able to work with other devices. This means that whatever is required for its operation or connection to other devices is available and that documentation and software are understandable. Customers also want the prices of higher-performance devices to fall as production costs decrease.

These things seem to be happening in the GPS marketplace. Most vendors respond quickly to customer needs and new applications.

Moving Maps & Cross-Sensory Aids

Figures for the integration of in-vehicle navigation systems into car designs range from a very conservative 4% to more than 20% by the year 2000. A University of Michigan study claims up to 50% of all new vehicles will be so equipped by 2011. With hundreds of millions of cars and trucks on the roads worldwide, even very small percentages represent huge potential markets for the moving maps, audible maps and databases that make them work.

Adding Time, Location & Velocity to Products

The market is ripe for devices that incorporate the three features of time, location and velocity, but time and locational coordinates are more easily added to products than a capability for determining velocity. GPS now makes the third option both possible and easy.

Velocity is measured by the rate of change of pseudo-ranges over time. In the case of GPS, it is equivalent to the rate of change of the distances from the satellites over time. In many cases, adding velocity-determining capability to a product will be accomplished simply by inserting a miniaturized GPS receiver into its casing.

Adding Mobility

Although it is technically easy to equip a vehicle with a navigation system, and vendors in many countries have coupled GPS positioning with CD-ROM or datacard units, bringing it to the customer's level ultimately depends on a vendor's ability to market and distribute what it sells and on the availability of good software to make it work.

Overseas vendors are usually good at capturing their home markets, but the U.S. market has not been favorable to manufacturers other than Sony and Pioneer. Japanese inroads are a result of their early integration of GPS technology into consumer products, particularly cars. Satellite-aided car systems have been big sellers in Japan for a number of years.

Miniaturization & New Materials

The all-digital world upon which electronics' manufacturers base much of their strategy will require individual units that are lightweight, small, impervious to heat and chemicals and resistant to myriad conditions. The flood of GPS units and accessories coming to market will add to the demands.

Miniature multichip GPS devices that can fit into casings the size of backgammon dice are being produced and will be used to add locational-precision features to many products. Miniaturized satellite systems are being studied as platforms for scientific experiments, engineering projects, planet exploration, communications and earth surveillance. Japanese researchers are designing very small GPS receivers as constituent elements of these systems.

Most consumer electronics products (as well as those for the military) will be housed in plastic, and demand will increase for more sophisticated compounds. Industry suppliers will be hard-pressed to find the technical answers to providing more resilient, affordable casing materials, especially those able to meet military specifications.

GPS-Related Service Industries

The opening up of GPS services presents a wide range of opportunities for new service industries. Also, subsequent mergers and alliances will lead to the introduction of new product lines by old companies. New ventures will be labor-intensive and capital-sparing, making them attractive to small-business entrepreneurs.

Equipment-Related Services

If it works, it might break, and if it breaks, someone has to fix it. A service segment will emerge to service the GPS equipment and components flooding the market. Demand is rising for specialists in:

✓ evaluation   ✓ calibration
✓ maintenance   ✓ testing
✓ repair   ✓ interfacing
✓ integration   ✓ system design

Cadres of marine and avionics equipment engineers, farming advisors, vehicle-navigation consultants and scientific-instrument support personnel will advertise and sell GPS-ready expertise.

Data & Databases

For persons knowledgeable in the collection and processing of data and in the management of databases, GPS accessibility brings with it ample opportunities for support services. These include data collection and preprocessing, creation of informational databases, database management and specialized mapping services.

Many North American and European companies already exist for collecting and preprocessing data. Field workers — very often specialists in the branch of science for which they are contracted — gather, sort and preprocess masses of data for subsequent delivery to other parties. Initial collection may be done on foot with handheld or portable GPS units, or it may be done with aircraft- or truck-mounted electronic surveying equipment.

Users of GPS-accurate information need to be able to retrieve the information in an easy and timely manner. Persons able to create user-friendly databases that meet clients' specific needs and those able to educate clients in effective use of the databases will become a significant part of the service community.

Task- or location-specific measurements can be gathered and sold as customized packages of digitized information for locational or navigational purposes. Database-management professionals will be called upon to upgrade existing databases to include GPS coordinates and to organize and manage new collections of GPS-gathered data.

Independent satellite systems may be launched to provide mapping services for farmers and environmentalists. By measuring light reflection off crops, experts can provide farmers with frequent, regular updates on the conditions of their crops.

The data received can also provide clues as to how other factors such as winds, flood or infestation may affect crop yield. Maps and information may be obtained on a one-time basis or by subscription.

Metrics

Providing measurement as a product will become an independent trade. Like a California house-seller's dependence on a termite inspector's release before a sale is final, other transactions may soon require confirmation of measurements to DGPS standards before becoming legally binding. The legal profession will become more reliant on GPS for settling territorial and zoning disputes and for establishing accurate bases for taxation, voting districts, etc.

Because the collection of data for applications for which GPS is suited is often labor-intensive, contractors will hire others to provide the measurements of subcentimeter precision that are needed. A capital-sparing, coordinates-for-sale industry will form quickly around certain types of projects, e.g., reconciliation of maps, evaluation of real estate, reconstruction of airport runways, compensation for earthquake damage, legal disputes and architecture.

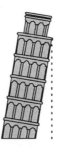

DGPS-ers will provide precision coordinates for walls and buildings, track the tilt of the Tower of Pisa or provide frequency traces for Josephson Array Voltage Standards in laboratories — for a price.

Satellite/Cellular Services

Early civilian satellite services seemed to focus on television distribution, and defense communications made up the basis of military use. Newer services will include networking and connecting customer-oriented control sites with mobile communications. Others may include broadcasting systems that use GPS locational fixes to aim radio programs directly to automobiles from space.

Reselling GPS time accuracy by routing it through commercial communications satellites could be the basis for an industrial time service. Microsecond timing could be bought on a single-time or subscription basis for tasks such as synchronized sampling and event recorders along power or telecommunications lines, or for various testing, measurement or fault-location purposes. Before this can happen on a cost-effective scale, however, standardization of data formats among the participants and the provider must occur.

Automatic vehicle-location services combine GPS technology with cellular phone services so that a vehicle can be tracked and voice contact can be established and maintained between the driver and a response center. Typical of systems being installed in new model automobiles is the Remote Emergency Satellite Cellular Unit (RESCU) from Ford. When activated (by phone or emergency button), the car component of RESCU transmits its geographic coordinates, its direction and its speed to a service center. The call and its particulars are forwarded to local 911 units, who go to the scene. Contact with a driver in distress may be maintained until rescue personnel arrive. Such relay stations could be established as commercial service centers for individuals on a subscription basis.

The integration of wide-area mobile communication with GPS has potential applications not even imagined when the technologies were evolving, particularly in developing countries. Economic sectors such as transportation, energy and natural resources will be affected by cost-effective solutions to many of their problems.

As applied to distance learning, the technology can provide teachers and students with better access to real-time communication with distant sites and mobile facilities. Fixed dispatching stations, acting as a hub for communications between sites, relay the wireless communications to mobile units equipped with GPS receivers.

Other types of applications that benefit from GPS-satellite/cellular connections include cellular auxiliary services, pay-per-listen digital satellite radio and satellite-cellular citizens-band (CB) services.

Timing & Synchronization

Pre-GPS satellite systems such as the Geostationary Operational Environmental Satellite System (GOESS) have provided timed signals accurate to 100 microseconds. The accuracy of the time code provided by the GPS satellite clocks is 100 times better than GOESS — under one microsecond.

Demand is growing for microsecond timing for the synchronization of sampling, relay testing, phase-angle measurement, fault location and event recorders. The universally accessible GPS signal can be used as the basis for a commercial industrial time service to satisfy that demand. Timing and synchronization services could be offered to subscribers for a fee.

Environmental Monitoring

GPS receivers are invaluable tools for mapping and surveying roads, trails, forests and water resources. They are also effective tools in the detection and prevention of fires. Sweden's use of GPS for forest inventory and management is an example of how the technology is being used to delineate old- and new-growth areas. (See Chapter 11, "GPS & the Environment," for more on this.)

Tracking the dispersion of hazardous waste material through the environment is becoming easier and more accurate. So, field workers will increasingly use GPS to generate progress maps and quantify the spatial accuracy of entries on old maps on a for-sale basis.

Research & Development

University research facilities can serve as enthusiastic subcontractors for GPS-related projects. In such a move, a Stanford University group developed an assortment of ground-based transmitters called pseudolites. Designed primarily to augment the FAA's precision-landing system, the innovative monitoring and control devices also seem ideal for parts and inventory tracking for factories.

The timing and locational accuracies of GPS are providing the bases for hundreds of research projects at schools and universities across the United States and around the world. At Trenton State College in New Jersey, portions of the GPS payload were simulated in the programming language BASIC. Autonavigation features and spatial dynamics of the 24-satellite constellation were done in MATLAB.

At Ohio State University, researchers are developing GPS-based techniques for mapping roadways and other parts of the civil infrastructure, and student environmentalists from universities and colleges have been given receivers and enlisted by the Environmental Protection Agency to spot and track endangered species.

Purdue University researchers are investigating the use of GPS for photogrammetric projects for Indiana's Transportation Department. There, GPS techniques are being implemented and tested using a Cessna airplane, an aerial camera and GPS receivers.

Education & Training in the Use of GPS

As more people use GPS, there will be a viable market opening for education and training in the many uses of the technology at all levels and for the creation of curricular and self-help material. Current civilian offerings of marine, recreational and avionics' use of GPS will be expanded to include professional services, as well.

Projections for the Industry

Projections made about future activity in any industry are inherently flawed by their dependency on assumptions. One of the first assumptions this author makes is that persons interested in GPS-generated business will gather information in the context of their own expertise and apply their own insight to its probability.

Educated, research-based guesses do, however, provide fuel for brainstorming. In that spirit, some expectations are included here.

With that said, it is predicted that GPS-related industries will become a $30-billion business early in the 21st century. According to reports from the U.S. Global Positioning System Industry Council, the worldwide market for GPS receiver equipment alone is expected to grow to more than $8 billion by the year 2000.

Prices for consumer-grade GPS devices have fallen since 1991 from about $1000 to around $200 in 1995. It is expected they will cost no more than half that by the year 2000. The integration of basic GPS components with other devices will help bring prices down.

Even a conservative estimate of penetration into world markets by GPS products and services reveals its potential for enormous impact on business activity in a number of sectors. Varying percentages of existing marine, land and air vehicles, for example, will be retrofit with GPS products and services, and most future systems will feature integrated GPS components. The sheer numbers of military vehicles worldwide ensures there will be a lot of business generated for years to come.

One of the biggest markets being opened up by GPS is that of air-traffic control. Seamless navigation and guidance for worldwide aviation and the management of air space have been predicted by market analysts to reach $200 billion by the year 2004.

This example is only one of many brought forward by researchers and venture capitalists underlining the expected effect on the market of GPS technology and techniques. Announcements are often accompanied by quite valid justification for funding. Indeed, as DGPS becomes the preferred means of navigation, crashes and near-misses resulting from wrong coordinates for approach or a pilot not knowing for sure where he or she is in the air will be greatly reduced.

This author does not intend to issue predictions per se or distribute ones attributed to others. You may, however, gain quick insight into the potential effect of GPS on markets by looking at a particular segment for a set time frame. The table below provides figures for illustrative purposes. For those market segments in which you are interested, plug in the most currently available figures.

MAKING AN EDUCATED ESTIMATE OF THE POTENTIAL EFFECT OF GPS ON A MARKET SEGMENT		
ESTIMATING MARKET SIZE	TRUCKS	SURVEYORS
Number of potential customers (people, vehicles, etc.) already existing	120 million	40,000
Estimated percentage of existing entities that will probably buy devices	5% (6,000,000)	35% (14,000)
Number of anticipated new entrants into the market or replacements within a set time frame (e.g., three years)	10,000,000	10,000
Percentage of new entrants that will probably incorporate GPS features	20% (2,000,000)	75% (7,500)
Average cost of unit for segment	~$500	~$30,000
Potential market size for the time frame	$4,000,000,000	$645,000,000

GPS Activities around the World

Supplying the growing population of GPS-equipment users with receivers and related paraphernalia will keep large sectors of industry busy for a long time, and there will be a great deal of competition — and collaboration — in the global marketplace. U.S. companies lead the world today in designing and manufacturing sophisticated navigation equipment, but consumer demand for low-end GPS products will prompt many others to go into business.

Nations around the world can boast of innovative applications of their newly obtained access to the Global Positioning System and GLONASS. Acceptance of the technology has spread very quickly, especially due to the affordability of receivers and their ease of use.

Among topics being addressed, long-standing local and regional problems seem to have priority and are being studied with an eye toward resolving them through the use of the better mapping, better measuring and better timing capabilities now provided by GPS. A glimpse into some of the applications being developed and producing results is provided below.

European GNSS

In Europe, concern is being expressed about reliance on a system controlled by the American military — and one under which users may be misled about their true positions. Not to discriminate, the EC expresses equal concern about potential total reliance on GLONASS, especially since it has exhibited frequency-interference problems. Supporting this motivation for independent European development is the widespread belief that the other system of navigation available to users in the northern hemisphere, LORAN-C, may disappear as an option.

Northwest European Loran-C System (NELS)

In anticipation of this lessened maintenance of LORAN-C and migration to GPS by the U.S., a number of European countries are joining together to assume operations of the Northwest European Loran-C System (NELS). These networks, formerly operated by the U.S. Coast Guard, will be upgraded and extended to join other networks in Europe.

Another approach, the European complement to GPS (CE-GPS), is an overlay to the U.S. system intended to minimize or overcome the constraints of a system subject to policy decisions by a foreign power. CE-GPS does, however, have a drawback in that it is a regional, not a global program.

Specially-designed, 10-channel GPS receiver stations have been set up in France, French Guyana and South Africa to work with the European Complement to GPS (CE-GPS). The aim of this project is to establish a GPS-aided sole-means navigation system for nonprecision approaches. Rather than direct use of GPS satellites, the system uses transponders on Inmarsat satellites to synchronize their clocks with GPS time signals. GPS-like signals are then generated and transmitted to users via the Inmarsat constellation.

Regional GPS Networks

Established in 1993 by the National Land Survey and Onsala Space Observatory, SWEPOS is Sweden's nationwide network of 21 permanently installed GPS stations. These reference stations (most of which are heated), are strung from above the Arctic Circle to Sweden's southernmost city of Kiruna. Each houses a 12-channel receiver and antenna and broadcasts real-time Differential-GPS data (sometimes via an FM-radio service) to users in the field.

The Geodetic Institute of Finland is establishing a permanent GPS network that will be part of a larger Scandinavian system. Initially, twelve stations were located in areas of different geological structures so that bedrock stability could be tested and monitored. Other plans include GPS networks for monitoring radioactive waste disposal sites.

Aviation

Overall, in aviation, GPS is currently being investigated in Europe as both a primary means of navigation and as a nonprecise approach-phase system. In France, Differential-GPS is being tested with wide-bodied transport aircraft for precision instrument approaches, and German engineers are examining the system's ability to meet availability and integrity criteria for Category-III landings. Other tasks being augmented by GPS include routing, inertial positioning for automatic landing and hybrid DGPS systems. For example, autonomous, non-powered missiles like the glide bombs described in Chapter 8, part of Germany's defense arsenal, are now equipped with GPS/INS components for higher accuracy.

Geodetic Reference Systems

According to research literature, European efforts in the area of geodetic reference systems seem to focus on establishing a common geodetic grid for civil aviation, computing precise measurements of the geoid and unifying the many vertical and horizontal datums currently used.

Although the ECAC member states have long been reluctant to adopt a standard geodetic reference system for civil aviation, the Eurocontrol Agency is now leading efforts to implement the WGS84 datum as that standard. Customized software is being used to convert coordinates from disparate datums to the WGS84 grid.

Increasingly stringent demands for accuracy in geodesy, geophysics, oceanography and engineering have caused the International Geoid Commission to focus efforts on the computation of precise measurements of the geoid, and a subcommission was appointed to derive a new European geoid model. Its center for data collection, evaluation and computing is located at the Institut fur Erdmessung (IfE) at the University of Hannover.

Coordinate reference datums are also the focus of attention at the Nottingham University Institute of Engineering Surveying and Space Geodesy in the United Kingdom, where engineers are developing software to convert all national geodetic datums to WGS84, the GPS Datum. Obstacles to conversion have included the inaccuracies and imprecision of published coordinates used by accepted navigation aids and the incomplete or inadequate states of available databases.

Typical of regional programs being implemented in Europe is one entitled the Baltic Sea Level GPS Campaign, which was launched in 1990 by the countries around the Baltic Sea. The aim of this international collaboration was to promote the unification and reconciliation of vertical datums of that particular area to GPS-accuracy standards. Efforts are being extended to reconcile other datums, as well.

Modeling

The International Geoid Commission was prompted to act because most geoid models available for Europe were based on calculations done from the 1950s through the 1980s. They did not meet today's higher standards for spatial resolution and accuracy, which require precision of ± 1-10 cm (± 0.39-3.90 inches) over distances from 100-1000 km (± 62-620 miles). GPS is being used to correct the situation. Modeling can help reduce the gaps and faults in geodetic references, the most known of which is the World Geodetic Survey (WGS-84) grid. Normal observation techniques may fail to cover all areas, and computer modeling is used to minimize error on the terrestrial grids — especially that attributed to the troposphere, which quickly and significantly distorts accuracy.

German researchers are working on solutions combining GPS observations with terrestrial measurements, and the operational software that models GPS observations also provides a means for evaluating observations in the context of their relevance to other applications. Observables include satellite signal quality and description, clock type, orbits, atmospheric effects and mathematical equations and compensation factors. Among conditions considered are kinematic or static positioning, variations among the types of receivers and model speed and reliability.

Map Creation & Positioning Service

Differential GPS has been used in the establishment and maintenance of control-point networks for European Survey Agencies' mapping efforts. Compared to traditional methods and facilities, the DGPS-based positioning service affords real economic advantage, as well as providing more precise measurement.

Demand for high precision in mapping and in the field of measurement in general has also extended offshore — to marine applications using GPS connected to the Electronic Chart Display and Information System, ECDIS.

Japan's Research Efforts

Japanese research and business communities are involved in many GPS-related projects and in efforts to agree on standards and unify international time-calibration techniques. Japanese researchers are collaborating with the Bureau of International de Poids et Measures (BIPM). Different sites in Japan are linked with laboratories in North America and Europe for the transfer of GPS-gathered differential time delays. A survey of the literature revealed descriptions of:

- a GPS-enhanced navigation system that was installed in Japan's first nuclear-powered ship in 1990 to verify its propulsive performances and maneuverability. During extensive sea trials, the system provided locational precision, calculation of speed and tests of turning.

- real-time Differential-GPS navigation systems developed by Japan's National Aerospace Laboratory and being tried out at the Sendai airport for terminal-area operations. In tests comparing it to standard GPS, DGPS proved far superior

- employment by Japanese environmentalists of techniques like those being used in the U.S. for tracking wildlife and monitoring endangered species. Data collected from individual studies are being used to build up a national database.

Other research efforts have been directed at:

- miniaturization;
- utilization of GPS for satellite rendezvous and docking;
- land mobile applications and innovative dual-antennae designs;
- detailed bottom topography in the Nanseishoto Trench Area;
- disaster prevention measures;
- time calibration;
- precise measurement of currents using drifting buoys; and
- exploration of geothermal resources.

SAMPLING OF GPS-RELATED ACTIVITY AROUND THE WORLD
(OUTSIDE THE U.S.)

NORTH, CENTRAL & SOUTH AMERICA

CANADA
- multidimensional spatial data reference services via electronic bulletin board
- evaluation of attitude (roll, pitch, heave) of oceangoing vessels
- navigation, rms errors, bathymetry and handling
- hydrographic data collection using deep-ocean logging platform
- integrated, automatic Arctic (& Desert) Navigation System for all-weather off-the-road use and backup systems for military

CENTRAL AMERICA & MEXICO
- typing forests and mapping distributions
- modeling forest cover for resource analysis
- image classification and verification
- reconciliation of maps

SOUTH AMERICA
- minimization of tropospheric wet path delay measurements
- effects on water-vapor calibration on precision

EUROPE

BELGIUM
- space geodetic program at Royal Observatory to determine Earth's rotational parameters and geocentric coordinates of terrestrial sites

FINLAND

- permanent GPS Network to study regional crustal deformation pattern
- investigation & remediation efforts for radioactive waste disposal sites

GERMANY

- modeling
- aviation, establishment of specifications for aviation equipment, techniques and certification for ICAO Cat-III
- kinematic GPS
- dual-frequency measurement
- inertial measuring systems
- hybrid DGPS
- map creation & connection to ECDIS
- development & assessment of GPS-equipment stability
- fishery & harbor applications
- modular construction sets for ITS fleet management
- geodesics and modeling for filling in gaps in geodetic references (esp. WGS-84)

ICELAND

- development & installation of systems for the broadcast of differential-GPS (DGPS) radio signals for sea, land and air use
- reference stations, integrity monitors and communication controls for sea, air and land

NORWAY

- Norwegian offshore industry
- GPS manpack receiver for high latitudes
- influence of ionospheric activities on frequencies and corrections
- guidance and control for space-station rendezvous operations
- North Sea and English Channel radar altimeter measurement and calibration, sea leveling, tides, storm surges and geoid

SAMPLING OF GPS-RELATED ACTIVITY AROUND THE WORLD

POLAND

- replacement of current aviation aids with DGPS combined with inertial units
- use of GLONASS

SWEDEN

- SWEPOS network of 21 permanently-installed DGPS stations for broadcast of real-time differentials
- synchronization and time reference system for multistatic radar (MSR)
- environmental management & control

THE UNITED KINGDOM

- coordination of reference datums used in the national AIP's of ECAC states
- assessment of the scale of effort and difficulties in re-surveying airports
- development of standards, methods, field procedures and specifications for aerodrome surveys
- development and sale of products for research and rescue missions, mine countermeasures, anti-surface-vessel applications, and antisubmarine warfare applications
- airborne radar
- mobile data-acquisition systems

AFRICA

EGYPT

- regional DGPS network for land, marine & air navigation

ASIA

JAPAN

- consumer products
- review of research conducted worldwide; guidance & control technologies
- utilization of GPS in space (rendezvous & docking technologies)
- standardization & unification of international time-calibration techniques
- estimation of controlling performance of watercraft, including locational precision, calculation of speed and tests of turning of nuclear-powered ships
- DGPS for airplane terminal area operations
- precise measurement of currents in lagoonal waters using GPS drifting buoy
- land mobile GPS receiver with dual antennae
- miniaturized satellite systems consisting of miniaturized constituent elements, including GPS receivers
- orbit determination & orbital re-entry software
- prediction of reservoir-hydrothermal variations using GPS gravity measurements

CHINA

- map making, sea & inland-water transport and ship anchorage positioning
- tracking, positioning & guidance for with aviation and low-orbit satellites
- dispatch systems for highway and railroad transport vehicles
- vehicle management for railroad hubs, harbors, air fields & cities
- precise coordinates for photographed spots in remote-sensing imagery
- high-precision navigation guidance systems along China's coasts

INDIA

- wide-area mobile communications services
- software factories

SAMPLING OF GPS-RELATED ACTIVITY AROUND THE WORLD

NEPAL HIMALAYA

- horizontal and vertical measurements of tectonic plate collision of Asian/Indian plates

AUSTRALIA

AUSTRALIA,
NEW SOUTH WALES

- development of small, low-cost satellites for independent communications, sensing and global-positioning enterprises, particularly for Pacific rim countries
- positioning and classification of land cover
- cartographic reconciliation of remotely-sensed images of vegetation with GPS coordinates

15

COSTS, POLITICS & STANDARDS

A panel of the National Academy of Public Administration and a committee of the National Research Council have recommended that the President establish explicit goals to guide government policy regarding the implementation and regulation of the Global Positioning System.

The Costs of GPS

The figures published for to-date costs of GPS range up to $10 billion.   However, since methods of calculation differ among information providers and among government agencies, exact numbers are probably unobtainable.

Some estimates include costs associated with secondary payloads such as nuclear detonation sensors; some do not.   In addition, proprietary agreements between the government and industry often preclude the publication of certain data.

Anyone referring to estimates of how much GPS has already cost and will continue to cost should be aware that the numbers may:

- have been adjusted to 1995 dollars;
- cite spending-year dollars;
- calculate only through the current date;
- extend through dates in the future; or
- not include hidden costs (e.g., maintenance, launch, payloads).

For example, in a 1994 Selected Acquisition Report submitted to the U.S. Congress by the Department of Defense, projections of GPS costs through the year 2016 put the eventual price tag at $14 billion, but this figure does not include costs for launching the satellites. Separate compilations of available data push the accumulative figure well over $21 billion. A breakdown of the figures is shown in the table on the next page.

Impact of Budgetary Decisions

For 1994 and 1995, the Department of Defense obtained more than $1 billion for its GPS budget. The Department of Transportation, the U.S. Coast Guard and the Federal Aviation Administration were each allotted smaller sums for their GPS projects.

Increased pressure to reduce federal spending bodes ill for most administrations. In 1996, the Department of Defense got only $221 million, from which it must purchase a number of new GPS satellites. Some of the $13 million awarded the Coast Guard in 1996 is slated for the Navigation Information Service, and the FAA's 1996 allotment of $93 million includes funds for the first year of WAAS.

Administrations operating under the umbrella of the Department of Transportation (DoT) are especially hard-hit. Individual units responsible for highway and transit systems, airports and airways and that of ports and waterways will have to vie for bigger portions of shrinking dollars.

*APPROXIMATE COSTS OF THE GLOBAL POSITIONING SYSTEM

	Government Fiscal Years 1974-1995	Government Fiscal Years 1996-1997	Balance through 2016
DEVELOPMENT & DEPLOYMENT			
Satellites	$3.4 billion	$0.5 billion	$7.3 billion
User Equipment	$3.0 billion	$0.9 billion	$2.2 billion
MISCELLANEOUS			
**Boosters & Launch	$1.5 billion	$0.4 billion	$1.9 billion
Payloads	$0.4 billion	$0.2 billion	$0.2 billion
	GFY 1974-1995	*GFY 1996-1997*	*GFY 1997-2016*
PERIOD TOTALS	$8.3 billion	$2.0 billion	$11.6 billion

TOTAL PROJECTED THROUGH 2016: $21.9 billion

* In year-of-spending dollars rounded to nearest tenth of one billion.

 Data compiled from U.S. government Selective Acquisition Report (SAR), RAND Critical Technologies Report & Aviator's Guide to GPS.

** Actual or estimated figures not available for some future

In 1996, the government appropriated DoT over \$35 billion to ensure "safe and efficient movement of people and goods and cost-effective investment in the nation's infrastructure." In 1997 and beyond, however, the department's responsibilities include the installation, implementation and expansion of GPS techniques and equipment — affecting air and sea, as well as surface transportation. As a result, the various administrations will not only have to work under budgetary constraints but will have to accommodate increased involvement with other agencies such as the Coast Guard and the Federal Aviation Administration.

Security vs. Free Access

Debating the Issue of Selective Availability

Selective availability has sparked a number of issues and debates. A choice to release the optimal power of the GPS to civilians, however, seems less schizophrenic and less heavy a decision on a moral or ethical basis as did, for example, the atomic bomb or, in the case of today, genetic manipulation.

Delays by the government to acknowledge the reduced effectiveness of downgraded signals may serve only to aggravate the public's perception of selective availability as an expensive nuisance. Pros and cons for eliminating selective availability include:

- Because the degradation can be corrected by technology in the public domain, justification for selective availability as a security measure is no longer convincing. (Enemies sophisticated enough to launch guided missiles could easily set up a signal-correction system.) Although its elimination has been recommended and phase-out is planned within 10 years, exactly when it will happen is somewhat contingent upon how well other security techniques such as the Y-code are able to deny precise positioning capabilities to enemies during war.

- Currently, a deterrent to quick certification of GPS or GLONASS navigation for civil applications in air traffic may be a perception (in Europe, particularly) of the political subjectivity of the systems.

- Political limits to the transfer of military science and technology to the public sector challenge the implicit right of a participating (taxpaying) public to scrutinize science policy. Trends in technology often run counter to democratic ideals.

- Taking GPS from the lab, through testing and into widespread use in the real world has been such an expensive ordeal that only government and military priorities made it possible. It is understandable, then, that its original purpose (which was military advantage) not be diluted by civilian/consumer demands.

In the case of GPS, should the public voice demanding removal of selective availability be ignored, the exertion of consumer power will speak more loudly.

Circumventing Selective Availability

Differential corrections will increasingly be made to downgraded signals as use of GPS increases and consumer demands for circumventing SA grow. In the 1970s, the Federal Aviation Administration developed the microwave landing systems (MLS) to replace instrumented landing systems (ILS). However, it is now committed to DGPS as a viable alternative to both.

The Wide-Area Augmentation System (WAAS) is an FAA network of stations to measure and transmit Differential-GPS. Because the level of accuracy achieved decreases with the distance of a user from a station, there will be an increasing demand for local base stations. A technique called event time tagging may also be used with commercial GPS receivers to limit or eliminate the effects of selective availability degradation. (See Chapter 4 for more on DGPS.)

More signals yield higher levels of accuracy. Receivers now exist that integrate signals from both GPS and GLONASS, processing combinations of measurements across a wide range of frequencies. Using both systems, even in circumstances where some satellites are inoperable, is more effective than using GPS or GLONASS alone.

Standards & Organizations

International Civil Aviation Organization

The mission of the International Civil Aviation Organization (ICAO) is to promote satellite and aeronautical communications, navigation and surveillance (CNS) and to facilitate worldwide commitment to satellite CNS services. Because these services will function effectively only if implemented according to standards that work on a global scale, ICAO monitors transitions to CNS systems, addresses issues of coverage and institutionalization and pushes global specifications.

Federal Aviation Administration (FAA)

In the U.S., the Federal Aviation Administration (FAA) is changing the standards, certification and procedure requirements so that augmented GPS (i.e., DGPS) can be approved for flights within U.S. airspace and portions of FAA-managed airspace over the Atlantic and Pacific Oceans and Gulf of Mexico. Standards must also exist for the manufacture of aviation equipment, and criteria that comply with GPS technology must be established for obstacle clearance. For example, the use of DGPS minimizes the buffer airspace required to operate safely and to maximize airport capacity.

For all operations except Cat-II and -III precision landings, aviation mission standards will be based on current Minimum Operational Performance Standards (MOPS). These standards are communicated to industry and the public by the FAA. The agency also publishes manufacturer and supplier guidelines for the installation and certification of aviation equipment.

International Maritime Organization (IMO)

In 1995, following assurances by the U.S. Coast Guard, the International Maritime Organization met to study the features of GPS-SPS (along with GLONASS) as a component of a future civil and internationally-controlled global navigation system for maritime use. The group studied operational requirements and institutional arrangements, e.g., beaconing DGPS signals over marine radio. In 1999, DGPS will be mandatory on SOLAS ships.

Civilian Protection

Before GPS satellite technology fills the communication, navigation and surveillance needs of civil aviation in this next century, issues relating to overall civilian use (in areas other than aviation) need to be resolved. The job falls to a joint Department of Defense and Department of Transportation (DoD/DoT) task force that studies the implications that GPS security policy decisions have on civilians. The task force has formally recommended that any management decision-making structure provide for full civil representation.

Appendix A
NAVIGATION, TIME & TECHNOLOGY

FROM STARS TO SATELLITES

Navigation (plain-wrap style) is the act of guiding people or vehicles — planning and controlling their movement over land, on the sea, in the air and across space. This scientific art of getting from "here" to "there" has always been seasoned by men and women looking to the sky. The Global Positioning System has not changed that.

The Bible refers to people using the stars to determine North, South, East and West, and a bright star is reported to have led worshippers to the birthplace of Jesus. Even before that, traders used the stars as guides to sail between Crete and Egypt, and Phoenician sailors used the North Star to get to Cornwall. Homer's Odysseus, heeding the words of a goddess, held the stars of the Great Bear over his left hand as he bobbed across the sea to home. Later fascination with a plethora of earthly navigational instruments then brought our eyes back down to earth.

Today, though, we are looking again to orbiting celestial beacons for guidance — this time, a man-made constellation of artificial satellites, the Global Positioning System (or GPS). Using signals instead of stars, the GPS is providing a reliable, weatherproof, round-the-clock utility for pinpointing our location anywhere on earth.

Pre-1900s

Early mariner kits held an assortment of tools and traditions, as each generation of adventurers left behind its lore and learning for the next. The repertoire of navigational aids included ropes, compasses, sextants, chronometers and beacons, the use of which persisted for hundreds of years. Not until the 1900s did things pick up.

Speed through water was originally measured by attaching a knotted line to a log, throwing the log overboard, then counting how many knots passed through a seaman's hands in a half minute (as gauged by a sand-glass).

Present-day use of "knots" is remnant testimony to this early method, but today, a knot equals a distance of one international nautical mile (or 1852 meters or ~6,075 feet). Crewmen later replaced knots for determining speed by counting either propeller rotations or engine revolutions.

Early compasses, first used around the 1100s, were pieces of iron ore floating in a bowl of water. Even when skies were overcast, their orientation gave mariners a good indication of where "north" was. These later evolved into devices mounted on gimbals.

There were beacons, too, such as those from lighthouses that have guided ships for thousands of years. Generically defined as stationary guideposts that transmit signals in all directions, beacons are also known as nondirectional beacons (NDBs). In this, they differ from radiobeacons, which are sent out in particular directions. NDBs have long been used as waypoints along shorelines for sailors to help them get their bearings in inclement weather.

In the 1700s, the inventions of the sextant and marine chronometer established astro-navigation on the open sea as an art. The sextant, an instrument for measuring the elevation angles to the sun and stars (when the latter were visible), provided enough information to determine latitude — but failed to help with longitude. This is because, at the time, the best clocks on land lost one or two minutes every few days.

Clocks at sea were even farther off, often malfunctioning or stopping completely because of fluctuations in pressure or temperature. When it came to determining longitude, a two-minute difference in time could translate into a 56-kilometer (35-mile) error in location. Realizing the importance of this, the British Parliament, in 1714, issued a challenge and offered a £20,000 prize to anyone who could solve a ship's longitude problem to within 50 kilometers (31 miles).

The prize remained unclaimed for almost 50 years, until John Harrison, a modestly-schooled cabinet maker, came up with an ingenious little device by which longitude could be calculated. The marine chronometer (or "Mr. Harrison's Time-Keeper," as he called it) was able to stand up to the sways of the ship and compensate for changing temperatures. It was put to the test when his son sailed from London to Jamaica with a total error over six weeks of only 30 kilometers (19 miles) — and John collected the money.

Sextant and chronometer readings are used only occasionally today. The tasks of location and timing are being taken over by radio-based techniques.

Human expertise, too, has always been an invaluable navigational aid, especially so in the early days of navigation, when all tools relied on the eyes and hands of the user. Regardless of how much seamen illuminated the instruments, if visibility were poor, the navigator was at a loss. Some seamen, though, became quite adept at extrapolating from past experience and shore soundings just where they might be. By 1900, new instruments were developed and old ones so improved that they threatened to replace much of the art previously entrusted to the human navigator; yet, the human element will always be crucial. The reliability and accuracy of technology often depend on someone ensuring that the circumstances under which it is used are, indeed, those for which it has been designed.

Aids & Inventions: 1900-1950

Radio, a Great Invention

Users of personal computers may be familiar with the term 50, 66 or 75 MegaHertz (MHz) but unaware that it reflects back to 1880 and an experimenter named H. R. Hertz, who first succeeded in transmitting a signal across a distance of a few feet. Hertz didn't pursue the idea too much farther than his laboratory, but his work inspired Guglielmo Marconi, who added to the repertoire of communications twenty years later by sending a radio signal clear across the Atlantic.

Initially, sailors thought radio was useful only insofar as they could finally check their chronometers at sea. However, by the time World War I began, the possibilities of directional antennae had been realized, and engineers realized the potential of radio to augment the eyes of navigators. The propagation properties of radio waves could help people "see," even in inclement weather.

Loop Antennae & Radiobeacons

Direction Finding (DF) was originally accomplished with an antenna in the shape of a loop. As the angle of the loop changed with respect to incoming directional radio waves, so did the intensity of the detected signal change. Radio waves coming at right angles to the loop produce the most significant DF measurement — that of *no* signal at all. Waves hitting the loop at angles other than "right on" produce signals of varying intensity, and it is from these that direction can be determined.

Combinations of loop and conventional antennae allowed navigators to further determine from which direction radio waves were being picked up but, because early radio receivers had no amplification, readings were faint and had to be fed into meter-like instruments that concentrated them. Airplanes fitted with on-board loop antennae and radio compass equipment could 'hone in' on airfield beacons (the earliest automatic direction-finding (ADF) systems).

Radiobeacons are simply radio waves sent in specific directions. Technically, they are described as electronic navigation aids that provide position-fixing and homing capabilities to vessels fitted with radio direction finding (RDF) equipment. Radiobeacons are installed at lighthouses and other locations along U.S. coastal areas and the Great Lakes, and small craft use them primarily as a low-cost means of homing into harbor. They operate all the time in all types of weather, within ranges from 10 to 175 nautical miles in a frequency band from 285-325 kHz. Station IDs are transmitted in Morse Code at a rate of six words per minute, but mariners are given time during transmissions to make refinements to their bearings.

The value of a radiobeacon system lies in its reliability, simplicity of operation and relatively low cost to a user. A radio wave is sent out in a certain direction; if something obstructs it on its way, an echo ping is returned, and it is deduced that something is present in that direction. By knowing how fast a ping travels in the air (or other medium) and measuring the time it takes for it to return, a person can figure out how far away the obstruction is positioned. Today, in the U.S., the marine radiobeacon system is operated and maintained by the Coast Guard as a government-provided service to recreational boaters and commercial vessels. Responsibility includes providing the public with information regarding the locations, operation and use of the system. High-power radiobeacon installations are being upgraded to transmit DGPS signals.

The Flight Machine & Gyroscope

Just as radio added a new dimension to communication, the flying machine added its dimension to transport. Ironically, however, when the Wright brothers got their heavier-than-air machine off the ground at Kitty Hawk in 1903, the most important contribution brought to navigation had little to do with speed or 3-dimensional movement. It had to do with stability.

Early on in their tests, the Wrights realized that a manned flying machine could not be stabilized as easily as an unmanned model. Its instability required a control sensor very different from those used by ships or land vehicles. Fortunately, a control sensor was available — a toy gyroscope. What had started out as a plaything became an instrument of precision. The development of the gyroscope was paralleled by advances in the manufacture of other control devices for sea, air and space purposes.

Birth in Battle: SONAR & RADAR

Wars waged on the ground and in the air inspire wars of another kind — wars of wits. In 1916, Allied efforts to detect U-boats by placing microphones on their warships were thwarted simply by the enemies' shutting off their motors. Something better had to be done, and it had to be active, seeking out the enemy (and icebergs, too) rather than just passively picking up noise. SOund NAvigation Ranging — SONAR — became another of necessity's progeny.

Early SONAR consisted of electrically generated pulses of sound sent out from the seeker ships. When they hit something, echoed "pings" bounced back to the ship. The time it took for pulses to go, hit and ping back was measured, and distance ranges were calculated. Ways were then developed to send pulses out in beams so that direction could be found and to change the sound waves back into electrical signals so that they could be displayed.

Also, by 1930, the U.S. had already investigated the use of direction-finding signals to detect passing aircraft, and the Germans had started developing a ship-detection system. World War II speeded things up. A system was needed to detect enemies in the air. This led to RAdio Detection And Ranging — RADAR. Its basic principle is the same as SONAR except that signals are sent along radio beams, and echoes are picked up by a radio receiver. Returning signals are fed into CRT displays and appear as "blips" on the screen.

MICROPHONES   SONAR   RADAR

By 1938, a line of radar stations was in operation across southern England, even though Great Britain had not started work on radar until long after the U.S. This leap ahead was due, primarily, to Robert Watson-Watt, a man who saw radar only as part of a larger, much more comprehensive system, This established him as one of western civilization's first systems engineers.

After the war and proliferation of new methods, another problem arose — that of traffic control. Even people who knew where they were had to be kept from colliding. This ushered in an era of height-finding and airborne radar. These extensions included features for identifying objects, visually representing scenarios to resemble an operator's viewpoint and doing calculations with computers.

Radionavigation Systems

Development of radionavigation systems, which receive radio signals and use a mathematical technique called triangulation to determine position, began during World War II. Long-range missiles of that time, which were ground-based, were equipped with low-frequency (LF) or very-low-frequency transmitters to improve bombing accuracy. Low-frequency signals were not as accurate as high-frequency ones but were used because they are not blocked by topographical features (mountains, for example). High-frequency signals are effective only if transmitters are high enough in space to transcend topography.

A LOng-RAN (LORAN) direction-finding system provides positional data over a wide area, not just from specific points. Most LORAN transmitters, however, are located in coastal areas. LORAN was very important to the development of GPS because it was the first system to use the time-of-arrival (TOA) of a radar signal for navigation purposes.

During World War II, in the Pacific arena, LORAN's low-frequency radio waves and pairs of stations helped ships and airplanes establish their locations, and the system proved impermeable to Japanese efforts at jamming. A medium-frequency system was subsequently developed for the Normandy invasion.

New Antennae

The small, parabolic dishes available today for picking up digital television signals evolved from frustration with early radar antennae that were too cumbersome to fit on anything but ships. As soon as it became possible to transmit signals at higher frequencies, differently shaped antennae were developed. Small dishes were first used in 1942 by maritime patrol airplanes and then by fighter planes.

Determining whether a craft were manned by friend or foe required an addition to the signaling system. Thus, friendly craft were fitted with a piece of transmitting equipment that would recognize incoming radar and respond with a distinctive mark on the radar picture. These transmitting responders are called transponders.

During World War II, as electronic advances continued to provide military advantage, the war of wits escalated. With each measure and countermeasure, the edge of technology was honed. Germans used long-range beam systems for night bombing; the British succeeded in transmitting signals to shift German beams and cause the bombs to miss their targets. The British set up radar stations along their coastlines; the Germans succeeded in jamming them long enough to escape up the English Channel. And the story continues.

Precursors to GPS

In the 1950s and 1960s, it became obvious that an accurate, worldwide system was needed to standardize the inertial navigation systems of increasing numbers of nuclear submarines circling the globe. This coincided with the emergence of satellite technologies and led to the Navy's Transit program. Under this program, satellites were developed, the earth's gravity field was modeled so that orbits could be determined, equipment was built, and ground stations were established to monitor satellites and control operations.

Omega is a well-established but less frequently mentioned system than LORAN. Developed by the U.S., six other nations contribute to its operation. It is used primarily for ocean navigation and for non-navigation jobs such as hurricane tracking and weather balloons. Omega can achieve accuracies of 2-4 miles, and its receiver units for meteorological use are inexpensive compared to those required for DGPS.

However, most applications that use Omega today are better served by GPS or other systems, and it is no longer required for navigation. Its scheduled phase-out date is late 1997, when partner nations also plan to cease operations. Alternatives to its use include LORAN-C, VLF and GPS.

Modern Navigation

In a more technical sense than just getting from here to there, navigation is the process of determining one's position and velocity relative to a chosen reference point or frame. It can be one of two types, noninertial or inertial. Noninertial navigation is, basically, piloting — by means of celestial bearings; radio, radar or LORAN; dead reckoning or Doppler radar.

Inertial navigation is a sophisticated form of dead reckoning in which any movement of a vehicle (airplane, ship, spacecraft, etc.) is detected and used to determine the present position of a vehicle at any time. Inertial navigation uses mathematics to do this when a start point and velocities of the vehicle are known. It first gets the velocity from a combination of gyroscope, accelerometer and computers. The marriage of inertial systems with GPS timing and locational accuracies delivered an ease of use and performance superior to any previous radionavigation system.

A navigation system is usually the whole set of devices that determines the location of any vehicle carrying it. It does this by converting the space passed into measurements. If the whole process is automated, the system is called an autonavigator.

Another way to describe inertial navigation is navigation in which rotation is sensed and for which compensation is made. To so preserve a system's orientation, inertial navigation makes use of the computers, gyroscopes and on-board accelerometers. The accelerometer, mounted on what is called a stable platform, measures any increases in velocity along three planes, each mutually perpendicular to the others.

An on-board gyroscope keeps the accelerometer in fixed orientation, regardless of how the vehicle moves. The gyroscope first registers rotation by sensing the amount of shift or swing (called relative displacement) between its spin axis and its case. Signals corresponding to this displacement are then sent to drive a motor. The motor, in turn, adjusts the platform (in an "equal and opposite" way) to compensate for rotation.

Feedback between the gyroscope and the platform is continuous. From this process, inertial acceleration is computed and integrated with conditions that may vary (such as air pressure, density, etc.). This yields velocity and three-dimensional position for most aircraft, missile, spacecraft and submarine applications.

Inertial systems are very stable over the short term. They do, however, drift slightly over time, so need to be reinitialized regularly. Inertial systems function without regard for weather or radio interference and are valuable additions to ships, submarines and aircraft, but they are expensive. Military use of inertial navigation has been extensive.

As missiles were motorized, and automatic plotting devices traced points of light across charts to mimic a craft's movements, gyroscopes, too, were motorized, and rate gyroscopes allowed measurement of the rate at which pitch and roll were occurring. These were combined with long-range direction finding to become the precursors of intercontinental ballistic weapons systems (ICBMs).

Emergence of a Utility Constellation

The 1957 Soviet launch of Sputnik sparked a lot of thinking, and a good idea dawned on some scientists and engineers as their eyes were drawn to the sky. If radio signals from a known spot on earth could be used to determine a satellite's location in the sky, signals from satellites in well-defined orbits in the sky could be harnessed to indicate the position on earth of a receiver picking them up. The seed was thus planted for the U.S. Navy's "Transit" system. Developed and launched in the 1960s. Transit measured the Doppler shift of signals from a satellite passing overhead to calculate location.

By the mid-1970s, the U.S. Department of Defense was constructing the much more sophisticated Global Positioning System (dubbed GPS), a positioning and time-transfer system that would also benefit navigation. Designed specifically for U.S. military advantage, GPS would enable personnel on military transport (ships, aircraft and ground vehicles) to determine their location anywhere in the world. Today, civilian satellite navigation systems are so widespread that the International Civil Aviation Organization, in Montreal, dropped a mandate requiring all international airports to possess a microwave landing system by January1998 in favor of GPS or GLONASS.

TWINKLING SATELLITES

"The planets in their station listening stood..."
Milton

Artificial Satellites

Natural satellites are naturally formed masses orbiting a planet — like our moon. Man-made units put into orbit around a celestial body are artificial satellites.

Today, there are thousands of artificial satellites occupying space. Some are passive, merely reflecting signals — the earliest of which were appropriately named Echo. Others are active, "working" units designed to receive signals, amplify them and relay them to other satellites or stations.

The reconnaissance (spy) satellites of the 1960s and `70s were huge, heavy, working contraptions — up to 50 feet long. Yet, they worked well enough to convince people of the benefits of a technology that exploits a vantage point from space. The strategic advantages gained from space-based units surpassed those realized by U-2 missions, providing the United States with a heightened degree of independence. Orbiting high above the atmosphere, they did their job without violating other countries' airspace (though complaints were waged). More importantly, they could not be shot down.

These reconnaissance satellites' frequent runs around the earth (every 90 minutes or so) presented repeated opportunities to examine specific areas. Their equipment could, supposedly, pick out and photograph objects only 1-foot wide. Also, because they were launched from the U.S., the success of these early spy satellites did not rely on Allies' cooperation, as did the U-2.

Eventually, communication channels were established between reconnaissance satellites and other types of satellites, such as those monitoring the weather. If cloud cover were bad over a photo-target area, for example, weather satellites could be programmed to alert the spy satellite when it cleared up so that pictures could be taken. If necessary, the orbit and altitude of the reconnaissance satellite could be altered.

Today, reconnaissance by technological means is no longer considered espionage but surveillance. And today's little satellites, not excluding those of the GPS, are compactly fitted with state-of-the-art electronics and information-gathering sensors.

Subsystems

Each artificial satellite contains a number of systems. Some are linked to and are essential for basic operations, and some are piggybacked to perform other functions. Among the many types of subsystems found aboard satellites are sensors, computers, autonavigation features and electrical systems.

Remote sensors that scan vast regions of the earth's surface are often mounted on satellites in order to detect, evaluate and predict changes that might affect it or its inhabitants. These sensors may observe atmospheric phenomena, evaluate natural resources, analyze the impact of large projects on surrounding areas or assess damage caused by earthquakes, fire or flood. Highly sophisticated remote-sensing devices may be designed for defense purposes, e.g., to detect nuclear explosions, troop movements or heat patterns that may be weapons-generated. GPS satellites themselves are being used for remote sensing, as well. They carry nuclear-explosion detection devices used to monitor nonproliferation treaties.

Non-GPS satellites put into orbit for such purposes have been circling the globe for decades. What is new is that today's models are fitted with GPS antennae that pick up signals that not only define their own navigational information but time-tag collected data with precise location and time information. The GPS satellites' large solar panels provide the main source of energy for their operation. However, a backup electrical system is needed on each satellite to provide energy during eclipses, when the sun's angle is less than optimal or when satellite load demands are high. Therefore, nickel-cadmium batteries are included.

Since 1989, satellite models have included an "autonav" feature that enables it to operate for a limited time if contact with the ground is lost or interrupted. Early Block II versions could re-transmit the last-known navigation-message data for three days in absence of ground control. Later and current versions, however, are able to operate autonomously and maintain system accuracy for six months, generating and transmitting its own navigation-message data.

This capability of actually generating and transmitting new navigation-message data is possible through a sophisticated data-communication system and powerful onboard computers. As long as contact between the ground and a satellite does exist, the ground control segment continually feeds satellite computers with long-range predictions of the measurements. If contact is severed, the satellite has enough projected information to estimate quite closely what the navigation message would be.

Dilutions of Precision

A good receiver determines which configuration of satellites in view provides the combination of signals that produces the best result. However, for some applications, there is less tolerance for certain types of dilution than others.

For example, knowing the geometric dilution is especially critical for any applications in which altitude must be calculated. Aviators must be aware of a Vertical Dilution of Precision (VDOP) when attempting to make precision landings. In addition, airborne receivers must be able to determine general, 3-D Position Dilution of Precision (PDOP).

For marine navigation, since altitude is assumed to be at sea level, a more practical objective is to obtain and use the lowest Horizontal Dilution of Precision (HDOP) possible. If necessary, it can be done with fewer than four satellites.

The degree to which satellite configuration can affect the accuracy of time signals is called Time Dilution of Precision (TDOP). TDOP is important to scientists, engineers and military personnel using GPS signals to synchronize clocks.

Evolutionary History

An evolutionary history of the GPS constellation reflects how satellite design advanced over an extended period of time and gives us a glimpse of what is to come. "R" types are replacements or replenishments for satellites being taken out of service; "F" types are follow-on versions of satellites in use. A summary of the different "block" versions that have made up the configuration appears in the table below.

Evolutionary History of the Global Positioning System Constellation

BLOCK TYPE	#	FIRST LAUNCH	PURPOSE	CLAIM TO FAME	FATE
0	2	1974	experimental prototypes for GPS; validate time-based ranging concept, atomic-frequency-derived time, and spread-spectrum radio signaling	remodeled Timations; carried atomic clocks into space for first time.	short-lived, as planned
I	11	1978	testing platform	life expectancy 60 months; many lasting longer — one more than 11 years, one 13; Block I #6 first GPS satellite to carry nuclear-explosion detector.	launch failure; deteriorating clocks; failed attitude-control systems; sole survivor retired in 1995
II	9	1989	originally designed to deploy shuttles but decision rescinded as a result of Challenger disaster	able to operate and continue transmitting navigation message data for 3 or more days if contact with control segment interrupted or lost.	replacement, especially since accuracy deteriorates after 3½ days without control segment contact

IIA	19	1990	new design, electronics, anti-spoofing capability, error-detection features	able to operate autonomously for six months if control segment contact lost; set of 24 provided full operational capability	replacement when usefulness exhausted
IIR	21	as needed starting 1996	replacement units	autonomous navigation, i.e., can generate and transmit own navigation message data (NAV-msg) and maintain system accuracy independent of control segment for 180 days; next generation to incorporate continuous communication channel to disseminate critical information to tactical units in time of conflict.	replacement when usefulness exhausted
IIF	33	early to mid-2000s	replenishments	estimated cost in excess of $2 billion; longer life expectancy (6-10 yrs.) and higher performance level than IIF	eventual replacement by more sophisticated, more robust units
-	6	-	follow-ups to replace IIF satellites	procurement already planned by DoD Joint Program Office	

Orbits

An orbit is the path a natural or artificial body in space takes around a celestial object such as the path the moon or a satellite takes around the earth or the earth takes around the sun. Orbits of artificial satellites may be either permanent (and, thus, stable) ones or temporary and unstable.

A permanent orbit is high — well outside the earth's atmosphere for its entire path. The cause of a temporary orbit's instability is that the low point of its path crosses (either intentionally or accidentally) within the earth's atmosphere. This produces drag on the satellite, eventually slowing it down (referred to as orbital decay) until it has lost so much of its momentum that even its high point falls within the atmosphere. When that happens, it spirals down toward earth, usually burning up from friction with the atmosphere on the way.

Most early satellites were launched into space for specific, short-term research, and many were deliberately placed into temporary, self-destruct orbits. Had they not been designed to burn up, once their usefulness was over, they would have become no more than orbiting space trash.

Incidents have been recorded of intended temporary satellites assuming stable orbits and staying out there as clutter, and 8500 pieces of floating debris are being tracked by the Air Force Space Command in Colorado Springs in efforts to avoid collisions with space stations or satellite units.

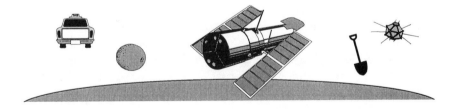

A satellite may be deliberately placed in a lopsided orbit, as well. This is useful when greater surface coverage of certain areas is more important than others. An example of this is a satellite placed in what is called a "Molniya" orbit, high over the northern hemisphere (to increase the amount of coverage there) but dipping lower over the southern hemisphere (which may not be the focus of that particular launch).

Almost all of today's working satellites need to stay put and function indefinitely; so, they are launched into high, stable orbits. How high any satellite is placed depends on its intended use. Also relevant is the amount of surface area to be covered. The surface area of earth that a satellite can cover depends directly on the height of its orbit. To blanket the earth's surface, many low-orbit satellites are needed; far fewer satellites are needed if placed in very high orbits.

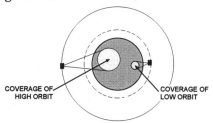

Low-orbiting satellites, up to 1600 kilometers above the earth, are the most suitable for detecting visual or infrared radiation from the earth, affording detailed images of the earth's surface for photoreconnaissance, electronics-intelligence and ocean-surveillance purposes. Medium-height orbits range from 1600 to a few thousand miles above the earth.

All 24 satellites of the Global Positioning System are placed in six very high orbital planes — from low points of about 12,552 statute miles (20,200 kilometers) to high points of about 12,614 statute miles (20,300 kilometers) above the earth.

Geosynchronous & Geostationary Orbits

The earth has a rotational period of 24 hours. An orbit whose period of rotation is some multiple or sub-multiple of that is referred to as a "geosynchronous" orbit. If a satellite is synchronized to match up in some way with the earth's rotation, it will pass over the same point on earth at a given time (or at given times) each day.

Geostationary orbits are a special case. If an orbiting body is placed 22,300 miles above the earth at the equator, it, too, will take 24 hours to make one complete rotation. By thus mimicking the earth's rotation, it will remain over the same place. These are described as geostationary orbits.

GPS satellites are in geosynchronous orbit with an orbital period of 12 hours a sub-multiple of the earth's 24-hour period. This means it circles the earth in the same orbit twice every 24 hours.

Time

Any consideration of location, change or motion ultimately depends upon a study of time, and GPS' reputation as a location-finding technology depends upon its functioning as a precise time-transfer facility. In our highly technical, industrialized world, we are surrounded by advances made possible only through the precise measurement of time and the synchronization of events.

Both Concept & Spatial Unit

Time can be hostage to the limitations of concept. For example, societies undominated by time (such as some African tribes, the Hopi Indians and Australian aborigines) possess few or no direct, grammatical references to what we call "time," though they have ways of reckoning its passage.

Some philosophers, notably Kant, presupposed the idea of worldwide time but did not think it applied to things that transcended experience (particularly the universe) — describing it, instead, as part of our mental apparatus for visualizing the world. In the context of the industrialized world, time is a catalyst, the standard by which social and business activities are organized. In science, time is a tool used to determine distance and speed and to synchronize the operation of machines or events.

Humans' earliest intuition of time came not from thoughts of duration or passage but from an innate sense of rhythm, of things repetitious and simultaneous. Certain things were done and repeated at certain times — and were usually associated with nature's intervals of solar days, lunar cycles and solar years. The appreciation of eternal cosmic rhythm by Mayan priests of the 6th and 7th centuries was so fine-tuned as to be seminal to the establishment of leap-year corrections even more accurate than today's Gregorian calendar. The solar day, beginning in light and retiring in darkness, closely matched our natural human cycle and served as our earliest block unit of time. Division into spatial parts (e.g., east, west, north, south) also fit segments of the day (i.e., morning, afternoon, evening and night), forming another basis for measurement.

Indeed, the Greek and Latin roots from which the word *time* evolved — *templus* and *templum* — signify intersection or bisection. The practical measurement of time depends on such spatial concepts as these. For the purposes of this book, time is defined as a unit of spatial division.

Measuring Time

There are three different aspects of time measurement and management — finding time, measuring time and keeping time, and interesting, innovative devices for each have cropped up over the years. Finding time by observing rotations of the earth relative to the stars was helped by dials, astrolabes and sextants.

Measuring time intervals has been done with sandglasses, water clocks, fire clocks, mechanical devices and atomic clocks. In ancient China and Japan, even the sense of smell was used — human timekeepers burned small pieces of distinctly scented incense in sequence, broadcasting aromatic signals of change to sensitive noses. Inventions of clocks and watches (mechanical, electric, quartz) finally made timekeeping easy and portable.

The familiar clockface unit, 12, has been used since as early as 2100 B.C., when drawings inside coffins depicted nights divided into 12 segments. This division originated, perhaps, from an ancient Egyptian custom of gauging time by the rising of stars on the horizon. Day and night were each divided into twelve "temporal" units. However, as the periods of light and darkness varied with the seasons, the length of segments varied, as well; one-twelfth of a shortened winter day was considerably shorter than one-twelfth of a summer day.

Temporal hours were abandoned by all but astrologers when the mechanical clock offered the constancy of equal "hours." The mechanical clock's future was secured when monastery monks realized it was more dependable and less trouble than other devices for summoning people to prayer and announcing events — and, wonderfully, it could be made to strike a bell.

People eventually started organizing their time by the hourly ringing of bells, and our word "clock" is derived from "clocca," a Celtic word for the sound made when a hard object is struck. Not until sometime around the 15th century did day-to-day civilian activities demand that someone come up with smaller divisions of time.

Astronomers, however, had long had to deal with small fractions of an hour and had already devised a system based on 60 primary minutes and 60 secondary minutes. These were adopted for domestic and civil use and the nomenclature shortened to "minutes" and "seconds." By the 16th century, clocks showing minutes and seconds were beginning to appear, but accuracy was not achieved until pendulums and spiral balances came into use in the 1800s.

Time & Longitude

When it became possible to keep accurate time, scientists were very enthusiastic, and one of the first tasks they tackled was that of determining longitude. Since the earth rotates a full 360 degrees every 24 hours (1440 minutes), it rotates one degree every 4 minutes. So, differences in longitude could be found by comparing differences in time between two locations.

But there was a problem. There was no standard for public time. Communities often determined local time simply by noting the position of the sun at noon or by some other imprecise method — sorely inadequate for scientific purposes.

In 1851, however, scientists at Harvard College started a public time service by telegraphing clock beats and distributing them across the expanses separating communities. Suddenly, there was a standard by which emerging industries could be regulated. This need for standard time became even more pressing as railways became popular and schedules had to be maintained.

By 1884, the world had been divided into 24 time zones, and the Prime Meridian was established at Greenwich, England. Most countries then adopted Greenwich Mean Time (GMT) as the standard upon which local times would be calculated. By the 1920s, electromechanical clocks kept time at most observatories, but discovery of possibly using the oscillations of quartz crystal as a frequency standard was gaining interest. By 1939, a quartz crystal clock replaced the electromechanical model at Greenwich and, within eight years, the first atomic-beam cesium clock was developed.

The atomic clock has surpassed all others for accuracy. Now, via GPS, the accuracy and stability of the best atomic clocks can be transferred to remote sites.

Atomically Clocking Time

"The atomic clock ticks faster..."   J. Robert Oppenheimer

There are several little atomic clocks in every GPS satellite. Only one operates at any one time; the others serve as back-ups. When one fails, the next takes over. Timing by these extremely accurate and precise atomic clocks and an exact knowledge of the orbits of the satellites are what make the Global Positioning System work.

With the introduction of atomic time over the last decades, time metrics have moved from milliseconds to picoseconds. The calculation of frequency has been extended from nine significant digits to sixteen, and it owes it to the energy states of atoms.

The energy states of atoms change, and the atomic clock is based on the measurement of those changes in certain chemical elements. Although rubidium and hydrogen are often used for atomic clocks in laboratories and navigational systems, the chemical element most suitable is cesium (aka caesium), a shiny, soft, gold-colored metal that produces a sky-blue ("caesius") color in the spectrum. Because cesium is strongly photoelectric — losing electrons easily when struck by light — it has long been used in spectrographic instruments, photoelectric cells, infrared devices, counters for scintillators and radio tubes.

Cesium's frequency has now been harnessed as the time standard for the atomic clocks aboard GPS satellites. (Rubidium clocks ride along as redundant standards.)

Phenomenal activity lies behind GPS' precision timing, and it all happens within a clock casing not much larger than a matchbox. In it, a little chunk of cesium (or rubidium) is heated enough to cause some of its outer atoms to separate from the rest. The outermost electron of each of these individual atoms spins in either the same direction as (parallel to) the spin of the atom itself, in which case it is a low-energy cesium atom — or in the direction opposite (anti-parallel) to the spin of the atom, indicating a higher state of energy.

A magnet is used to separate the two kinds. The low-energy atoms are then directed into a special chamber called a resonant cavity, to be zapped by microwaves (at specific frequencies and with a lot of fine tuning).

Being radiated excites the electrons of some of these low-energy atoms, causing their parallel spins to actually change direction — and go anti-parallel to the spin of the atom. Thus, low-energy atoms are changed into high-energy atoms.

How fast one type of atom absorbs energy is called its frequency (or resonance frequency). The rate at which this happens is different for each element and can be measured. The cycle of low-energy cesium being changed to high-energy cesium occurs 9,192,631,770 times per second.

Such very small, accurate measurement units are ideal as time standards. Also, since external things like pressure or magnetic fields don't change an atom's frequency, it remains constant. In other words, each oscillation can be translated into a constant time-transfer standard smaller than one 9-billionth of a second, the best achievable yet. (Based on these, it would take a million years before timing would be off by a mere second.)

This said, another point must be considered. Atomic time is not related to the earth's rotation but to the laws governing the transmission of energy in atoms. For accurate results in navigation and surveying, however, oscillation-derived atomic time must somehow be linked and coordinated to the earth's rotation.

Three things are involved:

1. **TAI**, Temps Atomique International, the average rate of atomic clocks worldwide;
2. **UT1**, time determined by observation of the heavens; and
3. **UTC**, Universal (Atomic) Time Coordinated.

The atomic second, adopted in 1967 as the international standard unit of time measurement, corresponds to the transition time between the two hyperfine levels of the ground state of the cesium-133 atom.

Atomic time, referred to as TAI (Temps Atomique International), is based on the average rate of a number of atomic clocks around the world. The International Bureau of Weights and Measurements in Paris coordinates world atomic time signals (TAI) with time determined by observation of the heavens (called UT1 time). This derived atomic time (called Universal Time Coordinated or UTC) is always kept within nine-tenths of a second of UT1 time.

TAI *coordinated with* **UT1** → **UTC**

Basically, atomic time coordinated with celestial time yields coordinated atomic time. It is the reference time scale for all scientific and technologic work; so, it must be as stable, accurate and reliable as possible. Also called broadcast time, UTC is the time announced over the radio and television.

GPS clocks have been employed to synchronize the reference clocks of AT&T's telecommunications networks across the U.S. The result is an ultra-stable, verifiable timing signal 100 times better than that required by international standards and doesn't require continuous tracking of satellites.

Time-of-Arrival Ranging

The amount of time between the transmission of a signal and its reception somewhere else (i.e., travel time) is called the time-of-arrival (TOA) value. Determining this accurately requires precise timekeeping and the synchronization of all the timekeepers involved (at both sending and receiving ends).

Some of us may have used the time-of-arrival concept during thunderstorms, counting the seconds between seeing a flash of lightning and hearing thunder. This time span is the TOA range. Combining this with the known speed of sound (about 1/5 mile per second) people have been able to figure out approximately how far away lightning occurs.

Time-of-arrival ranging is the basis of how GPS works, but its ranging relies on the speed of radio waves — traveling at the speed of light — rather than at the slow speed of sound waves. The radio signals are sent from an atomic clock aboard each satellite as digital strings of "1s" and "0s," which can be read by computers. They are broadcast over two radio-band frequencies ("L-bands").

RELATED DISCIPLINES

Kinds of Information Used with GPS

Today, much of the information, data and knowledge we use is digitized. That is, it is converted into electronic combinations of 1s (ones) and 0s (zeros) that can be handled, filed and stored on computers. Data are individual items or bits of information.

A database is a collection of these facts and figures stored in some semblance of order so that people can find things. Collections of knowledge are referred to as knowledge bases, and datasets are files or parts of files kept as resources for particular subjects. All data relevant to a topic are kept as a set, and the natures of datasets can vary from scientific, geographic, cultural or financial to recreational. An aviation dataset, for example, contains waypoints, aviation terms, formulae, maps, etc. — in other words, assembled facts and figures useful to someone flying a plane.

Scientific and technical datasets often have arrays or tables of data that can be read by many types of computers. Hardcopy lists of datasets available to the general public would comprise many telephone books, but they are becoming available in digital format on tape, CD-ROM, floppy disk or datacards that can be used with various kinds of equipment.

Specific information for a job at hand (such as navigation) is gathered and/or found in specialized databases. These can be merged with other databases, upgrading them both qualitatively and quantitatively, and they can be stored and shared via data warehousing.

Scientific databases contain the bulk of scientific information, data and knowledge that has been saved. Some are broadly defined and encompass views across many disciplines; others are narrowly defined datasets. As geologists, chemists, physicists, biologists and astronomers add to these stores of specific data, they contribute to the composite database of scientific knowledge from which researchers extract what they need.

Task-specific databases are collections of information, data and knowledge needed to accomplish certain tasks — the techniques or data relevant to car repair, for example. Such a database would contain a compilation of what can go wrong with a car, how to diagnose a problem and specific steps that can be taken to fix it. A preventive maintenance database would be a database relevant to the task of anticipating potential problems and the steps necessary to prevent them. Simply put, a task-specific database is a superset of all the instruction guides and procedure manuals on the topic. What is needed to do a job can be extracted from it.

Conceptual databases incorporate the elements of information, data and knowledge that are relevant to a user's world and how he or she wants to use them. It is a high-level abstraction of the world in which a person works and embodies a user's perception of how material should be defined and stored. Domain-specific databases are compiled by experts in a field.

Government-compiled public databases provide easy-to-access, consistent sources of information to private citizens, the media and professional organizations. Countries are consolidating information and establishing databases on issues such as health, security benefits, welfare, environment, public safety and law enforcement. Public databases also serve as dispatching agents for federal-to-local assistance or communication.

Attorneys access and use electronic legal databases to search for precedents, tax information and contract and trade regulations, as well as U.S. and foreign laws. As resources, legal databases are so valuable that many law schools now require students to become familiar with them. The same holds for databases compiled and kept by medical specialists and scientists.

Financial investment and financial services databases provide detailed information and data on quotes from the floors of the stock exchanges, business and economic news, prices of stocks, options and exchanges. Specific databases may contain corporate earnings estimates, Standard and Poor's ratings or summary data for corporations. Real-time visualizations of economic trends, for instance, would have to be connected to a database that contains that information and that changes dynamically in real time.

Expert (intelligent) databases or systems incorporate ways of representing knowledge and a capability to draw inferences from what is stored. Expert systems also help people find information across myriad research sources. An intelligent database provides a semblance of the real world in which a person works and is so organized that a user can easily manipulate and manage the information stored there. Some incorporate features that determine a user's pattern of use and adjust responses to appropriate levels.

Some things make sense only in a spatial context, i.e., in the right location. A real-space database contains coordinates and data for real locations and defines things such as altitude, latitude and longitude. Images can then be displayed (e.g., on a GPS or computer screen) according to their real-world-based coordinates. Coordinates control whether a real-space image is displayed or removed. The establishment of accurate real-space databases is, therefore, important to the spread of GPS positioning and navigation.

People can buy access to databases through subscription, by connecting and downloading information via modem or by getting it in hard copy, on floppy disc or CD-ROMs. On-line, "live" access to commercial databases is expensive; so, it is used primarily for information that changes quickly or is not available from other sources, such as news updates or stock prices.

Signaling Frequencies

Radio signals, such as those used by GPS, travel at the speed of light from a transmitter to a receiver (or a sender to an observer). As a transmitter moves toward a receiver, the number of waves measured per unit of time increases — as if many waves are compressed into a smaller and smaller distance. This measures as a higher frequency. As the transmitter moves away, fewer waves will be measured per unit of time — as if being stretched, resulting in a measurement of lower frequency (Doppler shift). If the user is moving, the frequency of the signal received by the user will also undergo a corresponding Doppler shift.

In the Transit system, the user must be at rest to get an accurate position; if in motion, he or she must correct the signal received from the satellite by the amount of his or her motion's induced Doppler effect. With GPS, appropriately designed user receivers can use the receiver-induced Doppler effect to compute the velocity of the user relative to the earth or the ground over which movement is taking place.

Appendix B
MEASUREMENTS & CALCULATIONS

"Ancient travelers guessed; modern travelers measure."
Dr. Johnson

TRIANGULATION

Triangulation takes advantage of the relationships between the sides of a triangle and the angles bounded within it. A short mapping exercise is used here to illustrate the steps involved.

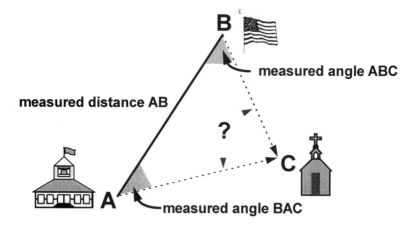

1. Measure one distance, from A to B, for example.

2. From A, then use a transit to "sight" C and determine angle (BAC).

3. Sight C from B and determine that angle (ABC).

You now have measurements for one side and two angles. A very simple formula from trigonometry allows you to use these known measurements to calculate the lengths of the unknowns, AC and BC. When sides AC and BC are known, the process can be repeated with other targets.

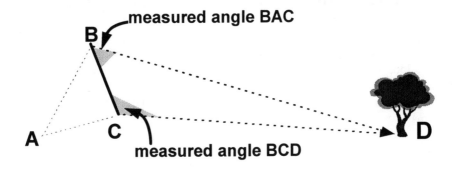

measured angle BAC

measured angle BCD

1. Sight D from B to determine angle (CBD).

2. Sight D from C and determine that angle (BCD).

3. Use the formula to find lengths of new sides, BD and CD.

4. Keep going until all relevant targets are mapped.

The difference with GPS is that most of the action takes place above ground, in space. Each satellite knows its distance from each of the others, and all the relevant angles are computed. These become part of the satellite almanac. The user's receiver is their common target.

Measuring the time delay between the code received from each satellite and the similar code it generates — and multiplying it by the speed of light, a receiver calculates how far the signal traveled to get there. For computational purposes, this is one side of a triangle. The process is repeated for each of the satellites in view.

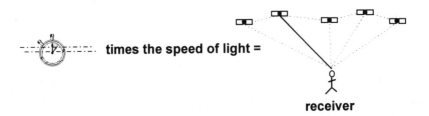

times the speed of light =

receiver

ERATOSTHENES, EARTH-MEASURER

The study of geodesy has come a long way. Though some of Columbus' contemporaries still believed the earth to be flat, some observant fellows very long before that had noticed ships disappearing over the horizon and had surmised that the earth was round. One of these was Eratosthenes, a Greek Keeper of the Scrolls in Egypt at around 220 B.C., who took it upon himself to find out just how big a sphere it was. Eratosthenes was also a mathematician, and his approach was geometric, but wells and camels became part of the equation.

To calculate the circumference of the earth, he needed three things, a base line (approximating one side of a triangle) and two angles (that were equal and opposite), which he set out to obtain, one at a time. The base line would be a north/south route from Alexandria to a place on the Tropic of Cancer, where he knew the sun's rays are perpendicular to the earth on the longest day of the year. If one such ray could be extended, it would pass through the center of the earth, giving him his theoretical second side to his triangle and a base for his angles. The solution lay in angles and ratios:

$$\frac{\text{Distance from Alexandria to Syrene}}{\text{Circumference of the Earth}} = \frac{\text{Difference from 0° in Alexandria sun's angle}}{\text{Total angle around any circle}}$$

Distance from Alexandria to Syrene
(which he was going to measure)

Circumference of the Earth
(what he wanted to know)

Difference from 0° in Alexandria sun's angle
(derived from the slant of a shadow)

Total angle around any circle
(which he knew was 360°)

Eratosthenes decided to travel due south to Syrene, on the Tropic of Cancer, but needed a calibrated means of getting there. Armed with an hourglass, the Greek trekked across the sands, diligently measuring and recording how far a camel would go in an hour. By the time he started out, he knew exactly how much ground a calibrated camel would cover over any stretch of time. Arriving at Syrene, he determined that he had covered 5000 stadia (~500 nautical miles or ~575 statute miles) long (his base line, the distance from Alexandria to Syrene).

Looking down a well shaft, he confirmed that the sun was directly overhead because its rays shone straight down to the bottom. Pleased, he returned to Alexandria, where he next had to figure out how "un-parallel" the sun's rays were at Alexandria on the longest day of the year. Then he would have a proportion to work with.

From geometry, Eratosthenes knew that, if he erected a post in Alexandria and measured the angle of its shadow also on the longest day of the year (the next summer solstice and, incidentally, when the shadow would be at its shortest), its angle would equal that between the intersecting lines at the center of the earth. With this last piece, he could solve his puzzle.

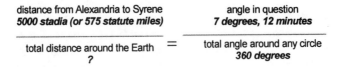

The angle he got was 1/50th of the total angle around the circle; so the distance of 5000 stadia would be, proportionally, 1/50th of the total distance around the earth.

Using those numbers, the circumference of the earth would be 50 × 575 or 28,750 statute miles — about 16% off today's accepted figure of 24,860 miles. Eratosthenes the Geodesist's persistence and ingenuity paid off with an impressive finding for the time.

Today's geodesists have the Global Positioning System to help them.

Appendix C
ORIGINAL EQUIPMENT MANUFACTURERS
& Sources of GPS Systems & Software

As GPS tools and techniques find their way into almost every area of our lives, increasing numbers of people are venturing into GPS-related manufacturing, sales and services. Of the companies supplying today's fast-growing demand, some are large, long-established technical-instrument manufacturers; others are small, specialized providers; others are consultants selling expertise and metrics. Keeping track of them is difficult, but regularly updated vendor information can be obtained from sourcebooks or via visits to websites.

A short listing of manufacturers and their product-line focus is given here simply for the convenience of readers. It is not meant as endorsement, nor is the list all-inclusive. At the time of printing, addresses were current.

3S Navigation
4 Executive Circle, Suite 200
Irvine, California 92614
http://www.3Snavigation.com
GPS/GLONASS, aviation, timing

Allen Osborne Associates, Inc.
756 Lakefield Road, Bldg. J
Westlake Village, California 91361
aoa@netcom.com
land, military, survey, timing

Ashtech, Inc.
1170 Kifer Road
Sunnyvale, California 94086
http://www.ashtech.com
combined GPS/GLONASS, OEM, aviation, land, military, survey

Del Norte Technology, Inc.
P. O. Box 696
1100 Pamela Drive
Euless, Texas 76039
farming, aviation, survey, software

Eastman Kodak Company
Commercial & Government Systems
1447 St. Paul Street
Rochester, New York 14653
kodakcsg@catdir.com
digital GPS cameras

II Morrow Incorporated
2345 Turner Road SE
Salem, Oregon 97302
http://www.iimorrow.com
aviation, land, marine

Magellan Systems Corporation
960 Overland Court
San Dimas, California 91773
http://www.magellangps.com
OEM, aviation, land, marine

Northstar Technologies
Division of CMC Electronics
30 Sudbury Road
Acton, Massachusetts 01720
http://www.northstarcmc.com
aviation, land, marine

Litton Systems, Inc.
Guidance & Control Systems Division
5500 Canoga Avenue
Woodland Hills, California 91367
http://www.littongcs.com
OEM, defense, GPS/INS, sensors,
land, marine, air

Premier GPS, Inc.
1003-D 55 Avenue NE
Calgary, Alberta T2E 6W1, Canada
(51° 06' 06.21" N, 114° 02' 21.21" W)
tabsha@premier-gps.com
OEM, aviation, land, marine, military,
survey, timing

Sextant Avionique
25 rue Jules Vedrine
26027 Valence Cedex, France
aviation

Sokkia
9111 Barton, Box 2934
Overland Park, Kansas 66201
(38° 57' 49.020" N, 94° 42' 57.540" W)
http://www.sokkia.com
survey, software

Techsonic Industries, Inc.
#3 Humminbird Lane
Eufaula, Alabama 36027
land, marine

Topcon GPS Products Division
65 West Century Road
Paramus, New Jersey 07652
http://www.Topcon.com
OEM, aviation, land, marine, military,
survey, timing

Trimble Navigation Limited
2105 Donlay Drive
Austin, Texas 78758-4534
OEM, aviation, land, marine, military,
survey, timing

Canadian Marconi Co.
600 Dr. Frederic Phillips Blvd.
Ville St. Laurent, PQ H4M 2S9
Canada
OEM, aviation, land, military

Carl Zeiss, Inc.
Geschaftsbereich Vermessung
7082 Oberkochen, Germany
survey

Communication Systems Int'l.
1200-58 Avenue S.E.,
Alberta T2H 2C0, Canada
OEM, aviation, land, marine, military,
survey, technical

Dassault Sercel NP
46 Rue de Bel Air, BP 433
Carquefou Cedex, 44474 France
OEM, aviation, land, marine, military,
survey, technical

Eagle Electronics
P.O. Box 669
Catoosa, Oklahoma 74015
OEM, aviation, land, marine, military,
survey, technical

GARMIN Corporation
1200 East 151st Street
Olathe, Kansas 66062
OEM, land, marine, aviation

Geotronics of North America Inc.
911 W. Hawthorne Drive
Itasca, Illinois 60143
OEM, aviation, land, marine, military,
survey, technical

ITT Avionics
100 Kingsland Road
Clifton, New Jersey 07014-1993
military aviation

Leica AG, Navigation & Positioning
23868 Hawthorne Boulevard
Torrance, California 90505
earth-moving machinery, OEM, marine,
military, survey

Leica Heerbrugg AG
9435 Heerbrugg
Heerbrugg CH-9435, Switzerland
OEM, survey

Micrologic, Inc.
9610 DeSoto Avenue
Chatsworth, California 91311
aviation, land, marine

Motorola, Inc.
1301 East Algonquin Road
Schaumberg, Illinois 60173
land, marine, military, survey, timing,
OEM

NARCO Avionics
Fort Washington, Pennsylvania 19034
OEM, aviation, land, marine, military,
survey, timing

Navsys Corporation
14960 Woodcarver Road
Colorado Springs, Colorado 80921
military

OMNISTAR, Inc.
8200 Westglen
Houston, Texas 77063
OEM, aviation, land, marine, military,
survey, timing

Peacock Systems, Inc.
Jet Aviation Terminal
Bedford, Massachusetts 01730
OEM, aviation, land, marine, military,
survey, timing

NovAtel Communication Ltd.
1020 64th Avenue NE
Calgary, AB Canada
OEM, GPS/GLONASS, timing

Rauff & Sorensen Shipmate
Ostre Alle 69530
Storinig, Denmark
marine

S-Tec Corporation
946 Pegram
Mineral Wells, Texas 76067
OEM, aviation, land, marine, military,
survey, timing

SEL
Lorenzstrasse 10
D-7000 Stuttgart 40, Germany
land

STC Navigation Systems
Brixham Road, Paignton
Devon, U.K.
OEM, aviation, land, marine, military,
survey, timing

Sagem
27 rue Le Blanc
Cedex 15, Paris, France
aviation

Silva U.S. Marine
33 Faulkenburg Road, Bldg. D-401
Tampa, Florida 33619
OEM, aviation, land, marine, military,
survey, timing

Terra Avionics
3520 Pan American Freeway NE
Albuquerque, New Mexico 87107
OEM, aviation, land, marine, military,
survey, timing

U.S. Coast Guard Information

MAIL	Commanding Officer Navigation Information Service (NIS) U.S. Coast Guard Navigation Center 7323 Telegraph Road Alexandria, Virginia 22315-3998
INTERNET	http://www.navcen.uscg.mil ftp:/ftp.navcen.uscg.mil
FACSIMILE	(703) 313-5931 (703) 313-5932 Navigation information is available via NIS's Fax-on-Demand service.
BULLETIN BOARD SERVICE (BBS)	(703) 313-5910
modem speeds	300-28,800 bps
protocols	most common U.S. and international
parameters	8 data bits, no parity, 1 stop bit, asynchronous comms, full duplex.
24-HOUR RECORDING GPS OMEGA	 (703) 313-5907 (703) 313-5906
BROADCASTS via RADIO	 frequencies: 2.5, 5, 10, 15, 20 MHz WWV, 14-15 minutes past each hour WWVH, 43-44 minutes past each hour
via PHONE	(303) 499-7111
BOATING SAFETY INFORMATION LINE	1-800-368-5647

Information provided by the U.S. Coast Guard Navigation Center.

BIBLIOGRAPHY

Listed below are a few particularly useful sources of information about the Global Positioning System. Additional topic-related references are given under chapter headings.

Dunnigan, James F., <u>Digital Soldiers: the Evolution of High-Tech Weaponry and Tomorrow's Brave New Battlefield</u>, Thomas Dunne Books, St. Martin's Press, New York, 1996.

Getting, I. A., "Perspective/Navigation: The Global Positioning System," <u>IEEE Spectrum</u>, Vol. 30, No. 12, Dec. 1993.

Kaplan, Elliott D., Ed., <u>Understanding GPS: Principles and Applications</u>, Artech House, Boston/London, 1996.

Leick, Alfred, <u>GPS Satellite Surveying</u>, John Wiley & Sons, New York, 1990, 1995.

Letham, Lawrence, <u>GPS Made Easy, Using Global Positioning Systems in the Outdoors</u>, The Mountaineers, Seattle, Washington, 1996.

Pace, Scott, Gerald Frost, Irving Lachow, David Frelinger, Donna Fosum, Donald K. Wassem, Monica Pinto, <u>The Global Positioning System: Assessing National Policies</u>, report prepared for the Executive Office of the President, Office of Science and Technology Policy, RAND Critical Technologies Institute, Santa Monica, California, 1995.

<u>Federal Radionavigation Plan</u> (FRP), United States Departments of Defense and Transportation; available from the National Technical Information Service (NTIS), Springfield, Virginia.

<u>Global Positioning Technology: Opportunities for Greater Federal Agency Joint Development and Use</u>, U.S. General Accounting Office Report GAO/RCED-94-280, Washington, D.C., Sept. 1994.

<u>Science and Technology: a Five-Year Outlook</u>, The National Academy of Sciences, Washington, D.C., 1979.

<u>U.S. Coast Guard Radionavigation Bulletin</u>, semiannual publication, Department of Transportation, Washington, D.C.

<u>Use of the Global Positioning System in the National Airspace System (NAS)</u>, Memorandum of Agreement between the Department of Defense (DoD) and the Federal Aviation Administration (FAA), signed March 1992.

<u>U.S. Government Selected Acquisition Report</u> (SAR), RCS:DD-COMP (Q&A) 823, Dec. 1994.

<u>FAA Aviation News</u>, published periodically by the Federal Aviation Administration.

SELECT CHAPTER REFERENCES

CHAPTER 2. GPS RECEIVERS

Bevis, M., S. Businger, T. A. Herring, C. Rocken et al., "GPS Meteorology: Remote Sensing of Atmospheric Water Vapor Using the Global Positioning System," Journal of Geophysical Research, Vol. 97, No. D14, Oct. 1992.

Cosentino, B., "Testing the Precision Lightweight GPS Receiver," Proceedings, IEEE Position Location and Navigation Symposium (PLANS`94), Las Vegas, Nevada, Apr. 1994; also, IEEE, New York, 1994.

Daher, J. K., J. M. Harris & M. L. Wheeler, "A Look at the Radio Frequency Susceptibility of Commercial GPS Receivers," Proceedings, IEEE National Aerospace and Electronics Conference (NAECON), Dayton, Ohio, May 1994; also IEEE, Vol. 1:164-170, New York, 1994.

Harris, J. M., M. L. Wheeler & J. K. Daher, "Commercial GPS Receiver Susceptibility Evaluation," Symposium Record, IEEE International Symposium on EMC (Compatibility in the Loop), Chicago, Illinois, Aug. 1994; also, IEEE, New York, 1994.

Hughes, David, "USAF, GEC-Marconi Test ILS/MLS/GPS Receiver," Aviation Week & Space Technology, Vol. 143, No. 23, Dec. 1995.

Hwu, S. U. B. P. Lu, R. J. Panneton & B. A. Bourgeois, "Space Station GPS Antennas Multipath Analysis," Symposium Digest, IEEE Antennas and Propagation Society International, Newport Beach, California, June 1995.

Karcz, P. J., "Global Positioning System: Arrival in the Fleet, a GPS AN/SRN-25 (V) Receiver Assessment," Vitro Technical Journal, Vol. 8, No. 1, Winter 1990.

Global Positioning Systems Technology and Its Application in Environmental Programs, GIS Technical Memorandum, U.S. Environmental Protection Agency, Office of Research & Development, EPA/600/R-92/036, Wash., D.C., Feb. 1992.

CHAPTER 3. DIFFERENTIAL GPS (DGPS)

Donoghue, J. A., "What WAAS Will Be," Air Transport World, Vol. 32, No. 9, Sept. 1995.

Fulghum, David A., "JDAM Errors to Be Slashed," Aviation Week & Space Technology, Vol. 142, No. 9, Feb. 1995.

Johnston, "The Comparison of Two Multi-Site Reference Station Differential GPS Systems," Journal of Navigation, Sept. 1994.

Kee, Changdon & B. W. Parkinson, "Wide-Area Differential GPS as a Future Navigation System in the U.S.," Proceedings, IEEE Position Location and Navigation Symposium (PLANS`94), Las Vegas, Nevada, Apr. 1994; IEEE, New York, 1994.

Klass, Philip J., "FAA Delays Awarding D-GPS Network Contract," Aviation Week & Space Technology, Vol. 142, No. 5, Jan. 1995.

Loh, R. & J. P. Fernow, "Integrity Monitoring Requirements for FAA's GPS Wide-Area Augmentation System (WAAS)," Proceedings, IEEE Position Location and Navigation Symposium (PLANS`94), Las Vegas, Nevada, Apr. 1994; also, IEEE, New York, 1994.

Nordwall, Bruce D., "GAO Questions Schedule for GPS Augmentation," Aviation Week & Space Technology, Vol. 142, No. 25, June 1995.

Pasquay, J. N., "Multi-Site Reference Station Differential GPS System," Navigation, Vol. 43, No. 169, in French, Jan. 1995.

Federally-Funded R&D Centers: Use of Contract Fee by the Aerospace Corporation, U.S. General Accounting Office Report GAO-NSIAD-95-174, Washington, D.C., Sept. 1995.

CHAPTER 4. GPS ON THE ROAD & RAILS

Brown, A., J. Siviter & J. Kiljan, "An Operational Test of a Vehicle Emergency Location Service in Colorado," Navigation, Journal of the Institute of Navigation, Vol. 41, No. 4, Winter 1994-1995.

Dooling, Dave, "Technology 1996: Transportation," IEEE Spectrum, Vol. 33, No. 1, Jan. 1996.

Gerland, H. E., "Intelligence on Board: Modern Approach to Transit Fleet Management," Proceedings, Vehicle Navigation and Information Systems (VNIS`94), Yokohama, Japan, Aug.-Sept. 1994; also IEEE, New York, 1994.

Heintz, Christopher, "Rockwell Adds GPS, Hand-Held Holster to OBC," Fleet Owner, Truck supplement, Feb. 1996.

Johnson, William W., "Enhancing Intelligent Transportation with GPS," Satellite Communications, Vol. 19, No. 4, Apr. 1995.

Longmore-Etheridge, Ann, "Following the Fleet," Security Management, Vol. 39, No. 2, Feb. 1995.

Mattos, P. G., "Integrated GPS and Dead Reckoning for Low-Cost Vehicle Navigation and Tracking," Proceedings, Vehicle Navigation and Information Systems (VNIS`94), Yokohama, Japan, Aug.-Sept. 1994; also IEEE, New York, 1994.

Rothblatt, Martin, "Talking Stars and Talking Cars," Satellite Communications, Vol. 14, No. 6, June 1990.

Wilsterman, Doug, "The Art of In-Vehicle Navigation," ENR, Intelligent Highway Systems Supplement, Nov. 1994.

"HighwayMaster and Motorola Join Forces to Meet Communication Needs," <u>Fleet Equipment</u>, Vol. 21, No. 3, March 1995.

"Satellite, Cellular Phone Link Monitors Motorists in Distress," <u>Security</u>, Vol. 32, No. 6, June 1995.

CHAPTER 5. GPS OVER LAND

Ahmed, J. R. S., K. S. Rattan & O. H. Abdallah, "Adaptive Neural Network for Identification and Tracking Control of a Robotic Manipulator," <u>Proceedings</u>, IEEE National Aerospace and Electronics Conference (NAECON), Dayton, May 1995.

Anderson N. W..& M. W. Smette, "Automation of an Air Drill System," <u>Proceedings</u>, Computers in Agriculture 1994, 5th International Conference, Orlando, Florida, Feb. 1994; also, American Society of Agricultural Engineers, St. Joseph, Michigan, 1994.

Cai, L. & G. Song, "Robust Position/Force Control of Robot Manipulators during Contact Tasks," <u>Proceedings</u>, American Control Conference (ACC`94), Baltimore, Maryland, June-July 1994; also <u>IEEE</u>, Vol. 1:216-220, New York, 1994.

Dyer, D. J., D. J. G. Lewis & A.. Stevenson, "Control and Guidance of a UMA Using GPS," <u>IEE Colloquium Digest</u>, Control and Guidance of Remotely Operated Vehicles, London, U.K., June 1995.

Hu, J., M. Queiroz, T. Burg & D. Dawson, "Adaptive Position/Force Control of Robot Manipulators without Velocity Measurements," <u>Proceedings</u>, IEEE International Conference on Robotics and Automation, Nagoya, Japan, May 1995; also <u>IEEE</u> Vol. 1:887-892, New York, 1995.

Jaynes, D. B., T. S. Colvin, J. Ambuel et al., "Yield Mapping by Electromagnetic Induction, <u>Proceedings</u>, Site-Specific Management for Agricultural Systems," Second International Conference, Minneapolis, MN, March 27-30, 94 (pub. 1995), p383(12).

Lachapelle, G., M. E. Cannon, D. C. Penney & T. Goddard, "GIS/GPS Facilitates Precision Farming," <u>GIS World</u>, v9, n7, p54(3), July 96.

Mangold, Grant, "Mobile Computer Manages Inputs, Pays Off in Lower Fertilizer Bills," <u>Successful Farming</u>, Iowa Edition, Vol. 93, No. 4, March 1995.

McKenzie, R. C., G. Lachapelle & M. E. Cannon, "Soil Salinity Mapping with Electromagnetic Induction and Satellite-Based Navigation Methods," <u>Canadian Journal of Soil Sciences</u>, v74, n 3, p335(9), Aug. 94.

Proctor, Paul, "Helicopter Aid L.A.'s Crime-Fighting Force," <u>Aviation Week & Space Technology</u>, Vol. 143, No. 21, Nov. 1995.

Rus, D., B. Donald & J. Jennings, "Moving Furniture with Teams of Autonomous Robots," <u>Proceedings</u>, IEEE/RSJ International Conference on Intelligent Robots and Systems, Human Robot Interaction and Cooperative Robots, Pittsburgh, Pennsylvania, Aug. 1995; also <u>IEEE</u> Computer Society Press, Vol. 1:235-242, 1995.

Schell, S.P. & J. A. Lockwood, "Spatial Analysis Optimizes Grasshopper Management," GIS World, Vol. 8, No. 11, Nov. 1995.

Tyson, Peter, "High-Tech Help for the Blind," Technology Review, Vol. 98, No. 3, Apr. 1995.

Drug Control: Observations on U.S. Interdiction in the Caribbean, U.S. General Accounting Office Report GAO-T-NSIAD-96-171, Washington, D.C., May 1996.

CHAPTER 6. IN THE AIR

Braff, J. R., P. Odonnell, C. Shively & R. Swider, "FAA's DGPS CAT III Feasibility Program: Update and Test Methodology," Proceedings, IEEE Position Location and Navigation Symposium (PLANS`94), Las Vegas, Apr. 1994; IEEE, New York, 1994.

Christensen, Lee & Ken Krause, "Precision Farming: Harnessing Technology," Agricultural Outlook, Economic Research Service, No.. 218, May 95.

Clarke, Charles W. (Bill), Aviator's Guide to GPS, 2nd Edition, TAB Practical Flying Series, TAB Books, McGraw-Hill, New York, 1996.

Collins, Richard L., "GPS Reveille," Flying, Vol. 122, No. 3, March 1995.

Gorder, P. J. & J. Uhlarik, "The Role of Automation in the Integrated Cockpit of Tomorrow's General Aviation Aircraft," Proceedings, IEEE International Conference on Systems, Man and Cybernetics (Intelligent Systems for the 21st Century), Vancouver, British Columbia, Canada, Oct. 1995.

Gibbs, W. Wayt, "Coming in for a Landing," Scientific American, 272:4, Apr. 1995.

Gray, R. A. & P. S. Maybeck, "An Integrated GPS/INS/Baro and Radar Altimeter System for Aircraft Precision Approach Landings," Proceedings, IEEE National Aerospace and Electronics Conference (NAECON), Dayton, Ohio, May 1995.

Leva, Joseph L., Maarten Uijt de Haag & Karen Van Dyke, "Performance of Standalone GPS," in Kaplan, Elliott D., Editor, Understanding GPS: Principles and Applications, Artech House, Boston/London, 1996.

Oman, C. M., M. S. Huntley, Jr. & S. A. Rasmussen, "Pilot Performance and Workload Using Simulated GPS Track Angle Error Displays," Analysis, Design and Evaluation of Man-Machine Systems, Postprint Volume, Sixth IFAC/IFIP/IFORS/IEA Symposium, Cambridge, Massachusetts, June 1995.

Rogers, J. W., C. J. Tidwell & A. D. Little, "Terminal Area Surveillance System," Conference Record, IEEE International Radar Conference, Alexandria, May 1995.

Sachs, G., H. Moller & K. Dobler, "Synthetic Vision experiments for Approach and Taxiing in Poor Visibility," Proceedings, Synthetic Vision for Vehicle Guidance and Control, International Society for Optical Engineering (SPIE), Vol. 2463:128-136, Orlando, Florida, Apr. 1995.

VanGraas, F., D. Diggle, L. Lake & S. Newman, "Laboratory Testing of an Interferometric GPS Flight Reference System," Proceedings, 51st Annual Meeting, Institute of Navigation, San Diego, California, June 1995.

"Evaluation of a Computer Aided Low-Altitude Helicopter Flight Guidance System," AGARD, Combat Automation for Airborne Weapon Systems: Man/Machine Interface Trends and Technologies, Apr. 1993.

"GPS Multipath Errors in the Precision Landing Environment," NASA, Langley Research Center, Joint University Program, Air Transportation Research, Feb. 1993.

Various Articles in Aviation Week & Space Technology:

Hughes, David, "UPS, United Complete GPS Autoland Tests," "Four Teams Join Boeing in GPS Approach Tests" and "Airbus Concentrates on Category 1 DGPS," Vol. 141:18, Oct. 1994, Vol. 143:8, Aug. 1995.

Klass, Philip, "GPS to Be Tested for Category-3 Landings," Vol. 142:7, Feb. 1995.

Nordwall, Bruce D., "FANS-1 Benefits Near on Pacific Routes," Vol. 143:10, Sept., and "Road Map Leads FAA to 'Free Flight,'" 143:19, Nov. 1995.

Phillips, Edward H., "Mini 'Free-Flight' System to Debut at Atlanta Games," Vol. 144:14, Apr. 1996.

CHAPTER 7: ON THE WATER — SAILING & BOATING

Adam, John A., "Specialties," IEEE Spectrum, Vol. 32, No. 1, Jan. 1995.

Allen, Arthur, "GPS Capabilities for Self-Locating Datum Marker Buoys," On Scene, U.S. Coast Guard Publication, Vol. 95, No. 4, Winter 1995.

Daniels, D. & N.. Nazoa, "A Search and Rescue Transponder (SART) for Maritime Rescue," Microwave Engineering Europe, June/July 1992.

Greer, R. A., "The United States Navy Electronic Chart Display and Information (ECDIS) Development Project," Proceedings, IEEE Position Location and Navigation Symposium (PLANS`94), Las Vegas, Apr. 1994; IEEE, New York, 1994.

Nordwall, Bruce D., "Outlaw Viking S-3B Extends Navy's Long-Range Tracking," Aviation Week & Space Technology, Vol. 142, No. 9, Feb. 1995.

Sabol-B.M, Shafer-D.J., & Melton-E., "Environmental Effects of Dredging. Mapping Seagrasses for Dredging Operations," report by Environmental Laboratory, Army Engineer Waterways Experiment Station, Vicksburg, MS, March 1996.

Stawell, W. B., "A Note on the Use of the Global Positioning System (GPS) for the Identification of Marine Radar Contacts," Journal of Navigation, 46:3, Sept. 1993.

"Final Results of the Baltic Sea Level 1990 GPS Campaign," Research Works of the SSG, International Association of Geodesy, 1994.

CHAPTER 8: DEFENSE

Bahder, T. B., "GPS for Land Combat Applications," Summary Report ARL-SR-40, Army Workshop at the University of North Carolina, Army Research Laboratory, Adelphi, Maryland, Aug. 1995.

Davis, Richard, Testimony to Select Committee on U.S. Intelligence, U.S. Senate, "Emerging Missile Threats to North America during the Next 15 Years," published in the National Intelligence Estimate 95-15, U.S. General Accounting Office Report GAO/NSIAD-96-225, Aug. 30, 1996;

Dougherty, J. J., H. El-Sherief & D. S. Hohman, "Use of the Global Positioning System for Evaluating Inertial Measurement Unit Errors," Journal of Guidance Control and Dynamics, Vol. 17, No. 3, May-June 1994.

Frost, G. & I. Lachow, "GPS-Aided Guidance for Ballistic Missile Applications: an Assessment," Proceedings, 51st Annual Meeting of the Institute of Navigation, RAND/RP-474, RAND Corporation, Santa Monica, California, June 1995.

Fulghum, David A., "JDAM Errors to Be Slashed," in Aviation Week & Space Technology, Vol. 142, No. 9, Feb. 1995.

Ioannidis, G., N. Walton, Pujara Neeraj & C. Bublitz, "GPS Exploitation for Precision Targeting a Relative Targeting System," Proceedings, IEEE Position Location and Navigation Symposium (PLANS`94), Las Vegas, Apr. 1994; IEEE, New York, 1994.

Junger, Ernst, Werke, Vol. 45, Stuttgart, 1963, translation, The Free Press, New York.

Keating, J. F., "The MXF-400 Series of Radios-Communications for the 21st Century," Proceedings, Tactical Communications Conference (TCC `94), Vol. 1, Digital Technology for the Tactical Communicator, Fort Wayne, Indiana, May 1994; also IEEE, New York, 1994.

Morrocco, John D., "Pentagon to Fund New ACTD Projects," and "Navy Primed for JSOW Critical Design Review," Aviation Week & Space Technology, Vol. 142, Nos. 9 & 12, Feb., March 1995.

Parra, M. Z. & R. G. McIntyre, "Global Positioning System (GPS) for the Army's Air Defense Operational Testing," Proceedings, International Telemetering Conference (ITC/USA/'91), Las Vegas, Nov. 1991; ISA, Research Triangle Park, 1991.

Paschall, R. N. & J. R. Layne, "Design and Analysis of an Integrated Targeting System," Proceedings, IEEE National Aerospace and Electronics Conference (NAECON), Dayton, Ohio, May 1994; also IEEE, Vol. 2:937-944, New York, 1994.

Pittman, D. N. & C. E. Roberts, "Determining GPS Anti-Jamming Performance on Tactical Missiles," Proceedings, IEEE Position Location and Navigation Symposium (PLANS`94), Las Vegas, Nevada, Apr. 1994; also, IEEE, New York, 1994.

Tralli, D. M. & S. M. Lichten, "Stochastic Estimation of Tropospheric Path Delays in Global Positioning System Geodetic Measurements," Bulletin Geodesique, 64:2, 1990.

Van Wechel R., & C. E. Hoefener, "The Role of the Global Positioning System in Advanced Air Combat Training Ranges," Proceedings, IEEE National Aerospace and Electronics Conference (NAECON 1990), Catalog No. 90CH2881-1, Dayton, May 1990; IEEE, New York, 1990.

CHAPTER 9. MAPPING & SURVEYING

Calais, E., V. Carrier & G. Buffet, "Comparison of Leveling and Global Positioning System Data: Application to the Determination of the Geoid in the Alpes-Maritimes," Comptes Rendus de l'Academie des Sciences, Serie II (Mecanique, Physique, Chimie Sciences del la Terre et de l'Univers), Vol. 317, No. 11, France, Dec. 1993.

Crow, Bill B., "Tangible Savings, Efficiencies Seen with Properly Positioned Data," Oil & Gas Journal, Vol. 92, No. 47, Nov. 1994.

Ewing, Clair E. & Michael M. Mitchell, Introduction to Geodesy, American Elsevier Publishing Company, Inc., New York, 1970.

Feeney, R., J. Bethel, B. van Gelder & S. Johnson, "Use of GPS to Enhance Mapping by Photogrammetry," Joint Highway Research Report, Purdue University, Lafayette, Indiana, May 1996.

Jarrett, Ian, "Surveying by Satellite," Asian Business, Vol. 31, No. 2, Feb. 1995.

Killeen, Patrick G., "The GSC's 31st Annual Survey of International Exploration Geophysics: Airborne Geophysical Surveying," Canadian Mining Journal, 117:1, 1996.

Lichten, S. M., S. L. Marcus & J. O. Dickey, "Sub-Daily Resolution of Earth Rotation Variations with Global Positioning System Measurements," Geophysical Research Letters, Vol. 19, No. 6, March 1992.

Lindqwister, U. J., A. P. Freedman & G. Blewitt, "Daily Estimates of the Earth's Pole Position with the Global Positioning System," Geophysical Research Letters, Vol. 19, No. 9, May 1992.

Mainville, A., R. Forsberg & M. G. Sideris, "Global Positioning System Testing of Geoids Computed from Geopotential Models and Local Gravity Data: a Case Study," Journal of Geophysical Research, Vol. 97, No. B7, July 1992.

Paris, Keith, "Five Steps to Simple GIS Application," American City & Country, Vol. 110, No. 13, Dec. 1995.

Tregoning, P., F. K. Brunner, Y. Bock, S. S. O. Puntodewo et al., "First Geodetic Measurement of Convergence across the Java Trench," Geophysical Research Letters, Vol. 21, No. 19, Sept. 1994.

Vigue, Y., S. M. Lichten, G. Blewitt, M. B. Heflin et al., "Precise Determination of Earth's Center of Mass Using Measurements from the Global Positioning System," Geophysical Research Letters, Vol. 19, No. 14, July 1992.

CHAPTER 10. GEOLOGY

Calais J. E. & J. B. Minster, "GPS Detection of Ionospheric Perturbations following the January 17, 1994 Northridge Earthquake," Geophysical Research Letters, Vol. 22, No. 9, May 1995.

Cohen, S., S. Holdahl, D. Caprette, S. Hilla et al., "Uplift of the Kenai Peninsula, Alaska, since the 1964 Prince William Sound Earthquake," Journal of Geophysical Research, Vol. 100, No. B2, Feb. 1995.

Dixon, T. H., "An Introduction to the Global Positioning System and Some Geological Applications," Reviews of Geophysics, Vol. 29, No. 2, May 1991.

Dixon, T. H., G. Gonzalez, S. M. Lichten, D. M. Tralli et al., "Preliminary Determination of Pacific North America Relative Motion in the Southern Gulf of California Using the Global Positioning System," Proceedings, Chapman Conference on Crustal-Scale Fluid Transport: Magnitude and Mechanisms, Balatonfured, Hungary, June 1990; Geophysical Research Letters, Vol. 18, No. 5, May 1991.

Ewert, John W., Thomas L. Murray, Andrew B. Lockhart & C. Dan Miller, "Preventing Volcanic Catastrophe: the U.S. International Volcano Disaster Assistance Program," Earthquakes and Volcanoes, Vol. 24, No. 6, Geological Survey, 1993.

Gray, Richard E., "Engineering Geology," Geotimes, Vol. 40, No. 2, Feb. 1995.

King, N. E., J. L. Svarc, E. B. Fogleman, W. K. Gross et al., "Continuous GPS Observations across the Hayward Fault, California," Journal of Geophysical Research, Vol. 100, No. B10, Oct. 1995.

Larsen, S. & R. Reilinger "Global Positioning System Measurements of Strain Accumulation across the Imperial Valley, California: 1986-1989," Journal of Geophysical Research, Vol. 97, No. B6, June 1992.

Larson, K. M., "Application of the Global Positioning System to Crustal Deformation Measurements; Results from the Southern California Borderlands," Journal of Geophysical Research, Vol. 98, No. B12, Dec. 1993.

Malla, R. P., S. C. Wu & S. M. Lichten, "Geocenter Location and Variation in Earth Orientation Using Global Positioning System Measurements," Journal of Geophysical Research, Vol. 98, No. B3, March 1993.

Owen, Susan "Rapid Deformation of the South Flank of Kilauea Volcano, Hawaii," Science, Vol. 267, No. 5202, March 1995.

Shimada S. & Y. Bock. "Crustal Deformation Measurements in Central Japan Determined by a Global Positioning System Fixed-Point Network," Journal of Geophysical Research, Vol. 97, No. B9, Aug. 1992.

Sigmundsson, F., E. Tryggvason, M. M. Alves, J. L. Alves et al., "Slow Inflation of the Furnas Volcano, Sao Miguel, Azores, Suggested from Initial Leveling and Global Positioning System Measurements," Geophysical Research Letters, 22:13, July 1995.

Sigmundsson, F., P. Einarsson & R. Bilham. "Magma Chamber Deflation Recorded by the Global Positioning System: the Hekla 1991 Eruption," Geophysical Research Letters, Vol. 19, No. 14, July 1992.

Straub C. & H.-G. Kahle, "Active Crustal Deformation in the Marmara Sea Region, NW Anatolia, Inferred from GPS Measurements," Geophysical Research Letters, Vol. 22, No. 18, Sept. 1995.

Stow, D., A. Hope, S. Phinn, A. Nguyen et al., "Monitoring Detailed Land Surface Changes from an Airborne Multispectral Digital Camera System," Proceedings, International Geoscience and Remote Sensing Symposium (IGARSS), Firenze, Italy, July 1995; also IEEE, Vol. 3:2103-2105, New York, 1995.

Williams, C. R., T. Arnadottir & P. Segall, "Coseismic Deformation and Dislocation Models of the 1989 Loma Prieta Earthquake Derived from Global Positioning System Measurements," Journal of Geophysical Research, Vol. 98, No. B3, March 1993.

"Satellites Track Plate Movement," Geotimes, Vol. 40, No. 3, March 1995.

CHAPTER 11: THE ENVIRONMENT

Global Positioning Systems Technology and Its Application in Environmental Programs, GIS Technical Memorandum 3, U.S. Environmental Protection Agency, Office of Research and Development, EPA/600/R-92/036, Wash., D.C., Feb. 1992.

Blodgett, J. C., M. E. Ikehara & G. E. Williams, "Monitoring Land Subsidence in Sacramento Valley, California, Using GPS," Journal of Survey Engineering - ASCE, v116, n2, May 90.

Collazo, Jaime A., "Accuracy Tests for Sonic Telemetry Studies in an Estuarine Environment," Journal of Wildlife Management, Vol. 59, No. 1, Jan. 1995.

Global Positioning Technology: Opportunities for Greater Federal Agency Joint Development and Use, U.S. General Accounting Office Report to Congressional Requesters, GAO/RCED-94-280, Washington, D.C., Sept. 1994.

Hughes, David, "Busy Storm Season Boost WC-130 Mission Tempo," Aviation Week & Space Technology, Vol. 143, No. 9, Aug. 1995.

Leffler, S., H. G. Reeser, E. Zaker, W. Hansen et al., "Global Positioning Site Environment Evaluator," Proceedings, Waste Management '90, Working towards a Cleaner Environment: Waste Processing, Transportation, Storage and Disposal, Tucson, Feb.-March 1990; University of Arizona, R. G. Post, Editor, Tucson, 1990.

Nordwall, Bruce D., "Enhanced GPS Spawns Innovative Applications," Aviation Week & Space Technology, Vol. 141, No. 21, Nov. 1994.

Norris, James G., Sandy Wyllie-Echeverria, Ronald M. Thom & Schafer, James, "Keep off the Eelgrass," GPS World, Advanstar Communications, Oregon, Feb. 1997.

Peterson, Darrel E., "Grizzly Country: GPS/GIS Help Monitor the Great Bear's Fragile Ecosystem," GeoResearch, Billings, MT; also GIS World, v9, n4, Apr. 96.

Sabol, B. M., D. J. Shafer & E. Melton, "Environmental Effects of Dredging. Mapping Seagrasses for Dredging Operations," Environmental Laboratory report, Army Engineer Waterways Experiment Station, Vicksburg, MS., March 1996

Schell, S. P. & J. A. Lockwood, "Spatial Analysis Optimizes Grasshopper Management," GIS World, Vol. 8, No. 11, Nov., 1995.

Strange, Wiliam E., "GPS Determination of Groundwater Withdrawal Subsidence," Journal of Survey Engineering-ASCE, Vol. 115, No. 2, National Geodetic Survey, MD, May 89.

Sylvander R., & H. Olsson, "The Use of the Global Positioning System for Effective Forest Inventory and Management: Experiences from the Swedish Boreal Forest Zone," Proceedings, IGARSS 1993 International Geoscience and Remote Sensing Symposium, Better Understanding of Earth Environment, Catalog No. 93CH3294-6, Tokyo, Aug. 1993; S. Fujimura, IEEE, New York, Vol. 2, 1993.

Ushio, Tomo-o, Wang Daohong, Zen-Ichiro Kawasaki, K. Matuura et al., "Synchronized Multipoint Measurements of Lightning Electric Field Changes," Proceedings, Fifth Annual Conference of Power and Energy Society, IEE Japan, Vol. 1, Institute of Electrical Engineering of Japan, Tokyo, Japan, 1994; also in Japanese in Transactions of IEEJ, Part B, Vol. 114-B, No. 11, Nov. 1994.

Yuan, L. L., R. A. Anthes, R. H. Ware, C. Rocken et al., "Sensing Climate Change Using the Global Positioning System," Journal of Geophysical Research, Vol. 98, No. D8, Aug. 1993.

CHAPTER 12: UTILITIES

Kezonuvic J. M. & B. Perunicic, "Automated Transmission Line Fault Analysis Using Synchronized Sampling at Two Ends," Proceedings, IEEE Power Industry Computer Application Conference, Salt Lake City, Utah, May 1995.

McLellan, James F., Todd R. Porter & P. S. Price, "Pipeline Deformation Monitoring Using GPS Survey Techniques," Journal of Survey Engineering, ASCE, Feb. 89, v115, n1, p56(11).

Piotrowski, T., "Synchronization of Telecommunication Network Using a Global Positioning Satellite," Symposium Record, IEEE PLANS '92, Position, Location and Navigation, 500 Years after Columbus: Navigation Challenges of Tomorrow, Catalog No. 92CH3085-8, Monterey, March 1992; IEEE, New York, 1992.

Schmid, U., "Synchronized UTC for Distributed Real-Time Systems," Proceedings, IFAC Workshop on Real-Time Programming, Lake Constance, Germany, June 1994.

Papers in Proceedings, IEE Colloquium on Developments in the Use of Global Positioning Systems (GPS) in Power Systems, London, UK, Feb. 1994:

Bates, G. A., "The Use of GPS in a Mobile Data Acquisition System"

Crossley, P., "Future of the Global Positioning System in Power Systems"

Gale, P. F., "The Use of GPS for Precise Time Tagging of Power System Disturbances and in Overhead Line Fault Location"

Jodice, J. A., & S. Harpham, "End-to-End Transient Simulation for Protection System Performance Testing"

Phadke, A. G., "Synchronized Phasor Measurements: Techniques and Uses,"

Taylor, P. L., "The Use of Global Positioning Satellites in the Location of Lightning Storms as Used by the Met Office's Arrival Time Difference Sferics Detection System"

CHAPTER 13: EXPLORATION

Ambrosius, B. A. C., E. T. Hesper & K. F. Wakker, "Application of the Global Positioning System for Hermes Rendezvous Navigation," Journal of Guidance, Control and Dynamics, Vol. 16, No. 1, Jan.-Feb. 1993.

Braden, K., C. Browning, H. Gelderloos, F. Smith et al., "Integrated Inertial Navigation System/Global Positioning System (INS/GPS) for Manned Return Vehicle Autoland Application," Symposium Record, IEEE PLANS '90, Position, Location and Navigation, The 1990s: a Decade of Excellence in the Navigation Sciences, Catalog No. 90CH2811-8, Las Vegas, March 1990; IEEE, New York, 1990.

Chao, C. C. & H. Bernstein, "Onboard Stationkeeping of Geosynchronous Satellites Using a Global Positioning System Receiver," Journal of Guidance, Control and Dynamics, Vol. 17, No. 4, July-Aug. 1994.

Fraile-Ordonez, J. M., A. Jansche & N. Lemke, "DGPS Positioning of the Russian MIR Station: Analysis of Visibility Conditions, Measurement Error Sources and Ground Requirements," Proceedings, DSNS `94, 3rd International Conference of Differential Satellite Navigation Systems, London, U.K., Apr. 1994

Goodchild C. & D. Kerr, "An Unmanned Underwater Vehicle Navigation and Guidance System," IEE Colloquium Digest, Control and Guidance of Remotely Operated Vehicles, London, U.K., June 1995.

Hein, G. W., H. Landau & H. Blomenhofer, "Determination of Instantaneous Sea Surface, Wave Heights and Ocean Currents Using Satellite Observations of the Global Positioning System," Marine Geodesy, Vol. 14, No. 3-4, July-Dec. 1990.

Johnson, Will, "Attitude Adjustment: GPS Innovation Keeps Satellites Oriented," Satellite Communications, Vol. 19, No. 6, June 1995

Kelecy, T. M., G. H. Born, M. E. Parke & C. Rocken, "Precise Mean Sea Level Measurements Using the Global Positioning System," Journal of Geophysical Research, Vol. 99, No. C4, Apr. 1994.

Lichten, S. M., B. J. Haines, L. E. Young, J. Srinivasan et al., "Using the Global Positioning System for Earth Orbiter and Deep Space Tracking," Proceedings, IEEE National Telesystems Conference (NTC`94), San Diego, California, May 1994; also, IEEE, New York, 1994.

Muzzi, R. W. & M. J. McCormick "A New Global Positioning System Drifter Buoy," Proceedings, OCEANS 94, Oceans Engineering for Today's Technology and Tomorrow's Preservation, Brest, France, Sept. 1994; IEEE, New York, 1994.

Osborne, M. L. & R. H. Tolson, "GPS Attitude Determination Using Deployable-Mounted Antennas," Joint Institute for Advancement of Flight Sciences, Hampton, Virginia, March 1996.

Pavlis, E. C., "Comparison of GPS S/C Orbits Determined from GPS and SLR Tracking Data (Orbit Determination and Analysis)," PSD Meeting Record, COSPAR Technical Panel on Satellite Dynamics, Thirtieth COSPAR Scientific Assembly, Hamburg, Germany, July 1994; also in Advance in Space Research, 16:12, 1995.

CHAPTER 14: MARKETS & OPPORTUNITIES

Arora, R. K.& A. K. Sharma, "Global Positioning Technology and Applications," Proceedings, IEEE 1994 Position Location and Navigation Symposium, Catalog No. 94CH3358-9, Las Vegas/New York, Apr. 1994.

Dooling, Dave, "Technology 1996: Transportation," IEEE Spectrum, Vol. 33, No. 1, Jan. 1996.

Eckert, R. C., "Report on Common Modular Architecture (CMA) for the Embedded GPS Receiver," Proceedings, IEEE Position Location and Navigation Symposium (PLANS`94), Las Vegas, Nevada, Apr. 1994; also, IEEE, New York, 1994.

Gale, Philip, "GPS Market Expected to Grow," Transmission & Distribution, Vol. 47, No. 13, Dec. 1995.

Goad, C. C., "Positioning with the Global Positioning System Satellites," Proceedings, GIS/LIS '91, Atlanta, Oct. 1991; Vol. 1, American Society of Photogrammetry & Remote Sensing, Bethesda, 1991.

Kassam, J. A. M. & B. S. Hlasny, "The British Columbia Active Control System: Realization of a New Spatial Data Infrastructure," Proceedings, Ninth Annual Symposium on Geographic Information Systems in Natural Resources Management, Vancouver, British Columbia, Canada, March 1995; also GIS World, Fort Collins, Colorado, Vol. 2:862-871, 1995.

Kurland, M. & H. Rawicz, "Involving Students in Undergraduate Research and Development: Two Perspectives," Proceedings, Frontiers in Education 1995, 25th Annual Conference, Engineering Education for the 21st Century, Atlanta, Nov. 1995.

Marais, E. L., "The Proposed Use of GPS to Provide the Frequency Traceability for a Josephson Array Voltage Standard," Conference Digest, Precision Electromagnetic Measurements, Boulder, Colorado, June-July 1994; also, IEEE, New York, 1994.

Mattos, P. G., "3-Volt Matchbox-Sized Transputer GPS for Vehicles and Portables," Proceedings, World Transputer Congress, (Transputer Applications and Systems '94), Como, Italy, Sept. 1994; also IOS Press, Amsterdam, Netherlands, 1994.

Morgan, Stephen Lee, "Australia Provides Access to Asian Satcom Markets," Satellite Communications, Vol. 19, No. 1, Jan. 1995.

Nordwall, Bruce D., "Avionics Market to Improve in '96," "GPS Technology Ripens for Consumer Market," "Small GPS Receivers Open New Possibilities" and "New Contracts to Speed GPS Expansion," Aviation Week & Space Technology, Volumes 141-143, Dec. 1994 - March 1995.

Oman, H., "Global Positioning System, Opportunities and Problems," IEEE Aerospace and Electronics Systems Magazine, Vol. 10, No. 7, July 1995.

Patton, Robert, "Pioneer Takes GPS to U.S." Electronics, Vol. 68, No. 2, Jan. 1995.

Reason, John, "Survey Vehicles Carry GPS, Lasers, Video — the Works," Electrical World, Vol. 209, No. 8, Aug. 1995.

Sennedot, D. & F. Hubert, "The NELS Network: Northwest European Loran C System," Proceedings, Oceans Engineering for Today's Technology and Tomorrow's Preservation (OCEANS'94), Brest, France, Sept., 1994; IEEE, New York, 1994.

Smock, Doug, "Consumer Electronics Pushing the Envelope," Plastics World, Vol. 53, No. 2, Feb. 1995.

Smuk, J., P. Katzin, V. Aparin & M. Shifrin, "Miniature GPS Translator Module," Digest of Symposium Papers, IEEE Microwave and Millimeter-Wave Monolithic Circuits, Orlando, Florida, May 1995.

Westfall, P., "AFIT Provides Satellite Learning for Military," Communications News, Vol. 31, No. 3, March 1994.

Federally-Funded R&D Centers: Use of Contract Fee by Aerospace Corporation, U.S. General Accounting Office Report GAO-NSIAD-95-174, Wash., D.C., Sept. 1995.

"GIS Project Opportunities in the World Bank," published by U.S. Trade and Development Agency, Rosslyn, Virginia, June 1996.

CHAPTER 15: COSTS, POLITICS & STANDARDS

Anderson, John H., Jr., Director of Transportation Issues, DOT's Budget: Safety, Management, and Other Issues Facing the Department in Fiscal Year 1998 and Beyond, testimony before Subcommittee on Transportation, U.S. House Committee on Appropriations, General Accounting Office publication GAO-T-RCED-96-88.

Fisher, K. P., "Activities of GNSS in the International Maritime Organization (IMO)," Proceedings, IEE Colloquium on the Implementation of GNSS, London, Nov. 1995.

Schrogl, K. U., "The New Structure of the ITU: Responses to Rapid Technological and Political Change," Space Communications, Vol. 12, No. 1, 1994.

Publications of U.S. General Accounting Office, Washington, D.C.:

DOT's Budget: Challenges Facing the Department in Fiscal Year 1997 and Beyond, U.S. General Accounting Office Report GAO-T-RCED-96-88, Washington, D.C., March 1996.

Federally-Funded R&D Centers: Use of Contract Fee by Aerospace Corporation, U.S. General Accounting Office Report GAO-NSIAD-95-174, Washington, D.C., Sept. 1995.

APPENDIX A: NAVIGATION, TIME & TECHNOLOGY

Jaduszliwer, B. & J. P. Hurrell, "Second Harmonic Level Monitors in Cesium Atomic Frequency Standards," Proceedings, 48th Annual IEEE International Frequency Control Symposium, Boston, Massachusetts, June 1994.

O'Connor, Leo, "Navigating with Gyroscopes and GPS," Mechanical Engineering, Vol. 116, No. 11, Nov. 1994.

Shlain, Leonard, Art & Physics: Parallel Visions in Space, Time & Light, William Morrow and Company, Inc., New York, 1991.

Toffler, Alvin & Heidi, War and Anti-War, Little, Brown and Co., New York, 1993.

Union of Concerned Scientists, Fallacy of Star Wars, Vintage, Random House, New York, 1984.

Whitrow, G. J., The Natural History of Time, Clarendon Press, Oxford, 1980.

The Director's Series on Proliferation, U.S. Department of Energy.

Additional Sources of Information

Ashkenazi, V., W. Chen, W. Y. Ochieng, C. J. Hill et al., "Design Tools for GNSS," in Colloquium Record, IEE Colloquium on the Implementation of GNSS, London, U.K. November 1995.

Bogdanov, P. P., Y. G. Gouzhva, A. G. Gevorkyan, A. B. Bassevich et al., "GLONASS On-Board Time/Frequency Standard-Architecture and Operation," in Proceedings, 48th Annual IEEE International Frequency Control Symposium, Boston, Massachusetts, June 1994.

Budznya, Tom, "Pager Warning: Concept Needs GPS Interface," ADA, Air Defense Artillery, Volume 96, No. 1, Army Air Defense Artillery School, January/February 1996.

Cameron, M. & A. Brown,, "Intelligent Transportation System Mayday Becomes a Reality," in Proceedings, IEEE National Aerospace and Electronics Conference (NAECON), Dayton, Ohio, May 1995.

Chadwick, D. J., "Applications of the Global Positioning System to Intelligent Vehicle Highway Systems," Proceedings, 1993 National Telesystems Conference, Commercial Application and Dual-Use Technology, Atlanta, June 1993; IEEE, New York, 1993.

Daly, P., "Progress towards Joint Civil Use of GPS and GLONASS," in Symposium Record, IEEE Position Location and Navigation Symposium (PLANS`92), 500 Years after Columbus — Navigation Challenges of Tomorrow, Monterey, California, March 1992; also, IEEE, New York, 1992.

Davis, Richard, "GPS Installations: Communication is the key to successful field approvals," FAA Aviation News, Vol. 35, No. 4, Federal Aviation Administration, May/June 1996.

Donahoe, Jamie M., "Emergency Resource Recordation: GPS may be your best bet." CRM, Vol. 19, No. 1, 96-23504-8, National Park Service, 1996.

Eggen-McIntosh, S., K. B. Lannom & D. M. Jacobs, "Mapping Forest Distributions of Central America and Mexico," Proceedings, Geographic Information Systems and Land Information Systems `94, Phoenix, Arizona, 1994; American Society of Photogrammetry & Remote Sensing, Bethesda, MD, 1994.

El-Saadawy, H., "The Impact of DGPS on Land, Marine and Air Navigation in Egypt," Proceedings, Third International Conference of Differential Satellite Navigation Systems (DSNS `94), London, U.K., April 1994; also in Journal of Navigation, Volume 47, No. 3:332-7, September 1994.

Foster, Dan A., "The Position of GPS in Wildlife and Habitat Mapping." <u>Mapping Tomorrow's Resources, Vol. II</u>, Proceedings, Natural Resources and Environmental Issues, National Park Service, Bryce Canyon, UT. 1993.

Gibbs, W. Wayt, "Coming in for a Landing," <u>Scientific American</u>, Volume 272, No. 4, April 1995.

Gray, Richard E., "Engineering Geology," <u>Geotimes</u>, Vol. 40, No. 2, February 1995.

Jackson, M. E. & R. Bilham, "1991-1992 GPS Measurements across the Nepal Himalaya," <u>Geophysical Research Letters</u>, Vol. 21, No. 12: 1169-72, June 1994.

Jackson, Willie, "Global Positioning System 'deploys' to Bosnia," <u>Army Communicator: Voice of the Signal Corps</u>, Volume 21, No. 3, Army Signal Center, Summer 1996.

Jarlemark, P. O. J., G. Elgered & J. M. Johansson, "Remote Sensing and Characterizations of Temporal and Spatial Variations in the Wet Refractivity and the Wet Delay," in <u>Proceedings</u>, International Geoscience and Remote Sensing Symposium, Firenze, Italy, July 1995; also <u>IEEE</u>, Vol. 3:2129-2131, NY, 1995.

Kilroy, Bill, "Improved Autonomous Accuracy for Forest Service GPS Receivers" <u>Engineering Field Notes</u>, Volume 28, U.S. Forest Service, May/August 1996.

Kobayashi, K., F. Munekata & K. Watanabe, "Accurate Navigation via Differential GPS and Vehicle Local Sensors," in <u>Proceedings</u>, IEEE International Conference on Multisensor Fusion and Integration for Intelligent Systems, Las Vegas, Oct. 1994.

Lehr, William et al., "Oil Spill Monitoring Using a Field Microcomputer-GPS Receiver Combination," <u>Proceedings</u>, Second Thematic Conference on Remote Sensing for Marine & Coast Environments, New Orleans, LA, Jan. 31-Feb 2, 1994.

Lindler, Bert, "Satellites Hunt the Hunters: Elk Hunting Research in Montana," <u>Forestry Research West</u>, #267, 96-46701-1, U.S. Forest Service, December 1995.

McCaskill, T. B., M. M. Largay, O. J. Oaks, W. G. Reid et al., "Measurements and Analysis of the Frequency Stability of GPS Navstar Clocks," in <u>Proceedings</u>, Conference on Precision Electromagnetic Measurements, Boulder, Colorado, June-July 1994; also, <u>IEEE</u>, New York, 1994.

Moorer, Daniel F., Jr., "Accepting and Understanding Space Capabilities," <u>Military Review: The Professional Journal of the U.S. Army</u>, Vol. 75, No. 3, 95-63006-9, Army Command and General Staff College, May/June 1995.

Mullins, Jerry L., "Global Positioning System Surveying, Aerial Photography and Mapping Program of the U.S. in Antarctica," <u>Antarctic Journal of the U.S.</u>, Vol. 29, No. 5, 96-07501-23, National Science Foundation, 1994.

Nashashibi, F., P. Fillatreau, B. Dacre-Wright & T. Simeon, "3-D Autonomous Navigation in a Natural Environment," in Proceedings, IEEE International Conference on Robotics and Automation, San Diego, California, May 1994; also, IEEE Computing Society Press, Los Alamitos, California, 1994.

Ngai, Hing-On, Lam Wa-Kwai & Lam Wong-Hing, "Study of the Performance of the Global Positioning System (GPS) in City Streets of Heavily Built-Up Areas for Future Vehicle Navigation Systems," Proceedings, Third International Symposium on Consumer Electronics, Hong Kong, November 1994; IEE Volume 2, 1994

Popiel, Jerome A., "Global Positioning System: the Truth for Boat Operators," On Scene, Volume 95, No. 4, U.S. Coast Guard, Winter 1995.

Pryke, C. L. & J. Lloyd-Evans, "A High-Performance GPS-Based Autonomous Event Time-Tagging System with Application in a Next-Generation Extensive Air Shower Array," in Nuclear Instruments & Methods in Physics Research, Section A (Accelerators, Spectrometers, Detectors and Associated Equipment), Volume 354, No. 2-3, January 1995.

Schell, Scott P. & Jeffrey A. Lockwood, "Spatial Analysis Optimizes Grasshopper Management," GIS World, Volume 8, No. 11, November 1995.

Simon, D. & H. El-Sherief, "Real-Time Navigation Using the Global Positioning System," in IEEE Aerospace and Electronics Systems Magazine, Volume 10, No. 1, January 1995.

Singh & Ackermann, "High-Accuracy GIS Data Base Georeferenced on GPS Aerial Triangulation," in Proceedings, GIS/LIS `95 Annual Conference and Exposition, Nashville, Tennessee, November 1995.

Szacsvay, S., "To Catch a Train: Train Location Systems for Railway Signalling," in Proceedings Preprint, Electrical Engineering Congress (EEC), Enabling Technologies, Developing Industry, Sydney, New South Wales, Australia, Nov. 1994.

Tiemeyer, B., M. E. Cannon, G. Lachapelle & G. Schanzer, "Satellite Navigation for High-Precision Aircraft Navigation with Emphasis on Atmospheric Effects," in Proceedings, IEEE Position Location and Navigation Symposium (PLANS`94), Las Vegas, Nevada, April 1994; also, IEEE, New York, 1994.

Till, R. D., W. Wanner & J. R. Evangelos, "Wide-Area Augmentation System (WAAS) Test and Evaluation Concepts," in Proceedings, IEEE National Aerospace and Electronics Conference (NAECON), Dayton, Ohio, May 1995.

Tsai, T., D. Jamieson, B. Whitten & B. Mee, "Testing of Rail Vehicles for Higher Speeds on Existing Lines," in Proceedings, IEEE/ASME Joint Railroad Conference, Baltimore, Maryland, April 1995.

Viljoen, P. C. & P. F. Retief, "The Use of the Global Positioning System for Real-Time Data Collecting during Ecological Aerial Surveys in the Kruger National Park, South Africa," journal article, Koedoe, Vol. 37, No. 1, 1994.

Proceedings, First Federal Geographic Technology Conference (GIS in Government), Exposition and DataMart, Washington, D.C., Sept. 1994.

Applications of GPS in Operation Desert Clean Sweep, short report, National Air Intelligence Center, Wright-Patterson AFB, OH, April 1996.

FAA Aircraft Certification Human Factors and Operations Checklist for Standalone GPS Receivers (TSO C129 Class A), final report, ADA2970739XSP, Federal Aviation Administration, February 94-March 95.

Space Support at the Operational Level: How Have We Learned the Lessons of Desert Storm, final report, ADA3073335XSP, Naval War College, Joint Military Operations Department, Newport, RI, Feb. 1996.

"GPS Compliance Checklist," FAA Aviation News, Volume 35, No. 4, 96-35507-8, Federal Aviation Administration, May/June 1996.

"GPS for Express Delivery," Telecommunications (International Edition), Volume 29, No. 3, March 1995.

"GPS Kit Improves MK. 80-Series Accuracy," Aviation Week & Space Technology, Volume 142, No. 7, February 1995.

"Satellites Track Plate Movement," Geotimes, Vol. 40, No. 3, March 1995.

"Troposphere's Effects on DGPS Accuracy Studied," Aviation Week & Space Technology, Volume 142, No. 11, March 1995.

"Where on earth are we going? A Look at the Planet's Ever-Changing Face," Frontiers, 95-47511-3, National Science Foundation, Oct. 1995.

GLOSSARY

A

accelerometer: device for measuring increases or decreases in speed of a vehicle, machine or projectile.

access: entry into or permission to use.

active satellites: working units designed to not only receive signals but to amplify and relay them to other stations.

adapter: device used to convert one type of equipment to another so that it can be used differently or can operate compatibly with others.

airborne GPS: multimode GPS receiver, usually coupled with ILS/MLS capabilities; designed for in-flight use.

algorithm: formula for a sequence of steps to solve a problem, do computation or make something happen; mechanical, recursive computational procedure.

almanac (satellite): navigation message with positioning data and the health status of all satellites; data obtained from satellites and stored in receiver so that it can calculate its own position.

alongtrack displacement: positioning error along a specified flight track.

antenna: wire or metal conductor used to pick up energy of radio signals being sent from remote source; for GPS usually microstrip-patch or qudrifilar-helix type.

anti-spoofing: AS; encryption of code or implementation of security measures to prevent unauthorized access or tampering.

area navigation: RNAV: methods appropriate to operate aircraft within certain limits or system capabilities; works standalone or with VORTAC or VOR/DME.

atmosphere: gaseous layers surrounding the earth; usually classified in layers differentiated by temperature, pressure and density.

atmospheric drag: deceleration of orbiting body from friction with atmosphere.

atomic clock: device used for timing signals emitted from GPS satellites; has chamber in which low-energy cesium (or rubidium) atoms are radiated to change them into high-energy atoms, oscillations of which are used as standards time units.

atomic second: international standard unit of time measurement; corresponds to transition time between 2 hyperfine levels of the ground state of cesium atom.

atomic time: time based on laws governing transmission of energy in atoms rather than related to earth's rotation; linked and coordinated to the earth's rotation for accurate results.

auditory display: device or means to relay information to persons via their ears; hearable prompt.

automatic vehicle location: technology by which motorists can summon help to their location or fleet managers can identify and locate vehicles from a control site.

autonavigation: feature enabling vehicle to operate independently for limited time if contact with ground or central control is lost or interrupted.

autonomous: self-contained; independent of ground control.

autopilot: computerized navigational control; in aircraft, control mechanism to automatically maintain altitude, course and stability..

aviation database: information, data and waypoints specific to flight.

aviation waypoint: geographical guidepost used by pilots; defined by latitude and longitude (degrees, minutes, seconds).

B

base line: line pre-established as a basis for measurement or comparison.

beacon: stationary guidepost that transmits signals in all directions; also called nondirectional beacon.

bearing: direction between two points relative to magnetic or true north (azimuth); compass direction of travel.

black-box unit: screenless receiver or other device; may be hooked up to display screen of another device.

block satellites: design versions that have been or are part of GPS configuration.

boundary survey: cadastral survey limited to one piece of property.

broadcast approach (marine ID): transmission by all ships of their identification and GPS-derived locations on a regular basis to all others within reception range.

broadcasting: transmitting signals (typically, radio) across a wide area.

C

cadastral surveys: surveys done for the specific purpose of establishing legal and political boundaries, e.g., for ownership, representation or taxation.

calibration: checking, adjusting or standardizing the scale or markings of an instrument of precision; quantitative measurement.

cartographer: map and chart artisan; mapmaker.

Category-I approach & landing (Cat-1): relatively easy instrumented aircraft approach for heights above touchdown of at least 200 feet with a minimum runway visual range of 1800 feet.

Category-II (Cat-2): approaches in which height above touchdown is at least 100 feet and the minimum runway visual range is 1200 feet.

Category-III (Cat-3): basically, "Look-Ma-no-hands!" approach in which aircraft is automatically guided and brought down onto the runway under stringent conditions; pilot cannot see runway until airplane touches down

Category-IIIa (Cat-3a): applies to landings with a minimum runway visual range of 700 feet but with no height minimum.

Category-IIIb (Cat-3b): applies to landings with a minimum runway visual range of 150 feet and no height minimum.

Category-IIIc (Cat-3c): refers to highly difficult landings under stringent conditions with neither height nor runway visual range restrictions applying.

CD-ROM: Compact-Disk, Read-Only Memory storage, information- or media-delivery device; capacity of each about a bookcaseful of text.

cesium: (aka caesium) Cs; shiny, soft, gold-colored metal that produces a sky-blue ("caesius") color in the spectrum; used in atomic clocks for GPS.

cesium atomic clock: clock using the frequency of oscillations of radiated cesium atom (9 billion times per second) as its time standard.

channel: electronic signal-sensitive component of a receiver; part that tunes in and relays signals to its processor.

chart plotters: devices used to create map graphics from navigation data.

circular orbit: path forming circular shape (as opposed to elliptical).

clock warm-up: how long it takes after a user first turns on the receiver until it begins calculating position; up to 6 minutes.

Coarse/Acquisition code: C/A; altered signal provided civilians under selective availability; easily acquired; accurate to at least within 100 meters; relatively short sequence of numbers sent over a relatively narrow bandwidth.

Coast Guard DGPS: network of 51 installed or planned differential base stations operated by U.S. Coast Guard along the Atlantic, Pacific and Gulf coasts of the U.S., around Alaska, along shores of Great Lakes and on Puerto Rico and Hawaii.

compass: small instrument for determining geographical direction; typically, magnetic needle(s) mounted horizontally, free to pivot until aligned in a N/S direction (conforming to magnetic field of the earth).

configuration: arrangement; formation (geometric, perhaps) or identity that a group of items seems to assume when observed as a set, e.g., "Big Dipper," GPS.

constellation: stellar objects, properties or individuals grouped either structurally or functionally; configuration of stars or satellites, e.g., Orion, GPS.

continuous, multichannel receiver: receiving device that has at least 4 channels (and up to as many as 12) and can track a number of satellites simultaneously and provide immediate readings on position and velocity.

control point: point used as a reference to measure other points' positions relative to an accepted grid or standard; a constant for verifying or regulating variables.

control segment: network of earth-based facilities (Master Control Station and several monitoring stations) responsible for overall operation of GPS — telemetry, tracking, controlling, up-loading and generation of messages.

control sensor: device used to measure how much things vary from an accepted norm; something designed to relay signals to other devices when quantitative or qualitative thresholds are exceeded.

coordinates: numbers (and/or letters) that reference known grids; for GPS, associated with latitude, longitude and altitude; sets of numbers defining location of point, line, curve or plane in space of given size.

coordinate system: a grid and methodology used for assigning numbers to positions.

Coordinated Universal Time: UTC; derivation of time kept by atomic clocks aboard satellites adjusted to Greenwich Mean Time.

course-change waypoints: virtual markers calculated as a flight path changes.

coverage: amount of surface area or volume of space penetrated or reached by signals that allows a user to obtain accurate positional fixes.

creep: shift that occurs gradually; geologically, slow slippage out of place of land mass as a result of pressure or wear.

crosstrack tolerance: allowance for displacement to left or right of a flight track.

cruise missiles: small, ground-hugging pilotless vehicles that can carry warheads over thousands of miles before releasing them.

crustal deformation: subtle shifts of only a few millimeters over great portions of the earth's crust, making it possible to study plate dynamics and locations of earthquake-prone areas with new vigor.

D

data: special-purpose facts and figures organized to facilitate analysis and from which conclusions may be drawn; used in the plural.

data processors: components (computer chips) that interpret signals and display the information numerically or graphically.

data warehousing: accumulating, storing and sharing digitized resources

database: data collected and stored in ways that facilitate access to information; electronically-stored data.

database integrity: maintaining quality control of the database when map sources of varying scales and resolutions are used and combined. Engineering-level quality control align measurements and waypoints

datacard unit: device with a slot for readable card that contains electronic data.

datasets: files or parts of files kept as resources for particular subjects.

datum: uniquely named mapping system referencing grids that cover areas of the earth; usually tagged with the year of its last update; not the singular of data; pluralized as datums.

Dead-Reckoning: DR; essentially, calculation or navigation based on educated guesses; applying course and distance traveled to previous position in order to estimate current position.

delayed transmission: sending data sometime after having been collected and stored in a processor.

DGPS-ready: can be modified to work around selective availability; has slot for attaching special equipment that enables receiver to process corrected signals transmitted by differential station.

differential antenna: antenna able to pick up signal corrections transmitted by a DGPS station; must come with or be added to receiver.

differential beacon receiver: device designed to tune in to signals transmitted from differential stations; the means by which a GPS user obtains corrections for selectively-available signals; must be either built in or added to civilian receiver.

differential correction: adjustment made to civilian (C/A) signal to overcome degradation effects of selective availability; transmitted to users equipped with DGPS receivers via precisely coordinated base stations.

Differential Global Positioning System: DGPS; Differential GPS; Coast-Guard-developed network of reference stations that transmit signals allowing persons using civilian receivers to adjust fixes for more accuracy; differential determined by measuring amount of adjustment needed to align degraded signals with known station coordinates.

differential-ready: upgradeable to work around selective availability; has slot for attaching equipment that enables receiver to process signals from DGPS stations.

digital communicator: small device used for field communication; portable processor, GPS receiver and pager; also called tactical automated situation receiver.

digital maps: maps electronically created and displayed (via streams of computerized binary digits of 0s and 1s).

digitized: converted into electronic combinations of 1s (ones) and 0s (zeros) that can be handled, filed and stored electronically on computers.

Dilution of Precision: *DOP; distorting effect that satellite configuration has on results obtained from GPS; can be geometric, positional, horizontal, vertical or time-related; ideal dilution of precision (distortion) is zero.

Direction Finding: DF; determining the source of a signal using a radio receiver and rotating antenna.

directional antenna: antenna adapted to send or receive signals from particular direction(s).

dispatch system: means of communication used to locate and send someone or something to specific location (or direct them to a task).

display unit: any means used for delivering information or output to a user of a device; usually visual (via screen), may be auditory (via earphones or speakers) or proprioceptive (via touch or sensors).

Distance-Measuring Equipment: DME; used to keep track of distance traversed by aircraft or vehicle; usually combined with navigation system.

dithering: intentional variance; done by DoD to precise time sent from clocks aboard satellites to GPS receivers; a means of imposing selective availability.

domain-specific database: digitized compilation of data specific to a domain, e.g., waste remediation, tariffs; usually put together by experts in a field of study;

Doppler effect: apparent increase in the frequency of sound, light or radio waves as its source approaches a receiver and a decrease as it moves away; named after Austrian physicist.

Doppler radar: dead reckoning using a radar signal reflected off the earth and being changed.

double-channel sequencer: one channel monitors positioning data while the other contacts the next satellite.

downloading: collecting electronic data from external source for processing and/or storage in other device (e.g., computer).

Dr. Johnson: Samuel Johnson, 18th c. English lexicographer and author.

Dynamic Environment Communications Analysis Testbed: DECAT; analysis software for modeling orbital and structural dynamics of space vehicles; determines which GPS satellites are available and calculates resultant geometric and positional dilutions of precision for configurations.

E

earth-orientation variation: daily estimates of changes in the earth's pole position over a three-week period; nearly continuous centimeter-level measurement.

eclipse: partial or total obscuring (from a particular point of view) of an orbiting body by another; for GPS, the period during which earth blocks the sun's energy from reaching the solar-array panels on a satellite.

ecosystem: inseparable interdependency between a biotic community and its physical environment; includes source of energy (usually sun), consumers (animals and some plants) , producers (plants), reducer organisms (bacteria, fungi) and nonliving chemicals (minerals, gases, water).

Electronic Chart Display Information System: ECDIS; system that allows a navigator to retrieve and view specific information along a route.

electronic navigation system: ENS; digitized information system used to augment published charts.

electronic toll-collection system: ETC; smart cards enhanced with GPS-receiver capabilities. register coordinates of entry and exit points of vehicle along a highway, along with fee schedules, payments and debit according to length and rates for particular segments traveled.

e-mail address: unique name and path for electronic communication.

Enhanced Navigation Reference System: ENRS; hybrid system of strapdown inertial navigation system (INS) with features of CIRIS and DGPS measurements.

ephemeris data: orbital data; regularly updated tables of computed positions of satellites, moon, sun, planets and stars; necessary for astronomy and navigation; very accurate information (up to 16 different measurements) regarding the position of the satellite and its velocity; sent as part of NAVmsg.

epicenter: place on the surface of the earth directly above the focus point (or source of greatest movement) of an earthquake.

estuarine near-shore habitat: roosting and breeding area located at a lower, tide-widened portion of a river, usually at its mouth.

European Complement to GPS: CE-GPS; regional overlay (to U.S. system) designed to minimize or overcome possible constraints of U.S. policy decisions.

event recorder: device designed to automatically collect data or information; means of recording history of an event or process.

expert database, expert system: digitized package of knowledge or expertise and the means for a user to draw inferences from contents; electronic domain in which a person works; may incorporate user-profiling to adjust level of responses.

external antenna: antenna placed away from receiver unit.

external interface: means for a user to control or interact with a device, e.g., display, control buttons, joystick.

F

F (block type): follow-on versions of satellites in use.

FAA Network: Federal Aviation Administration's augmentation network of 734 Differential-GPS stations; covers mainland United States.

fault (geologic): fracture in rock formation caused by movement of one section of earth's crust relative to another; also called rift.

fault (transmission): cause of interruption in a line, e.g., high-frequency pulses.

Fault-Tolerant Inertial Navigation GPS: FT IN/GPS; integrated navigation and control system for next-generation vehicles.

FEDERAL (United States Government)

Aviation Administration: FAA; controlling interface for civil aviation in U.S.

HighWay Administration: FHWA; maintains national highway systems.

Radionavigation Plan: FRP; U.S. government radionavigation-systems policy statement published by the Departments of Defense and Transportation; a consolidated plan for the management of civil and military radionavigation systems; available from National Technical Information Service (NTIS) and Government Printing Office.

fixed-station configuration: network of stations installed and arranged for a particular purpose.

fixed-station unit: device (e.g., receiver) permanently installed at a location.

flat-patch antenna: microstrip-type antenna commonly used for hand-held receivers; consists of flat strip of signal-sensitive material.

flight distance: amount of flight path between aircraft and next waypoint.

flight track: aircraft's entire route; full sequence of distances between waypoints.

free flight: pilot-managed air-traffic control. flight independent of ground control; allows a pilot equipped with GPS receiver and special type of radio to collaborate with similarly-equipped aviators in vicinity to determine routes;

frequency: how often something takes place over given span of time; can be measured in cycles, revolutions or pulses per second, minute, hour, etc.

G

geocenter: center of the mass of the earth.

geodesic: descriptive for any shape in which the principal normal of any point on its curve is the normal to the surface on which the curve occurs; like geodesic dome, vaulted structure of straight, lightweight elements forming interlocking polygons.

geodesy: science of the size and shape of the earth and influence of gravitational forces on them; surveying that takes the curvature of the earth into consideration.

geodetic datum: national records of horizontal and vertical measurements; reference source of geoidal data and representations of local or global ellipsoids.

geodetic survey: process for defining exact coordinates of points, lengths and directions of lines on surface of the earth; including effects of gravity; used by cartographers to establish reference networks or control points for mapping.

Geographic Information System: GIS; dynamically changing database containing information specific to the study of geography and the means for a user to draw relationships among them; may be local, national or global.

geography: study of the earth and its natural division via images; includes aspects of human distribution and activity.

geoid: hypothetical, "normal" level of the earth's surface, as if elevation and gravity were constant everywhere; imaginary near-sphere averaging of irregularities; coincides with mean sea level.

geological oceanography: study of ocean structure and bottom sediments.

geological survey: measurement of earth's surface structure in particular area.

geologist: specialist in the composition, structure and physical changes that occur on and in that part of the earth's crust accessible to human observation; expert in the deposition and distribution of metals and minerals and how strata reflect physical influences on the earth's crust.

geology: study of earth's history as a rocky-metallic body; includes layering, paleontology, mineralogy and petrology.

geometric configuration (GPS): geometric shape resulting from configuration of chosen GPS satellites.

Geometric Dilution of Precision: GDOP; distortion that geometry of satellites has on results obtained from GPS; ideal configuration = 1 satellite overhead, 3 satellites equally-spaced and close to horizon (but above mask angle).

geometrical geodesy: use of observation and measurement to determine the size and shape of the earth; determination of figures, areas and relative positions of portions of the earth's surface and figure of the earth as a whole.

geostationary orbit: orbit of satellite placed 22,300 miles above sea level moving eastward in path over the equator; keeps paces with earth's rotation so that space-based unit appears stationary.

geosynchronous orbit: orbit whose rotational period is some multiple or sub-multiple of 24 hours; synchronized with rotation of the earth.

Getting, Ivan A.: pioneered studies to explore possibilities of satellite-aided navigation in 1960s; put together team that won R&D funding from Defense Department to develop viable GPS for military.

gimbal: device for suspending object (e.g., compass, gyroscope, viewing apparatus) in such a way that it remains horizontal despite motion of its platform; involves 2 rings at right angles to each other.

glide bomb: bomb with no propulsion; glides to target after launch from aircraft.

global datum: reference for an ellipsoid approximating the shape of the entire geoid (total earth area).

Global Navigation Satellite System: GNSS; term used by ICAO to cover all navigation systems using satellite information to determine onboard position; only two formally registered — GPS and GLONASS.

GLObal 'naya Navigatsionnaya Sputnikovaya Sistema: GLONASS; Russia's space-based time and location-finding constellation.

Global Positioning System: GPS; U.S. military locator technology; accurate, 3-D (latitude, longitude and altitude) positioning and time-transfer system that operates from space; comprised of constellation of artificial satellites that transmit signals, network of ground stations and any number of user receivers.

global services: border- and language-independent services.

GPS receiver: receiving device that processes and displays locational and timing information from signals emitted by GPS satellites.

GPS User Equipment: UE; all devices used to obtain locational and timing information from signals received from GPS satellites.

Greenwich Mean Time: GMT; standard upon which local times are calculated; based on the meridian of longitude passing through Greenwich, U.K. from which each 15-degree meridian west has standard time difference (decrease) of 1 hour.

grid: lines on a map that divide areas into squares or rectangles; may differ from map to map depending on how curved areas of earth are converted to flat map; requires reference to specific set of coordinates.

grid coordinate reference: datum used as standard for a particular map; system or methodology that defines areas on maps.

ground antenna: permanently mounted, earth-based antenna; may be located at GPS monitoring station for sending data back to the satellites.

ground-to-air data link: communication venue used to transmit data from the ground to aircraft or satellite.

groundwater: water present in cracks and pores of earth's surface; source of wells.

gyroscope: fast-rotating flywheel mounted in such a way that it can rotate freely about any axis; when spinning quickly, forces of inertia (and torque) overcome gravity, providing its platform with stability and a resistance to movement.

H

half-life: indicator of how fast or slowly radioactivity of material lessens; time it takes for it to lose half its strength.

hand-held: small and portable; can be carried in user's hand.

Harrison, John: 17th c. English cabinetmaker-son of clocksmith; invented chronometer, first practical, accurate (to 10 miles) device for finding longitude at sea; awarded prize by British government.

head-mounted display: HMD; headpiece or head-held brace with viewing or optical-display devices located or suspended in front of a user's eyes to deliver information or stimuli; may also provide auditory clues.

head-up display: output device that does not require a user (a pilot, perhaps, or a blind person) to turn to look at a screen for information.

Hertz, R. H.: late 19th century German physicist; demonstrated electromagnetic (Hertzian) waves now known as radio waves; realized they travel at speed of light, are reflected, refracted and polarized (but failed to realize potential for signaling).

high-frequency radio signals: signals traveling from transmitter to receiver (or GPS to user) at speed of light; blocked by topographical features such as mountains; effective only if transmitters are high enough in space to transcend topography.

historical geology: study of the development of the planet in the context of the different life forms it supports.

horizontal accuracy: precision based upon latitude and longitude only.

horizontal datum: set of assumed or real reference points from which horizontal reckoning or scaling begins; of use to mariners.

Horizontal Dilution of Precision: HDOP; distorting effect that satellite configuration has on results obtained from GPS; important for marine use (for which altitude is unimportant); ideal dilution of precision is zero.

hydrologist: person who studies properties and distributions of water in soil, rocks and atmosphere, especially effect of water flow on earth's surface.

I

IFR-approved: approved for operation under Instrument Flight Rules, which govern approaches not meeting visual-flight-rule minimums. .

inertial navigation: sophisticated form of dead reckoning in which start point and any movement of a vehicle (airplane, ship, spacecraft, etc.) is detected and used to determine the present position of a vehicle at any time.

Inertial Navigation System: INS; combination of computers, gyroscopes and on-board accelerators for guiding and maintaining craft or missile on predetermined course.

information: random collections of unsynthesized, unanalyzed material.

infrastructure: substructure

input: anything put into system or device or used in its operation to achieve results; usually data or information; can be funds, energy, etc.

Instrument Landing System: ILS; passive, short-range system used with radar for precision approach navigation; still used for precision approaches by commercial airline industry and Defense Department.

Instrumented Flight Rules: IFR; regulations governing any landings not meeting visual-flight-rule minimums.

Intelligent Transportation System: ITS; vehicles equipped with locator systems (GPS antenna and receiver), wireless communications systems (cellular phone) and sensors plus equipment and control sensors installed along highways.

Intelligent Vehicle Highway System: IVHS; master plan for an intelligent transportation system coupling GPS with onboard sensors, highway sensors, automatic mapping and communication devices.

interfacing capability: measure of how easily a device works with others.

internal data processor — little built-in computer.

International Civil Aviation Organization: ICAO; agency to promote satellite aeronautical Communications, Navigation and Surveillance (CNS) and facilitate worldwide commitment to satellite CNS services.

international datums: sets of reference grids reliable and detailed enough to become de-facto standards for particular uses; often established (e.g., between North American/European datums and Tokyo/North American datums) to provide more extensive, consistent reference bases.

in-vehicle navigation: anything driver does within a vehicle to get it from one place to another; includes choosing route, changing direction and responding to road and traffic conditions.

ionosphere: dispersive layer of atmosphere where free electrons are generated from gas molecules by sun's ultraviolet rays; causes time delay of signals passing through.

isotope variability: difference in the number of neutrons atoms may have (even if number of protons is equal).

J

jammer-to-signal tolerance J/S: degree to which a signal can resist interference by external electronic attack.

Joint Program Office: JPO; GPS operations site at Headquarters Space Systems Division, Los Angeles Air Force Base, California; oversees satellite development and production; conducts field tests for GPS equipment and techniques used by DoD.

K

kilometer: 1000 meters or ~0.62137 mile.

kinematic: referring to pure motion not influenced by mass or force.

knot: 1852 meters or ~6,075 feet or nautical mile; remnant of speed measured by tying knotted line to a log, throwing log overboard, then counting how many knots passed through a seaman's hands in 30 secs.

knowledge: accumulated understanding gained primarily through experience or study; cognitive/intellective sum of things perceived, discovered or inferred.

knowledge base: knowledge that is cloned, enhanced, augmented, stored or transmitted for use in problem solving and from which inferences may be drawn; usually digitized, stored, accessed and transmitted via electronic interface.

L

L1 and L2 frequencies: 1575.42 MHz and 1227.6 MHz, respectively; wave bands for radio signals picked up by GPS receivers on earth; Link 1 carries both P (precise) and C/A codes; Link 2 carries P-code (but may be modulated for C/A and Y codes).

labor-intensive: requiring many hours for completion (as opposed to capital-intensive that requires high monetary investment).

laser terrain-profiling: using laser beams to measure and topologically map portions of the earth.

latitude: imaginary lines drawn parallel to earth's equator as part of a spherical coordinate system; measured in degrees (parts of 360°), minutes and seconds (north and south) as measured from equator.

level: cross-haired telescope mounted on a tripod, augmented by cross bars and plumb lines for adjustment to a true horizontal line.

Liquid Crystal Display: LCD; type of flat screen used in calculators and digital watches; produced by electric field being applied to surface of liquid crystal molecules and orienting them to act as polarized light filters; less clear but more energy-saving than Cathode-Ray Tubes (CRTs) used for television.

Local Area Augmentation System: LAAS; local-area base stations to provide closer-in corrected signals for precision landings in Categories I, II and III.

Local Differential Global Positioning System: LADGPS; same as above.

LOng-RANge direction-finding system: LORAN; U.S. long-range system using low-frequency radio waves and paired stations; signals parallel earth's contours, unobstructed by topology; can be picked up thousands of miles away; provides positional data over a wide area, not just from specific points. LORAN-C, a non-FAA system operated by the U.S. Coast Guard, transmits from (24+) shore stations.

longitude: imaginary lines drawn from pole to pole as part of a spherical coordinate system; measured in degrees° (parts of 360°), minutes' and seconds" east or west of meridian at Greenwich, U.K. (designated as 0°).

loop antenna: antenna in shape of a loop, angle of which affects intensity of signal detected from incoming directional radio waves.

low-frequency radio signals: fewer radio waves per unit of time; not blocked by topographical features.

low-frequency transmitter: device that sends low-frequency radio waves.

low-orbiting satellite: those up to 1600 kilometers above the earth.

M

manpack unit: lightweight, portable receivers that can be carried by an individual in a backpack or case.

map datum: compilation of data, coordinates and waypoints for a defined area.

map reconciliation: making map coordinates consistent with one another; adjusting references to conform to those on accepted grids.

map scale: degree to which measurements are reduced; ratio of proportions on which map is based, e.g., one inch = 1 mile.

Marconi, Guglielmo: sent radio signal clear across the Atlantic.

marine chronometer: sea-worthy timing device by which longitude can be calculated; "Mr. Harrison's Time-Keeper."

marine equipment system: devices used for on-water navigation

marine identification system: system using aircraft to notify command carrier (or individual vessels) of location and identities of vessels in their area or over the horizon.

mask angle: an angle (part of 360°) measured vertically from the horizon, below which accuracy of signals is dubious.

Master Control Station: MCS; aka Consolidated Space Operations Center (CSOC); Colorado location where data are analyzed and computations are done, and from which updated navigation messages are sent to satellites via ground antennae (usually once per day).

medium-height orbit: range from 1600 to a few thousand miles above earth.

medium-range missile: projectile with range of about 1000 km.

MegaHertz: MHz; an experimenter named H. R. Hertz, who first succeeded in transmitting a signal across a distance of a few feet.

menu-driven: process by which user of a system chooses options from a prepared list as opposed to issuing commands.

microsecond: one-millionth (10^{-6}) of a second.

millisecond: one-thousandth (10^{-3}) of a second.

missed-approach waypoint: points designated when approach fails to indicate exactly where it "missed," at which point turns must be executed and into which holding pattern the craft must go.

model, modeling: computer-generated simulation of something real; software that enables generation of realistic computer graphics for simulated scenarios.

Molniya orbit: high over the northern hemisphere (to increase the amount of coverage there) but dipping lower over the southern hemisphere (which may not be the focus of that particular launch).

mounting brackets: gimbals or stands that hold devices in a fixed position.

moving-map display: map on a screen that tracks movement (of the receiver alone or person holding it) in near-real time.

multimode receiver: MMR; type of receiver; basic types include 3-mode ILS/MLS/GPS and hybrid LORAN-C/GPS.

N

NATIONAL

Airspace System: NAS; U.S. airspace; navigation facilities, equipment, airports; information, maps, rules, procedures, material and personnel assigned to flight operation governed by U.S. jurisdiction.

Geodetic Survey: NGS; responsible for establishing network of reference or control points as bases for accurate land mapping.

Oceanic & Atmospheric Administration: NOAA; agency that creates and distributes assessments and predictions of weather, climate, space environment, ocean resources, living marine resources and nautical, aeronautical and geodetic events and systems; provides nautical charting data that serves as basis for U.S. nautical positioning.

natural satellite: naturally formed mass orbiting a planet, e.g., our moon.

Natural Systems Model: ecosystem database with analysis and modeling tool; used by scientists for calculating water surface slope, depth, velocity, flow, etc.

nautical mile (international): 1852 meters or ~6,075 feet or knot; one minute of arc of circle; preferred measurement for navigation; nm.

navigation: planning, monitoring and/or controlling movement of people or vehicles on land, at sea, in the air and in space; determining position and velocity relative to a chosen reference point or frame.

navigation message: NAVmsg; transmission from satellite of positioning data and health status of other specified satellites; allows receiver to determine where satellite was when signal was sent.

NAvigation Sensor System Interface: NAVSSI; U.S. Navy's version of ECDIS, an electronic charting display system.

navigation system: set of devices and techniques that can determine location of vehicle carrying it by converting space passed through it into measurements.

navigation warfare: art and science of navigation technology as strategic weapon.

Navstar System or Navstar GPS: name often used to describe GPS because its satellites are currently Navstar type.

network: configuration of interconnected facilities.

NonDirectional Beacon: NDB; guidepost that transmits signals in all directions.

non-GPS navigational aids: systems used, basically, for nonprecision approaches that outline minimum standards for altitude, visibility and final approach but have to be used under particular conditions, e.g., VOR, TACAN, RNAV, NDB, LORAN.

noninertial navigation: basically, piloting, by means of radio, radar, LORAN, celestial bearings, dead reckoning or Doppler radar.

nonprecision approach: approach and landing not governed by specific slope requirements; standard instrument procedure.

north-up display: directional display in which North is always at the top.

Northwest European Loran-C System: NELS; former U.S. Coast Guard network; scheduled for upgrade, extension and connection to other networks in Europe.

O

oceanography: study of the sea bed and its geologic idiosyncrasies.

Omega: system for ocean navigation and non-navigation jobs (e.g., hurricane tracking, weather balloons); operated by U.S. and six other nations; relatively inexpensive; accuracy of 2-4 miles; to be phased out.

Oppenheimer, Robert: American physicist, leader of WW II Army Corps of Engineers' "Manhattan Project" to produce atomic bomb.

orbit: the path a natural or artificial body in space takes around a celestial object. e.g., the path the moon or a satellite takes around the earth or the earth takes around the sun.

orbital data: ephemeris data; very accurate information (up to 16 different measurements) regarding the position of the satellite and its velocity.

orbital inclination: angle of tilt of the spatial plane of an orbit relative to the equator.

orbital period: time it takes an orbiting body to make a complete round.

oscillation: variations between extremes over a measured period of time, e.g., cycles per second.

output: information, energy, or work produced by a person or system.

P

panel-mounted: designed for permanent installation on vehicle panel or dashboard.

passive satellites: units capable of merely reflecting signals.

path in the sky: graphic representation of a trajectory via head-mounted display (HMD) to help a pilot visualize the scenario.

PC Mission Planner: training program used with personal computers for artillery placement, tracking troop movements, etc.

PCMCIA-slot card: credit-card-sized add-on for laptop computers; Personal Computer Memory Card International Association.

P-code: military-grade precision code; more accurate than C/A, well within 30 meters; pseudorandom, week-long number sequence transmitted over wide bandwidth; hard to acquire but less susceptible than civilian code to spoofing; requires military receiver.

P-code with AS: Y-code; precise GPS code (P-code) with anti-spoofing (AS) feature; encrypted military code.

permanent DGPS station: equipment and facilities installed in one place for 6 months or longer

permanent, stable orbit: orbit outside earth's atmosphere for its entire path.

photoelectric: loses electrons easily when struck by light.

photogrammetry: use of photography to make maps or scale drawings; precise measurement via photography.

physical geodesy: science of earth's gravitational field, rotation and movement on its surface of large plates of land mass; dynamic "geo-metry," or earth-measurement.

physical geology: the earth, what it consists of and how it changes.

physical oceanography: study of currents and circulation of the seas.

plate tectonics: movement of continents on the planet's surface as driven by forces within the crust.

plug-in cards: circuit boards or datacards that can be inserted into a computer slot to enhance its performance or capacity.

Position Dilution of Precision: PDOP; cumulative effect that satellite geometry has on latitude, longitude and altitude fixes.

positioning data: bits of information that help determine location.

Precise Positioning Service: PPS; Global Positioning System service provided select users (primarily military); within 20-meter accuracy.

precision approach: instrument landing subject to slope requirements.

Precision Code: P-code; GPS signal code designated for military use.

precision timing: timing within 10-millisecond accuracy.

Prime Meridian: 0°00' 00" longitude line passing through old Greenwich Observatory in Greenwich, England; set by international treaty in 1884 as basis for global time zones.

processor: computer to perform calculations on data it receives.

proprioreceptive: relying on and responding to touch or pressure.

pseudolites: configuration of ground-based transmitters, monitoring and control devices that serves as substitute visible satellites for aircraft in vicinity of airport to enhance accuracy.

public database: easy-to-access, consistent source of information to private citizens, media and professional organizations; consolidated information on issues such as health, security benefits, welfare, environment, public safety and law enforcement.

Q

quadrifilar antenna: type of antenna commonly used for hand-held receivers; signal-sensitive material in shape of a helix.

quartz crystal clock: timepiece using quartz crystal oscillations as frequency standard.

R

radar altimeters: radar-based devices for measuring altitude.

radio signals: wireless electrical signals sent over electromagnetic waves.

radioactivity: spontaneous emission of radiation (electrons, alpha particles, gamma rays, etc.) as a result of atom instability or nuclear reaction.

radiobeacons: radio waves sent in specific directions; technically, electronic navigation aids providing position-fixing and homing capabilities to vessels fitted with radio direction finding (RDF) equipment.

radiometers: instruments that measure water vapor along a line of sight.

radionavigation: use of radio waves to determine position for navigation.

radionavigation system: system capable of receiving radio signals and using triangulation to determine position.

Range Applications Joint Program Office: RAJPO; GPS-based range-tracking system for U.S. army, navy and air force.

ranging code: used by receiver to determine transit time of signal.

rate gyroscope: device used to measure rate at which pitch and roll occur in vehicle or trajectory.

real time: actual time something occurs; with computerized problem solving, time between putting data in and receiving solution; when response to input to a computer is fast enough to affect subsequent input.

real-space database: coordinates for objects that relate to and rely on a position relative to the real world for meaning; collection of specific, real-world-dependent altitude, latitude and longitude coordinates.

receiver: piece of equipment that can pick up and process signals transmitted from a distant source.

reconnaissance satellites: orbiting (spy) unit designed to examine and gather data from very small, very specific areas on earth's surface.

reference waypoints: specific control points from which the locations of other waypoints are computed.

Regional Control Station: RCS; GPS ground site used to record and archive data for specific region, assess operational performance, detect system malfunctions and provide status reports; emergency communication center for command and/or service changes.

regional databases: collections of digitized information specific to a region

regional datum: measurements of a geoid-shaped ellipsoid for particular region and related to a particular point in that region.

relative displacement: amount of shift between a spin axis and its case.

remediation: calculated attempt to restore the ecological balance of a site.

remote sensors: devices mounted on satellites or other units to detect, evaluate and predict changes that might affect it, its surroundings or targeted areas.

resonant cavity: special chamber in which the radioactive component of an atomic clock is housed.

resource management (land/forest): mapping and surveying of property corners, roads, trails and water resources.

robot: electronically controlled machine; programmable to navigate to precise locations and/or perform specific tasks; can be any size, shape or material.

S

satellite almanac: navigation message with positioning data and health status of all the other satellites.

satellite blocks: design versions of satellites; associated with different phases of the evolution of the GPS constellation.

satellite signals: radio emissions originating from aboard satellites

satellites: natural or manmade objects orbiting celestial bodies.

scale: reduce or increase size proportionately with regard to a fixed measurement.

sea-level datum: theoretically, level of the geoid; practically, mean sea level derived from average of tidal cycles over 1 year.

sea-surface positioning: calculating sea-level and measuring ocean waves.

Selective Availability: S/A; imposition of wandering, artificial error on precise time signal to prevent enemies from gaining the strategic advantage of high-accuracy positioning; also includes slowly changing errors introduced into orbit information contained in each satellite message.

self-location: determination by person in the field of his or her location; affirmation of launch location for projectile-type weapons.

sequencing receiver: device that tracks satellites, in sequence, one at a time, until enough readings are received to calculate position.

sextant: instrument for measuring elevation angles to sun and stars using mirrors and a calibrated gauge.

sheet flows: surface waters that vary only 1.4 centimeters from known control points; problem of low-relief terrain.

signals-in-space: SIS; radio signals broadcast in or from space.

simulation: process or apparatus to generate test conditions that approximate real or operational conditions, e.g., using flight simulators for pilot training; interactive software that generates sounds and forces in a simulated world.

single-channel sequencing receiver: receiver that uses only one channel to track several satellites, tuning in, one at a time, to make range measurements and monitor navigation messages; requires sequencing very quickly through all (four chosen) before position can be calculated.

smart cars: vehicles fitted with sensors and devices that aid navigation.

smart robots: remotely controlled machines fitted with sensors, receivers and measuring devices and designed to perform tasks.

software: coded programs that tell a computer what to do in order to perform a specific task; a set of logical, detailed instructions for operating a computer.

solar-array panel: arrangement of photovoltaic cells to convert solar energy into electrical energy.

sole-means navigation system: system incorporating capabilities matching or exceeding those of other systems; only approved system meant to replace all others.

sound-based navigational interface: software and hardware that provide a user with an acoustic (ear-based) gauge of surroundings; surround-sound headphones that deliver cues in the form of sounds that seem to come from different directions.

SOund NAvigation Ranging: SONAR; electrically generated pulses of sound sent out from the seeker ships to hit something, echo back so that distance traveled can be calculated from time lapse; pulses sent out in beams so that direction could be found; waves converted into electrical signals and fed into visual displays.

space element (GPS): segment from which users receive navigational and timing information; constellation of satellites broadcasting time signals; 21 working satellites and 3 spares (potentially more), along with components included in them;

spoofing: use of technology to dupe remote receiver into processing fake signals, e.g., transmitting counterfeit signals to lure aircraft into danger.

Sputnik: artificial satellite launched by the U.S.S.R. on October 4, 1957.

squittering: sporadically timing very quick announcements over a wide, robust radio channel as a means of minimizing collision among communications in flight.

stable orbit: high, permanent path well outside the earth's atmosphere.

Standard Positioning Service: SPS; civilian users with 100-meter accuracy

statute mile: standard mile; 5,280 feet.

strain accumulation: along faults in earthquake-prone areas

surveyor: a person who determines the boundaries, areas or elevations of a piece of land using the techniques of geometry and trigonometry.

synchronization: operating or coinciding in time or rate.

T

TACtical Air Navigation: TACAN; military's ultra-high-frequency, short-range, land-based system; scheduled for phaseout.

teleoperation or telemanipulation: computer-programmed control or remote control of robot technology to get something done; synchronized actions mimicked in a remote location; operation of equipment via electronic signals.

telescoping antenna: antenna that can be extended above treetops or other obstructions for signal acquisition and collapsed for transport.

temporary orbit: unstable path low point of which crosses (either intentionally or accidentally) within the earth's atmosphere, producing drag on the orbiting unit, eventually slowing it down into descent.

Temps Atomique International: TAI; average rate of atomic clocks worldwide.

Terminal Area Surveillance System: TASS; multifunction, ground-based radar system intended to replace current airport surveillance radars, Doppler weather radars and low-level wind-advisory systems.

terminal-area waypoints: guideposts provided specifically for safe maneuvering an aircraft within the limited space allotted for final approach and landing.

three-dimensional data: GPS data representing latitude, longitude and altitude; alternately, data representing three separate measurements.

Timation: U.S. Navy two-dimensional system

time delay (GPS): how far a receiver's code has to shift to align with a satellite's.

Time Dilution of Precision: TDOP; the degree to which satellite configuration can affect the accuracy of time signals.

Time-Of-Arrival: TOA; travel time between transmission of a signal and its reception.

Time-to-First-Fix: TTFF; how long it takes after a user first turns on a receiver until he or she gets positional coordinates.

topographic maps: maps showing mountains and valleys in relative elevations; U.S. Geological Survey standard scale of 1:24000; some also indicate locations of buildings, roads, sewers, wells, water and power lines.

topographic survey: measurement of heights and contours of particular regions or places; usually conducted by the USGS.

topography: art of representing features of the earth's surface

track-up display: display showing direction to be followed at the top of the screen.

trajectory: flight path

transceiver: device that both receives and transmits signals.

Transit: U.S. Navy two-dimensional system that took long time for processor to fix locations; good for low-dynamic platforms (e.g., ships) but not for high-velocity aviation; evolutionally comparable to Russian Tsikada, forerunner of GLONASS.

transit: most commonly used surveyor's instrument; a level mounted so that it can be angled at varying degrees and with which accurate measurements can be obtained.

transmitters: devices that send signals.

transponders: devices that send responses to signals

triangulation: mathematical procedure based on principles of geometry and the relationships among angles.

troposphere: portion of the atmosphere containing concentrations of water vapor that delay GPS signals.

turn-area adjustment: steps required for any change in flight direction over 150°.

U

UNITED STATES (U.S.)

Army Corps of Engineers: See Coast Guard/ACE.

Bureau of Land Management: BLM; organization responsible for surveying and mapping property to determine legal boundaries of public lands; gathers geographic data, provides fire-fighting support; relies on cadastral surveying

Coast Guard: USCG; developer of DGPS system to augment GPS; 51 installed or planned base stations; does for marine navigation what FAA does for aviation.

Coast Guard/Army Corps of Engineers: ACE; contributes 14 additional DGPS sites along the Mississippi and Ohio Rivers.

Committee on Extension of the Standard Atmosphere: group representing 29 U.S. scientific and engineering organizations.

Department of Defense: DoD; agency responsible for defense; developer of the Global Positioning System.

Department of Transportation: DoT; agency drawing up master plan for intelligent transportation system (ITS) based on GPS; funds IVHS.

Geological Survey: USGS; organization that designs, develops and implements plans for measuring elevations on the earth's surface, including topology data for calculating water surface slope, depth, velocity and direction of flow; publishes maps, oversees digitization for geographic datums for use in government and public domains.

Environmental Protection Agency: EPA; agency responsible for monitoring the environment and managing natural assets; surveying and mapping landfills, wells, outfalls and other facilities; quantifies spatial accuracy and maintains quality and map-scale control of GIS database; tests and evaluates equipment.

Federal Aviation Administration: FAA; controlling interface and certifying agent for all aspects of civil aviation in United States; inspects navigation equipment on flights; tests feasibility of new technology for approach and landing applications.

Forest Service: Agency responsible for nation's natural resources.

Pentagon: a 5-sided military-command site in Washington, D. C. that houses the Department of Defense and branches of the U.S. armed forces.

standard atmosphere: in geopotential height up to 90 km (300,000 feet) and in geometric height above 90 km.

Universal (Atomic) Time Coordinated: UTC; time standard derived from coordinating world atomic time signals (TAI) with time determined by observation of the heavens (called UT1 time).

unstable orbit: path of which low point path crosses within earth's atmosphere, producing drag on orbiting unit, slowing it down until loses enough momentum for high point to fall within atmosphere; causing unit to spiraling down towards earth.

update rate: how quickly information is revised; GPS-receiver range — once per second to once every ten minutes.

user segment (GPS): sum of people, antennae and passive receivers that convert and use GPS-satellite signals to determine position, velocity or time.

V

vehicle-based sensor: device mounted on moving vehicle to record data and feed the information to stationary control units or collection devices along routes; when used with GPS, can tag data with exact coordinates.

vehicular receivers: receiving devices with accessories such as an outside antenna, a dashboard-mounted map display or slots for inserting digital datum cards or CDs.

vehicular systems: units and accessories designed for moving vehicles.

velocity: rate of change of position over time; using GPS, the rate of change of distances from satellites over time

vertical accuracy: degree of precision based upon altitude only.

vertical datum: set of assumed or real reference points from which vertical reckoning or scaling begins; of use to aviators.

Vertical Dilution of Precision: VDOP; amount of vertical error introduced as a result of less-than-ideal satellite configuration.

Very-High-Frequency: VHF; 30-300 megacycles per second.

virtual-reality acoustic display: VR hearing-dependent apparatus for delivering information to a user.

visual display: sight-dependent means of delivering information.

Visual Flight Rules: VFR; regulations governing approaches and landings in which the pilot can see the runway.

VOR: FAA's Very-high-frequency OmniRange, point-to-point navigational system providing locational readings from transmitters to planes en route; in use since 1950s, combined with DME for flight within National Airspace System; to be phased out.

VORTAC: VOR (above) with military-provided (or TACAN) DME.

W

waypoint: coordinates for predetermined positions (expressed in degrees, minutes and seconds of latitude and longitude); virtual markers for defining routes and reporting progression along a path.

waypoint displacement area: rectangular area formed around and centered on the predetermined position of a waypoint.

waypoint segment: section of a flight track between two waypoints.

waypoint tolerance: amount of error tolerated for predetermined geographical positions (defined by latitude and longitude).

Wide-Area Augmentation System: WAAS; FAA network of stations used to measure and transmit differential-GPS corrections.

wide-area base station: node on WAAS network; 1 main and 2 backup units.

working satellites: active units designed to not only receive signals but to amplify them and relay them to other stations.

World Geodetic System 1984: WGS-84; common grid of absolute earth coordinates upon which military and civil positioning data are standardized; internationally accepted set of geodetic parameters; positions of points relative to center of earth's mass.

World Meteorological Organization: international entity responsible for monitoring and tracking weather; assigns names to regions and boundaries of the atmosphere up to 100 kilometers.

X, Y, Z

Y-code: P-code + AS; encrypted precise GPS code; decipherable by military receivers with special chip installed.

yield monitoring: process of overlaying farm yield data onto maps illustrating things that may affect crops.

ACRONYMS

ACE	Army Corps of Engineers; also, Aviation Capacity Enhancement
ADF	Automatic Direction Finding
ADW	Experimental Standoff (Weapon) Dispenser
AHD	Australian Height Datum
AMFM	Automated Mapping & Facilities Management
AS	Anti-Spoofing
autonav	AUTOnomous NAVigation
AUV	Autonomous Unmanned (or Underwater) Vehicle
AVL	Automatic Vehicle Location
BIPM	Bureau International de Poids et Measures
BLM	Bureau of Land Management
C/A code	Coarse/Acquisition code
Cat-1, 2, 3	Categories I, II and III (approaches and landings)
Cat-3a, b, c	Categories IIIa, IIIb and IIIc (approaches and landings)
CD-ROM	Compact-Disk, Read-Only Memory
CE-GPS	European Complement to GPS
CESA	Committee on Extension of the Standard Atmosphere
CG/ACE	Coast Guard/Army Corps of Engineers
CIRIS	Completely Integrated Reference Instrumentation System
CIS	Confederation of Independent States
CNS	Communications, Navigation and Surveillance
COMTESS	Combat Mission Training Evaluation & Simulation System
Cs	Cesium (aka caesium)
CSOC	Consolidated Space Operations Center
DECAT	Dynamic Environment Communications Analysis Testbed
DF	Direction Finding
DGPS	Differential Global Positioning System; (Differential GPS)
DMA	Defense Mapping Agency
DME	Distance-Measuring Equipment
DNC	Digital Nautical Chart
DoD; DOD	Department of Defense
DOP	Dilution of Precision

DoT; DOT	Department of Transportation
DR	Dead-Reckoning
ECDIS	Electronic Chart Display Information System
EMP	ElectroMagnetic Pulse
ENRS	Enhanced Navigation Reference System
ENS	Electronic Navigation System
EPA	Environmental Protection Agency
ETC	Electronic Toll-Collection
F version	Follow-on version
FAA	Federal Aviation Administration
FANS-1	Future Air Navigation Suite
FHWA	Federal HighWay Administration
FRP	Federal Radionavigation Plan
FT IN/GPS	Fault-Tolerant Inertial-Navigation/Global Positioning System
GAM	GPS-Aided Munition
GDOP	Geometric Dilution of Precision
GIC	GPS Integrity Channel
GIS	Geographic Information System
GLONASS	GLObal 'naya Navigatsionnaya Sputnikovaya Sistema
GMP	GPS Mission Planner
GMT	Greenwich Mean Time
GNSS	Global Navigation Satellite System
GOESS	Geostationary Operational Environmental Satellite System
GPS	Global Positioning System
GPSEE	Global Positioning Site Environment Evaluator
HDOP	Horizontal Dilution of Precision
HMD	Head-Mounted Display
HPPS	High-Precision Permanent Positioning Service (German)
Hz	Hertzian
ICAO	International Civil Aviation Organization
ICBM	Intercontinental Ballistic Weapons Systems
IEEE	Institute of Electrical and Electronic Engineers
IFR	Instrumented Flight Rules
ILS	Instrument Landing System

IMO	International Maritime Organization
INS	Inertial Navigation System
ITS	Intelligent Transportation System
IVHS	Intelligent Vehicle Highway Systems
J/S	Jammer-to-Signal
JDAM	Joint Direct Attack Munitions (program)
JPO	Joint Program Office
kt	knot
L1	Link 1 (L-band 1575.42 MHz frequency signal)
L2	Link 2 (L-band 1227.6 MHz frequency signal)
LAAS	Local-Area Augmentation System
LCD	Liquid Crystal Display
LDGPS	Local Differential Global Positioning System
LORAN	LOng-RANge (direction-finding system)
MCS	Master Control Station
MHz	MegaHertz
MLS	Microwave Landing System
MMR	MultiMode Receiver
MOPS	Minimum Operational Performance Standards
NAS	National Airspace System
NAVmsg	NAVigation message
NAVSSI	NAvigation Sensor System Interface
NDB	NonDirectional Beacon
NELS	Northwest European Loran-C System
NGS	National Geodetic Survey
NiCd	NIckel-CaDmium batteries
nm	nautical mile (international)
NOAA	National Oceanic & Atmospheric Administration
NPL	National Priorities List
NSM	Natural Systems Model
PCMCIA	Personal Computer Memory Card International Association.
P-code	Precision Code
P-code +AS	P-code with Anti-Spoofing (Y-code)
PDOP	Position Dilution of Precision

PLANS	Primary Land Arctic Navigation System (Canadian)
PPS	Precise Positioning Service
R type	Replacement or Replenishment (satellite block)
R&D	Research and Development
RADAR	RAdio Detection And Ranging
RAIM	Receiver Autonomous Integrity Monitor
RAJPO	Range Applications Joint Program Office
RCS	Regional Control Station
RNAV	aRea NAVtion
SA	Selective Availability
SIS	Signals-In-Space
SONAR	SOund NAvigation Ranging
SPS	Standard Positioning Service
TACAN	TACtical Air Navigation
TAI	Temps Atomique International
TASS	Terminal Area Surveillance System
TDOP	Time Dilution of Precision
TOA	Time-Of-Arrival
TTFF	Time-to-First-Fix
UE	User Equipment
USCG	United States Coast Guard
USGS	United States Geological Survey
UT1	Universal Time (as determined by observation of the heavens)
UTC	Universal (Atomic) Time Coordinated
VDOP	Vertical Dilution of Precision
VFR	Visual Flight Rules
VHF	Very-High-Frequency
VLBI	Very-Long-Baseline Interferometry
VOR	Very-high-frequency OmniRange
VORTAC	VOR with military-provided (or TACAN) DME
WAAS	Wide-Area Augmentation System
WGS-84	World Geodetic System 1984
XTE	cross Track Error
Y-code	P-code + AS (encrypted P-code)

Examples of Equipment Available in Today's Marketplace

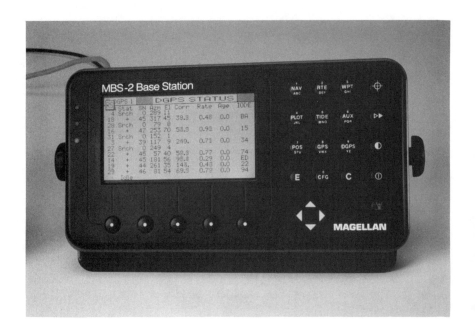

Magellan Base Station

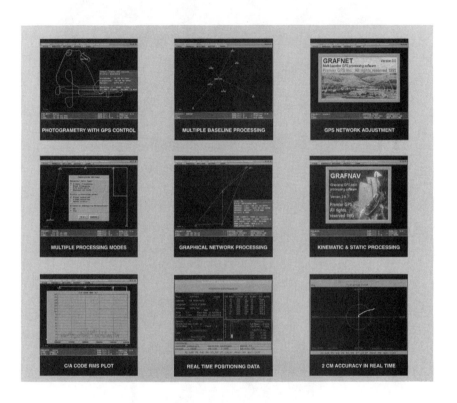

Premier Post-Processing & Kinematic Displays

Sokkia Spectrum

Sokkia GSR 2200

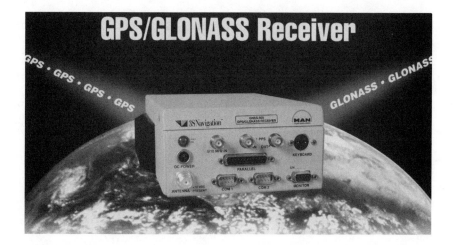

3S Navigation Combined GPS/GLONASS Receiver

Humminbird Marine Receiver & Antenna

Ashtech Ag Navigator

Magellan Marine Panel Unit

Ashtech Reliance Products for Surveying

By the same author:

THE VIRTUAL REALITY PRIMER
MCGRAW-HILL, INC.
NEW YORK

About the Author

L. Casey Larijani is a technical writer and consultant living in Manhattan. Trained as a teacher, Ms. Larijani is interested in investigating new technologies and fostering an understanding of them among laypersons in the fields of business, conservation and education. Ms. Larijani was previously Director of James Martin Research and Managing Editor of High-Productivity Software, Inc.

INDEX

B

C

G

H

S

ORDERING INFORMATION

Quantity discounts are available on bulk purchases of this book for educational or promotional purposes.

GPS for Everyone

L. Casey Larijani

To order, call (toll-free in the U.S.):

1-888-257-8830
1-800-898-3310

For more information or to find out about special editions, contact:

American Interface Corporation
Publishing Division
400 East 52nd Street, Suite 11A
New York, New York 10022-6423

1-800-898-3310